Negotiating Across Cultures

WITHDRAWN

Negotiating Across Cultures
Communication Obstacles in
International Diplomacy

Raymond Cohen

Foreword by Ambassador Samuel W. Lewis

UNITED STATES
INSTITUTE OF PEACE PRESS

Washington, D.C.

United States Institute of Peace
1550 M Street, N.W.
Washington, D.C. 20005

First published 1991

Printed in the United States of America

Library of Congress Cataloging-in-Publication Data
Cohen, Raymond, 1947–
    Negotiating across cultures : communication obstacles in
international diplomacy / Raymond Cohen : foreword by Samuel W.
Lewis.
        p.   cm.
    Includes bibliographical references and index.
    ISBN 1-878379-08-9
    1. Diplomacy—Cross-cultural studies. 2. Negotiation—Cross-
    cultural studies. 3. United States—Foreign relations—1945–
    I. Title.
JX1677.C63   1990
327.2′0973—dc20   90-24979
                                                           CIP

United States Institute of Peace

The United States Institute of Peace is an independent, nonpartisan, federal institution created and funded by Congress to strengthen the nation's capacity to promote the peaceful resolution of international conflict. Established in 1984, the Institute has its origins in the tradition of American statesmanship, which seeks to limit international violence and to achieve a just peace based on freedom and human dignity. The Institute meets its congressional mandate to expand available knowledge about ways to achieve a more peaceful world through an array of programs including grantmaking, a three-tiered fellowship program, research and studies projects, development of library resources, and a variety of citizen education activities. The Institute is governed by a bipartisan, fifteen-member Board of Directors, including four members ex officio from the executive branch of the federal government and eleven individuals appointed from outside federal service by the President of the United States and confirmed by the Senate.

Board of Directors

John Norton Moore (Chairman), Walter L. Brown Professor of Law and Director of the Graduate Program, University of Virginia School of Law

Elspeth Davies Rostow (Vice Chairman), Stiles Professor of American Studies Emerita, Lyndon B. Johnson School of Public Affairs, University of Texas

Dennis L. Bark, Senior Fellow, Hoover Institution on War, Revolution, and Peace, Stanford University

William R. Kintner, Professor Emeritus of Political Science, University of Pennsylvania

Evron M. Kirkpatrick, President, Helen Dwight Reid Educational Foundation, Washington

Morris I. Leibman, Esq., Sidley and Austin, Chicago

Sidney Lovett, retired United Church of Christ Minister, Holderness, N.H.

Richard John Neuhaus, Director, Institute on Religion and Public Life, New York

Mary Louise Smith, civic leader; former member, Board of Directors, Iowa Peace Institute

W. Scott Thompson, Professor of International Politics, Fletcher School of Law and Diplomacy, Tufts University

Allen Weinstein, President, Center for Democracy, Washington, and University Professor and Professor of History, Boston University

Members ex officio

J. A. Baldwin, Vice Admiral, U.S. Navy, and President, National Defense University

Stephen J. Hadley, Assistant Secretary of Defense for International Security Policy

Ronald F. Lehman II, Director, U.S. Arms Control and Disarmament Agency

Richard Schifter, Assistant Secretary of State for Human Rights and Humanitarian Affairs

Samuel W. Lewis, President, United States Institute of Peace (nonvoting)

For Rivka
The Song of Solomon, iv. 6–7

Contents

Foreword

"Ich bin ein Berliner," said President John F. Kennedy, wanting to show his solidarity with the citizens of West Berlin just after the Berlin Wall had been built. Unfortunately, that phrase actually translates as "I am a jelly-filled doughnut," a popular Berlin pastry! Kennedy's grammatical lapse probably caused no great harm, but it does illustrate how difficult it can be for people from different cultures to communicate, even when they have substantially similar cultural backgrounds. How much more difficult, then, must intercultural communication be between the United States and non-European countries.

In *Negotiating Across Cultures*, Raymond Cohen examines the ways in which cultural factors have affected the conduct and outcome of U.S. dealings with five increasingly significant non-European nations: Japan, China, Egypt, India, and Mexico. In my own diplomatic experience on three continents, I encountered frequently the kinds of intercultural obstacles to mutual understanding that Cohen describes in this volume. For example, when Americans cannot accept a proposal, they say "no" readily; Israelis are even less likely than Americans to leave their response ambiguous. However, most Latin Americans, Arabs, Iranians, and Japanese will go to extraordinary lengths to avoid ever giving a flat negative. Instead, they employ infinite delay in responding, or use creative euphemisms to convey their meaning, since a bald "no" in most Asian or Latin American countries is considered insulting. Americans often infer a "yes" from this ambiguity. When the real "no" finally becomes clear, they may feel betrayed. In analyzing this kind of cultural miscommunication, Cohen has produced a thoughtful, gracefully written book that should be valuable to many diplomats, government officials, and scholars.

As part of his investigations, Cohen analyzes numerous negotiations that have taken place over the past forty years, including several that are still making headlines. For example, he presents a wealth of material on the ongoing negotiations with Japan about minimizing trade barriers, and the continuing talks with Mexico about controlling illegal immigration and drug trafficking. But he also studies the drawn-out discussions with China that led to the breakthrough in Sino-American relations in the 1970s, the complex negotiations with Egypt and Israel leading up to the Camp David accords of 1978, and the conflict over the safeguards proposed for the sale of nuclear fuel to India in the early 1980s. Cohen doesn't confine himself to high-visibility encounters, however; he also devotes attention to more mundane but nonetheless important issues such as boundary and water-rights disputes with Mexico, air-transport agreements with India, and the American effort to arrange for the use of Egyptian military facilities.

Such an examination of the record is important, of course. More important, though, is the fact that Cohen goes beyond the mere presentation of examples to provide a theoretical framework for his analysis. He argues that there is no single, universal model for negotiation. On the contrary, he describes two quite different models, each equally valid in its own terms. Cohen defines the first model as "low context," the predominantly verbal and explicit style typical of individualistic societies such as the United States. The second model is "high context," a style associated with nonverbal and implicit communication more typical of interdependent societies.

Obviously, these distinctions are over-simplified, but they do serve to highlight the areas of conflict in intercultural encounters. And indeed the examples cited by Cohen provide persuasive evidence of the negative consequences of such conflict. Cohen does not claim that culture explains everything, but he does conclude that in extreme cases communication obstacles can contribute significantly to the failure of negotiations. More often, though, such cultural dissonance results in less dramatic consequences, such as a less-favorable agreement than might have been expected, or more generally, a loss of credibility or damage to the wider relationship.

Cohen notes that neither Americans nor their non-European protagonists have a monopoly on wisdom when it comes to negotiation. He finds much to commend in both the low-context and the high-context approaches: "Learning that there is more than one way to go about things is surely not only enlightening but also enriches one's palette of alternatives." It is not possible, therefore, to lay down hard-and-fast rules of how to negotiate. Nevertheless, there are certain obvious lessons to be learned from the information presented here, and Cohen summarizes them in the final section of the book, where he makes ten specific recommendations for the intercultural negotiator.

Appropriately enough, *Negotiating Across Cultures* is the first book from the Jennings Randolph fellows program to be published by the Institute. We believe it will make an important contribution to the study of diplomacy and international relations. Its combination of solid practical advice with an innovative theoretical framework fits well under the Institute's mandate to "strengthen the nation's capacity to promote peaceful resolution of international conflict."

Samuel W. Lewis, President
United States Institute of Peace

Acknowledgments

The research and writing of this essay were carried out at the United States Institute of Peace, where the author was a Peace Fellow in the Jennings Randolph Program during 1988–89.

I am very grateful to the members of the Board of Directors of the Institute and its president, Samuel W. Lewis, for the opportunity to carry on my work in a congenial environment. Michael Lund and his staff were, and are, instrumental in making the fellowship program a success. Kathleen Allison, Barbara Cullicott, Libby Diniak, Denise Dowdell, Darleen Hall, Gregory McCarthy, Charles Nelson, and Charles Smith gave me every administrative assistance. I would also like to thank the following friends and colleagues at the Institute for their help and advice: Hrach Gregorian, Priscilla M. Jensen, Gerry Jones, Paul Kimmel, Richard Lewis, David Little, Lewis Rasmussen, John Reinhardt, John Richardson, and Tim Sisk.

Many people in public life generously gave of their wisdom and assistance. Thanks are due to Adolfo Aguilar, Francesco Alberti, Diego Asencio, Lucius Battle, Timothy Bennett, Sergio Dias Briquets, Herbert Brownell, Carleton Coon, Martin Creekmore, Hermann Eilts, John Ferch, Roger Fisher, Joseph Friedkin, Robert Goheen, Herbert Hagerty, John Jova, Julius Katz, Herbert Kelman, Paul Kreisberg, Daniel Kurtzer, Steven Lande, Herbert Levin, Joseph Lorenz, Patrick Lucey, Thomas Mann, Doris Meisner, Joerg Menzel, Richard Parker, William Quandt, El Sayed Abdel Raouf El Reedy, Randy Ridell, Jeffrey Rubin, Nadav Safran, Harold Saunders, Robert Sayre, Howard Schaefer, Gordon Streeb, Lorand

Szalay, Viron Vaky, Christopher Van Hollen, Nicolas Veliotes, Peter Wallison, Robert Wilcox, and William Zartman.

Patricia Bandy, Mia Cunningham, and Dan Snodderly did a very professional editing and publishing job. My good friend Richard Smith read the manuscript and was particularly supportive during its preparation.

Negotiating Across Cultures

one

Prelude
The *Astoria* Affair

To the average American observer, whose impression of diplomacy is obtained from watching brief snatches of United Nations debates and the visits of foreign dignitaries to Washington on television, the most striking feature of the diplomatic scene is not the clash of cultures but the apparent existence of a universal diplomatic culture. Although the odd interpreter and the occasional item of exotic costume may hint at foreign origin, diplomats seem to belong to an exclusive fraternity. They dress in similar elegant suits, flash the same charming smiles at photo opportunity sessions, and often speak elegant Harvard- or Oxford-accented English. When they express themselves in those invariant and familiar phrases about "friendly and constructive talks," the inevitable conclusion presents itself: these people share a common (elitist) language, way of life, and outlook on the world; they are members of the diplomatic club.

My own initial assumption to that effect was reinforced by such classic texts as Sir Harold Nicolson's famous study, *Diplomacy*. According to Nicolson, there is a universal diplomatic language of specialized words and phrases used by diplomats when they communicate with one another.[1] Nowhere does he suggest that the polished and expert diplomat may ever be sucked into the whirlpools of miscommunication. Accuracy in the conveying and reporting of information is taken for granted as the point of departure, not the goal, of diplomacy. If this version is true, an important conclusion inevitably follows: disagreement is invariably based on an objective conflict of interests; wherever else one may seek the sources of international dissension and misunderstanding, they are not to be found in any recurrent breakdown or failure of the communication process. Such a conclusion is reassuring; although the timber of international relations may be warped, at least the carpenter's tools are true and sure.

The first seeds of doubt about the completeness of this authorized version were sown in my mind by an account I came across of the *Astoria* affair. In October 1938, Hirosi Saito, a former Japanese ambassador to the United States, died in Washington. As a mark of respect, President Franklin D. Roosevelt ordered the U.S. Navy to convey the late ambassador's ashes home to Japan. The cruiser *Astoria* was chosen for the mission. Roosevelt, whose enthusiasm for the Navy was famous, made the decision without consulting State Department experts and despite the grave state of U.S.-Japanese relations. Japanese aggression against China and infringement of American interests continued unabated. The president certainly did not intend to downplay these very real causes of friction, let alone hint at any new course in American foreign policy—which would have been quite unacceptable to public opinion, outraged as it was by Japanese atrocities against Chinese civilians and such incidents as the sinking of the USS *Panay*.

But he had not reckoned on how the gesture would be viewed through Japanese eyes. Extraordinary importance is attached in Japanese culture to paying respect to the dead. Elaborate rituals are associated with the practice, and Japanese homes often contain a small shrine to the family ancestors. Reverence for the deceased goes far beyond anything found in American culture. Against this background Roosevelt's act of courtesy acquired a resonance in Tokyo never intended in Washington. Ambassador Grew wrote in his diary at the time,

> The reaction here was immediately and inevitably political. The Japanese interpreted the gesture as of deep political significance, and a tremendous reaction, both emotional and political, immediately took place. Not only did the Government and people of Japan assume that a new leaf had been turned in Japanese-American relations and a wave

of friendliness for the United States [sweep] over the country, but there promptly developed a determination to express Japan's gratitude in a concrete way.[2]

The State Department and the Tokyo embassy were horrified and embarrassed by the whole affair. One cross-cultural complication followed another. A jeweler from Osaka gave twenty pearl necklaces for the wives of the officers of the *Astoria*. If they were accepted, American public opinion would be outraged; in American public life such a lavish gift has the connotation of a bribe. If they were rejected, Japanese opinion would be deeply hurt; gift giving is naturally accepted in Japan as part of that complex lattice of moral indebtedness, mutual obligation, and social duty that underpins the Japanese way of life; the direct refusal of a present may cause, as Ambassador Grew ruefully observed, "serious offense."

As the *Astoria* approached Yokohama, Japanese excitement intensified. Plans went ahead for a mass rally of the kind beloved in Japan, replete with national anthems, waving flags, regimented students, speeches, a demonstration of martial arts, and a baseball game between a local team and the American crew. All this fanfare could only give an utterly distorted impression of the true state of diplomatic ties. Participation by representatives of the United States in such effusive ceremonial would hardly accord with the firmness that U.S. diplomacy sought to convey in the face of the ruthless expansion of Japanese power and influence on the Chinese mainland. The reaction of the American people to all the ballyhoo, Grew noted, would be: "Show us your appreciation in acts, not words"(p. 242).

It required all of Grew's skills to disentangle the knot without causing an equally undesirable backlash in Japanese opinion. The episode posed "one of the most difficult problems" to face the ambassador since his arrival in Japan in 1932. A tone of restrained dignity was tactfully insisted upon. Extraneous festivities were quietly canceled or toned down; the necklaces were held in safekeeping for a while, then returned. Even so, to the Japanese, the visit spoke for itself. Moving and elaborate funeral rites went ahead. A shrine had been erected at the harbor to first receive the casket; the funeral procession marched through the densely lined streets of Yokohama; a special train conveyed the remains to Tokyo, where yet more intricate and ornate pageantry awaited the ambassador's remains. What had been intended as a simple mark of courtesy escalated into a major demonstration of international esteem. The Japanese foreign minister commended it as a "graceful act . . . an opportunity for the restoration of good relations." Emperor Hirohito himself received the bemused captain of the American vessel, informing him with emotion that he "had performed a great service which was deeply appreciated by himself and the nation."[3]

If, as will surely be agreed, interstate communication depends on governments conveying no more and no less than they mean, the dispatch of the *Astoria,* however well-intentioned, was a diplomatic blunder. Because of the quite different weight and meaning attached in Japanese and American cultures to such seemingly universal human concerns as showing respect for the dead and giving gifts, a gesture that was intended to transmit one message inadvertently transmitted another one entirely. By innocently and unconsciously failing to take cross-cultural differences into account, the president sent a misleading diplomatic signal.

Was the *Astoria* episode a colorful but basically exceptional one? Further research into American diplomatic history indicates that it was not. Although an exhaustive study of the effect of cross-cultural factors on the foreign relations of the United States will have to await another occasion, the following book will serve as a brief introduction to the subject. By focusing on the more limited, but still important, field of American diplomatic negotiation with selected non-Western states, I hope to demonstrate that the effects of cross-cultural differences—although not always malign, by any means—have been pervasive and consequential.

For a closing thought to this segment we may return to the hero of the *Astoria* affair, Ambassador Grew, whose memoir of his time in Tokyo contains many examples of the difficulties of communication, both verbal and nonverbal. In an address to the America-Japan Society, Grew reflected on the role of the ambassador. It was, he argued, to act first and foremost as an interpreter of the two countries to each other in a situation in which the written word was quite inadequate. "What really counts is the interpretation of the written word and of the spirit that lies behind it," he wrote. With an extraordinarily modern insight Grew then submitted the following radical proposition: "International friction," he suggested, "is often based not so much on radical disagreement as on nebulous misunderstanding and doubt" (pp. 229–30). It is in this spirit that we shall turn to consideration of the effects of cross-cultural differences on international negotiation.

two

Negotiation
The Cultural Roots

Negotiation defined

Diplomatic negotiation consists of a process of communication between states seeking to arrive at a mutually acceptable outcome on some issue or issues of shared concern. On the spectrum of diplomatic activity it is to be distinguished, on the one hand, from the simple exchange of views and, on the other hand, from the practice of coercive diplomacy by which one party attempts to impose its wishes unilaterally.

In an anarchic world without any overarching international authority that can resolve disputes and allocate resources among contending powers, it may be useful to think of negotiation as the primary mechanism for achieving peaceful and legitimate change. Indeed it might even be described, in quasi-anthropological terms, as the procedure legitimating the transition of nations from one state of affairs in their relationships to another. Put another way, diplomatic negotiation can be thought of as a kind of rite of passage, analogous to the ceremonies by which societies celebrate the transition of individuals or groups from one status to another. The relevance of negotiation in the transition from war to peace is self-evident: the choreography of the exchanges, implying mutual recognition and acceptance after the dislocation and alienation of war,

may be no less momentous than the content of the settlement arrived at. But even in less-momentous situations it is the mutuality,
the reciprocity, of the negotiation that is required to cast the mantle
of authenticity over the whole business. An arrangement reached
by negotiation, and hence by joint consent, is absolutely different
from one arrived at by the crude imposition of one party's will on
another.

Usually, but not always, diplomatic negotiation is made up of a
rather structured exchange of proposals between accredited representatives. This exchange may be conducted formally or informally, verbally or nonverbally, tacitly or explicitly, and may be accompanied by unilateral activities outside the chosen setting. What
cannot be disputed is that the goal of the process is an agreed rearrangement (prospective or retrospective) of some element of the
relationship. As we shall see, this rather abstract definition is necessary because different cultures may disagree on important details
of the nature and mechanics of the negotiating process.

The nature of culture

The problem to be explored in this book concerns the effect on
diplomatic negotiation of cultural differences between the negotiating parties. We must first clarify just what we mean by culture.
Any visitor to foreign parts is struck by the remarkable variety of
customs, manners, and forms of social organization developed by
the human race in the conduct of its everyday affairs. In essence,
the concept of culture was developed by anthropologists as a way
of accounting for this extraordinary richness. It has been argued
since the time of such pioneers in anthropology as Edward Tylor
that the life-style of a collectivity is not the result of random and
arbitrary accident. Rather, it is the outward expression of a unifying and consistent vision brought by a particular community to its
confrontation with such core issues as the origins of the cosmos,
the harsh unpredictability of the natural environment, the nature
of society, and humankind's place in the order of things.[1] Human
heterogeneity results when alternative answers are proffered to invariant questions.

A neat, one-sentence definition of culture can only mislead.
More helpful is an ostensive definition, intended to draw attention
to the main features of the concept. Amid the welter of formulations put forward in the literature, three key aspects of culture

have gained general approval: that it is a quality not of individuals, but of the society of which individuals are a part; that it is acquired—through acculturation or socialization—by individuals from their respective societies; and that each culture is a unique complex of attributes subsuming every area of social life.

From the first feature we may conclude that culture is not to be confused with innate personality, let alone with "national character." Take, for example, the institution of the vendetta or blood feud, the obligation found in clan-based societies to avenge a loss of honor to one's kith and kin perpetrated by members of another group. The duty is remorseless: a family member is killed, a woman dishonored, a relative abused. Whatever an individual's personal propensities, whether he is peaceably or violently inclined, he has no choice in the matter; he must join his fellow clansmen in the act of retaliation or be ostracized by the group—and in collectivistic societies ostracism is an unthinkable deprivation. Thus character has nothing to do with it. In societies where the feud is endemic, even the most outrageous homicide statistics cannot form the basis of conclusions about the personal traits of the individuals who make up that society.

The second feature of culture places emphasis on the methods by which a society implants its way of life in its members. Partly, these mechanisms are formal and conscious—education both religious and secular, creation of role models, propaganda and advertising, military service or its absence, and systems of reward and punishment (widely defined to include not only the courts and prison system, but also the salary scale and the ways communities honor their distinguished citizens, past and present). But, of course, the informal modes of influence that are present in the family home, playground, street corner, and workplace may be no less influential.

From the third ostensive feature of culture it follows that the concept is not restricted to exotic artifacts or rituals but equally subsumes material, intellectual, and organizational dimensions. The objects, decorations, homes, buildings, and towns we surround ourselves with are only part of the story, albeit a revealing part. How much about a culture can be learned from the things that are cherished, the spaces that are lived and worked in, the styles of dress and deportment! No less important, however, are a culture's intangibles: the etiquette of personal encounter, the manner in which relationships are conducted (the structure of the family and the obligations it entails, the nature of friendship, the way in which the multitude of social roles is defined), and, perhaps most important, the assumptions inculcated about how life's activities should and should not be conducted.

To Clyde Kluckhohn, culture is fundamentally a property of information, a grammar for organizing reality, for imparting meaning to the world. "Culture," he posits, "consists in patterned ways of thinking, feeling and reaction, acquired and transmitted mainly by symbols, constituting the distinctive achievements of human groups, including their embodiments in artifacts; the essential core of culture consists of traditional (i.e., historically derived and selected) ideas and especially their attached values."[2] Humankind can be thought of as displaying a rich selection of physical hardware. We come in a variety of shapes, sizes, and shades, but our capacities and potentialities are astonishingly similar. It is the programming of the human system, the "software," that translates potential into actuality, converting the American ideals of freedom, individuality, and migration into an inanimate object like a mobile home.

Human software, then, is made up of ideas, meanings, conventions, and assumptions. It molds our perceptions, so that where the city dweller sees only sand, the nomad picks up a host of clues about the nature of the terrain, the presence of wildlife, the weather, the availability of pasture, and the proximity of other tribes. It structures our ideas, so that one group sees work as the fulfillment of human destiny while another sees it as a curse. It shapes our actions, defining the rules of interaction for meeting, parting, bestowing hospitality, trading, begging, giving, and negotiating. Whereas artifacts and buildings are observable, the substructure of principles that underpins thought and behavior is less accessible to the casual observer. Because most social interaction takes place within, rather than among, cultures, we usually take all those assumptions and conventions for granted or assume they are of universal validity. "Surely," we tell ourselves in the West, "all men and women are self-evidently created equal." What a shock to discover societies dominated by caste, social class, or stratification on ethnic or sexist grounds!

Finally, it is worth remarking that a society's conduct of government and politics can hardly be supposed to lie beyond the scope of culture. I refer here not so much to the outward form of institutions established to govern—and often copied from national role models, such as the British Parliament or the U.S. Congress—but to the substance of political behavior. After all, communist states

have parties, national assemblies, and constitutions. More consequential are such factors as the prevalence of bribery, the ethics of
public officials, the real basis upon which representatives serve (to
promote the interests of a constituency, clan, or ethnic group), how
fresh blood is brought into the system (by co-optation, family ties,
success in business, or military record), models of patron-client relations, expectations of leadership, acceptance or rejection of the
adversarial system, and so on. Political culture, in brief, cannot be
understood in isolation from the wider culture, and it is a pity that
this artificial distinction has become widely accepted.

Problems of intercultural relations

It is not, however, the influence of culture on politics or diplomacy
as such that concerns us here. The emphasis of this book is not on
culture as a determinant of negotiating behavior—it is simply one
of a whole range of relevant variables—but of the effect on bilateral negotiation of the cultural gap between the negotiating parties. The problem is one of relative, not absolute, values. Of interest is the chemistry of the combination: what happens when
culturally dissonant traits react with each other? Take the concept
of "face," a prominent feature of both Chinese and Japanese cultures. In a Sino-Japanese negotiation, therefore, misunderstanding based on disparate assumptions about face is unlikely to loom
large.[3] Not so in a Sino-American negotiation, however, where the
relative gap is much wider. Although the need for saving face is
more or less appreciated in the West, the equal imperative in transactions with China of honoring or giving face is almost certainly
less familiar.[4]

A growing literature in the social sciences suggests that intercultural communication may be strongly influenced, and even hindered on occasion, by the confrontation of disparate assumptions,
not only about the role of language and nonverbal gestures, but
also about the nature and value of social relationships.[5] Unencumbered discourse, it is argued, rests on the interlocutors' possession
of a complex and extensive body of shared knowledge, conscious
and unconscious, of what is right and fitting in human communication and contact. When this knowledge is absent, inadvertent
confusion may result. Many aspects of cross-cultural activity have
been helpfully illuminated by this approach. The use of cross-
cultural insights and findings in eminently applied fields such as

medicine, psychiatry, education, social work, and marketing suggests that the perspective is of more than purely academic interest. Of particular relevance for our purposes are studies confirming the effect of cultural differences on business negotiations.[6]

In recent years there have also been a number of suggestive applications of the intercultural communication approach to the field of international negotiation. One application has taken the form of the detailed, historical case study. Marie Strazar examined the effect of cross-cultural elements in the negotiation of the 1951 San Francisco peace treaty between the United States and Japan. Her conclusion was that an important contribution to the success of the talks was made in this particular situation by the complementarity of cultural traits. The willingness of the Japanese to adjust uncomplainingly to their surroundings, an acceptance of hierarchy in social life, and familiarity with dependency (*amae*) relationships proved compatible, she argued, with the optimistic and manipulative American approach to nature, egalitarianism in relationships, and readiness to accept a role of responsible leadership.[7]

Another noteworthy case study was Hiroshi Kimura's analysis of the Soviet-Japanese fisheries talks held in Moscow in 1977. He argued that it was not just the objective intractability of the issues involved that weighed on negotiations; the clash of "culturally conditioned patterns of behavior and thought" also complicated matters. Whereas cultural differences acted complementarily in San Francisco, they proved antithetical in Moscow. Japanese status consciousness and acceptance of dependency evoked not indulgence and sympathy but exploitative and brutal treatment by a Soviet Union preoccupied with rank, power relationships, and the establishment of its own superiority.[8]

A second approach to culture and negotiation focuses not so much on the bilateral chemistry of a negotiation as on national negotiating styles taken as subjects of investigation in their own right. Michael Blaker published a good historical study of Japanese negotiating behavior in the twentieth century.[9] Richard Solomon's more conceptual account of Chinese negotiating style, although brief, is also particularly enlightening given the author's practical experience on the National Security Council.[10] Something like Solomon's briefing analysis must surely have been drawn upon by American negotiators. Originally published by the Rand Corporation, Solomon's analysis has also been included in a survey of the negotiating styles of six countries put out by the Foreign Service Institute of the U.S. Department of State.[11]

All these accounts are most useful to the researcher, and probably to the practitioner as well. Their one limitation is their static, one-sided nature compared with bilateral case studies. They tend to overlook the fact that negotiation is a game for more than one player. A comparison of the Strazar and Kimura studies confirms that the same cultural ingredients react differently in the presence of different cultural agents. In short, the nature of the intercultural chemistry depends on the properties of all the participants.

Samuel Lewis, former U.S. ambassador to Israel, has pointed out in this context that Egyptian negotiating behavior varies from region to region. Overbearing in Africa, where they draw on long institutional experience and prestige, Egyptian diplomats tend to deal with other Arabs in a special if superordinate way. Americans and Israelis come in for a quite different treatment.[12] Another former U.S. ambassador, with extensive experience of the Indian subcontinent, confirms the point with respect to India. Domineering in its treatment of small regional partners such as Nepal and Sri Lanka, India has displayed a painful and defensive sensitivity in matters of pride and status in relations with the United States. When one or both of the parties have a strong sense of hierarchy in international affairs, derived from social stratification at home, the relative status of the parties is likely to influence strongly the ambience of negotiations.

Avoiding the usual drawback of the national negotiating style approach, however, is a 1989 analysis of Soviet diplomacy written by a serving diplomat, Raymond F. Smith, who has had extensive hands-on experience of dealing with Soviet negotiators. In a nutshell, Smith argues that Soviet negotiating behavior is marked by three dominant features: preoccupation with authority, avoidance of risk, and imperative need to assert control. These features, he maintains, "provide the context within which specific issues on the table are negotiated, whether the negotiators are two Soviet citizens at the collective market or Soviet and American diplomats in Geneva." He goes on to make the original observation—usually overlooked by negotiating theorists—that negotiating style is not something neutral, like one's putting technique. On the contrary, the clash of negotiating styles between Americans and Russians may even lead talks to "break down in mutual bafflement and anger." Once this point is realized, it may be possible, by studying the differences between the two countries' approaches to diplomacy, to negotiate more effectively in the future.[13]

A third approach to culture and negotiation is provided by Glen

Fisher, a former foreign service officer with a background in social anthropology and sociology. His work is the first (and so far, only) attempt to construct a systematic, theoretical introduction to the subject. The more pronounced the cultural contrasts between the negotiating parties, he argues, the greater the "potential for misunderstanding" and the more time they will lose "talking past each other." Different values, mannerisms, forms of verbal and nonverbal behavior, and notions of status may block confidence and impede communication "even before the substance of negotiation is addressed." Within negotiation itself, he believes, culture impinges on negotiation in four crucial ways: by conditioning one's perception of reality, blocking out information inconsistent or unfamiliar with culturally grounded assumptions, projecting meaning on to the other party's words and actions, and possibly impelling the ethnocentric observer to an incorrect attribution of motive. Fisher compares and contrasts American, French, Japanese, and Mexican assumptions about such issues as the nature of the negotiating encounter; the importance of form, hospitality, and protocol; the choice of delegates; decision-making style; national self-image; methods of persuasion; and linguistic conventions.[14]

Methodology

In this study I have attempted to integrate elements of the case-study, national negotiating style, and conceptual approaches described in the preceding section. Within the loose conceptual framework of a process model of negotiation (preparatory phase, opening moves, intermediate phase, and final rounds), I examine the encounter and interplay of contrasting negotiating styles in the light of detailed historical examples. This historical material was obtained from the reconstruction and analysis of bilateral diplomatic negotiations in the postwar period between the United States and various non-Western states. Where possible, documentary evidence has been drawn upon, but secondary sources and also the autobiographical accounts of participants proved indispensable. When requested, I have withheld the identity of my interviewees. I also refrain from giving the names of past or present State Department officials when to do so might cause embarrassment.

A methodological word of caution: my only criterion for selecting a case was availability of evidence. Any negotiation that could be reconstructed in sufficient detail to bear historical analysis was deemed worthy of inclusion. Obviously the set of cases finally gathered is in no statistical sense representative. It is up to the reader to judge whether my findings are helpful. No exaggerated claim of definitiveness is made for this book. Because the events under investigation were unique historical occurrences, they can never be replicated in the laboratory, nor surrounding circumstances held constant while variables are manipulated. No control group of duplicate negotiations, with only the identity of the parties changed, is available. However, the comparative analysis of case studies can provide the kind of historical variation that the laboratory scientist tries to create artificially. What it cannot achieve is the degree of scientific precision available to the researcher of human behavior under controlled conditions. All it can do is propose more or less convincing explanations of otherwise puzzling phenomena. Still, skepticism should be one's constant companion. Atypical occurrences are to be eschewed and only those tendencies noted that repeat themselves over time, in varying situations involving a changing cast of actors and a repertoire of shifting issues. If a peculiar reaction is observed to recur, even though circumstances and participants change, one is justified in inferring that some underlying process is at work that is a property of the relationship rather than of the situation. In summary, results can be only probable, not certain. There is no pretension here of having uncovered laws of diplomatic behavior; there are simply suggestive tendencies—hypotheses for further research.[15]

In the final analysis, then, there can be no substitute for the skill and discrimination of researchers. Researchers must piece together a conventional narrative of what actually occurred and also attempt to provide a psychological reconstruction of what lay behind the outward train of events. In other words, they must open the clock case and peer into the inner world of the negotiators' perceptions, assessments, and anticipations.

For practical, not ideological, reasons this study takes the United States as the baseline culture against which other cultures are compared and contrasted: the project was funded by an American institution and was largely conducted in Washington; and material on contemporary diplomacy—archival, published, and oral—is much more accessible in the United States than in most other countries. The openness of American public life facilitates political research to a degree hardly found elsewhere. Because I am a citizen of none of the states mentioned in this book (and was obliged to learn about American culture "on the job") I feel that the one sin this study is not guilty of is ethnocentrism or cultural bias!

The partners of the United States in the bilateral negotiations discussed in this study (China, Egypt, India, Japan, and Mexico) were chosen as regional great powers with cultural identities quite distinct from those of the United States and its North Atlantic allies and cultural siblings. For convenience, I call them collectively "non-Western" states. From the outset, the checkered history of their relations with the United States over the years qualified them as potentially rewarding subjects of investigation. My initial plan was to present each relationship in a separate chapter. Unexpectedly, as my research progressed, the cultural dissonances that have marked U.S. negotiations with one or another of the five states were observed to recur with others as well. It turned out that shared cross-cultural contrasts underpinned the United States' diplomatic dealings across the board. Without ignoring individual variants, therefore, I decided in the end that it would be most interesting to weave my material together into an integrated narrative.

An "international diplomatic culture"?

One final objection to be addressed is the argument that although culture undeniably affects the customs and habits of society at the grass roots level, it does not necessarily influence the behavior of the foreign service. Highly educated and well traveled, should not diplomats, irrespective of their countries of origin, be considered members of an international diplomatic community with its own distinctive subculture? Indeed, may not diplomats from different countries be more like one other than like the fellow citizens they ostensibly represent?

In proposing precisely this case, William Zartman and Maureen Berman argue that "idiosyncratic differences" can be accommodated within a general model of negotiation. They readily accept that there are "national differences in negotiating behavior" and that culture affects "the perceptions and assumptions of negotiators." However, they maintain that "cultural aspects of communication" are "peripheral to the understanding of the basic negotiating process." They suggest two reasons for this: first, "that negotiation is a universal process, and that cultural differences are simply differences in style and language"; and second, "that by now the world has established an international diplomatic culture that soon socializes its members into similar behavior."[16]

A good argument can probably be made, if not for a single diplomatic culture, then at least for a set of functional cultures governing defined multilateral regimes, such as those concerning ocean issues, telecommunications, the General Agreement on Tariffs and Trade, and so on. When technical experts work together over extended periods, become personally acquainted, and develop a strong stake in the success of their joint endeavors, there is every likelihood that they will indeed acquire a common language, a sense of belonging to a professional fraternity.[17] But it is unclear whether this commonality generally occurs in bilateral negotiation, apart from exceptions such as long-running arms control talks.

Although only empirical research can ultimately resolve the question, there is prima facie support for the effects of cross-cultural dissonance on bilateral ties. Diplomats already quoted, such as Grew, Smith, Lewis, and Fisher, are clearly convinced of such effects from their personal experience. As Robert F. Goheen, former ambassador to India, said in a speech: "There are vast differences in the cultural background of Americans and Indians, which sometimes lead to differing expectations and ways of interpreting experience."[18] Others put it even more strongly.

There are two possible weaknesses in Zartman and Berman's case. One is that they restrict their purview to culture as a static variable rather than consider the intercultural chemistry that occurs when a culture gap opens up between the parties. Another is the equation of culture with national character. While they are right to reject "ridiculous stereotypes," such as inscrutable orientals and haggling Arabs, no serious student of culture would really propose such travesties. But is not the image of the cosmopolitan diplomat, free of all narrow cultural limitations, an equally questionable stereotype? Is the impact of culture really so superficial that it can be removed by a few years' foreign travel?

Why, in spite of their worldliness and expertise, diplomats should be influenced by their cultural backgrounds can be accounted for in various ways. Glen Fisher suggests three possible answers. First, no officials can completely escape the mindset of the parent society; it is too deeply woven by socialization into the warp and weft of their nature. No amount of professional training in later life can wipe away the deep-seated assumptions of childhood. Second, diplomats are not free agents: they cannot stray beyond "the public's tolerable limits of morality or self-image." Were they to do so, they would soon be looking for other work. Finally, it should be emphasized that negotiation is a group activity and therefore subject to cultural norms.[19] We might add that positions evolve within and between various government agencies, and negotiators continually refer to home base for instructions. The idiosyncratic character traits of individual delegates, as Gilbert Winham demonstrates, play much less of a role than is popularly assumed.[20]

An additional, perhaps decisive, consideration is that in the modern world professional diplomats are no longer the only, or even the main, actors in international negotiation. Officials from domestic agencies such as treasury, trade, defense, agriculture, customs, justice, science and technology, drug enforcement, and many others are just as likely to be involved in major or minor negotiating roles in present-day diplomacy. Some doubtless have international experience; many do not. Elected representatives, political appointees, and migrants from the private sector are even less likely to reflect the norms of an international diplomatic culture. When Harold Nicolson was an official in the service of His Majesty's Foreign Office (in the 1920s), diplomacy might have been restricted to a select elite. Those days are long since gone.

three

Intercultural Dissonance
A Theoretical Framework

So far, I have suggested that intercultural negotiation may be prone to misunderstanding. Some initial confirmatory testimony has been offered. But before proceeding to the empirical material that is vital to my case it will be useful to present the reader with a more systematic analysis of intercultural communication suggesting just why dissonance should occur at all. For this purpose I will use a particularly helpful model proposed by Lorand Szalay.[1] With very little modification it can provide a theoretical underpinning for my study. If it is accepted that a communicatory interaction—the exchange of messages, or proposals, to be more exact—lies at the heart of negotiation, then it follows that negotiation can be considered a special case of communication. Hence obstacles to communication in general may constitute hindrances to negotiation in particular.

The Szalay model

Szalay's point of departure is a distinction between the form or code in which a message is sent, and its content or meaning. Modern communication technology, with its mechanical vocabulary (such as "bits" or "packages" of information), may lead to the tempting but misleading conclusion that communication simply involves the transfer of hard, indubitable data—like so many billiard balls—from a sender to a receiver. According to this analogy, the main factor likely to compromise understanding is the physical quality of the message: is reception affected by "noise" on the line? Has part of the message been lost in transmission?

The trouble with this metaphor is that it overlooks the problem of decoding, peeling away the outer husk of a message to reveal its inner meaning. Let us assume that a message has been successfully transmitted at one end and picked up at the other, with no loss of information and no noise to confuse the issue. Is communication now complete? Of course not. Once a message has been physically received, it still has to be comprehended—and comprehension is a matter of psychology, not mechanics. Between human beings, unlike computers or radios, the difficult question is whether the receiver is able to discern the ideas contained within the message, the intention behind the words.

After all, as Szalay points out, "The idea itself does not really travel, only the code; the words, the patterns of sound or print. The meaning that a person attaches to the words received will come from his own mind. His interpretation is determined by his own frame of reference, his ideas, interests, past experiences, etc.—just as much as the meaning of the original message is fundamentally determined by the sender's mind, his frame of reference" (p. 135).

For a message to be correctly understood there must be sufficient similarity, if not identity, between the intention of the sender and the meaning attributed by the receiver. Put another way, the content encoded by the sender must be consistent with the content decoded by the receiver. If the parties involved are able to draw upon similar semantic assumptions, if they both use the same sort of code to convey a certain meaning, then they will be able to communicate successfully with each other. "Since the encoder and the decoder are two separate individuals," Szalay continues, "their reactions are likely to be similar only to the extent that they share experiences, that they have similar frames of reference. The more different they are, the less isomorphism there will be between encoded and decoded content" (p. 136).

Szalay now arrives at a key contention, which is also crucial to my own argument: for there to be real understanding—true communication in the normative sense of the term—the parties engaged must be able to draw upon matching semantic assumptions.

And this ability occurs optimally within the boundaries of a common culture. Because most communication does indeed take place within a given community, this condition usually holds. This is not to say that everyone within a particular culture must possess an identical outlook on life; within any community many factors go into forming an individual's lexicon of subjective meanings. However, intimate acquaintance with a culture presupposes familiarity with a wide range of possible subjective variations—"alternative life-styles"—on the dominant theme.

Within a given society, as any teacher knows, it is hard enough to reach beyond the imaginative constraints of generation and class. How much more difficult to communicate across cultural boundaries, where there is no organic compatibility between the frames of reference and the semantic assumptions of sender and receiver. Cultural strangers can rely on no shared experience of family, church, schooling, community, and country. Their national histories, traditions, and belief systems may or may not concur. When they communicate there can be no guarantee that the meanings encoded by one and decoded by the other are at all related. In Szalay's words: "Cultural meanings are basically subjective meanings shared by members of a particular cultural group. People in each country of the world develop their own particular interests, perceptions, attitudes, and beliefs, which form a characteristic frame of reference within which they organize and interpret their life experiences . . . Different cultural experiences produce different interpretations not shown in conventional dictionaries" (pp. 140–41).

To illustrate the point, Szalay shows how spontaneous word association tests uncover the culturally grounded meanings attached by Americans and Koreans to the word "corruption." For both groups the word has negative connotations. But at a more subtle level the word evokes very different associations to the two sides. For Americans, corruption implies immoral and criminal behavior. For Koreans, Szalay demonstrates, corruption is not considered morally wrong, although they accept that its social consequences are unfortunate. The explanation for this critical distinction lies in differing conceptions of public service. In the United States a civil servant is supposed to be impartial, not to take bribes, and to serve the whole community. In Korea it is accepted that one gives gifts to officials, who have obligations to friends and relatives that take precedence over any abstract duty to society. When Americans and Koreans talk to one other about corruption, therefore, they are unlikely to attach the same range of meanings to the word, even if it is correctly translated. This divergence is not accidental: it is a logical consequence of the different cultural frameworks within which the word is imbedded.

In the area of diplomatic negotiation the potential for dissonance inherent in intercultural communication finds its most sustained expression. Not the simple, unmediated conversation of tourist and local here, but a complex and sustained interchange of proposals over time, overlaid by level after confusing level of interagency consultation, political supervision, and media and legislative oversight. At every stage of negotiations the possibility for misunderstanding exists, whether about the procedure, the content, or the institutional setting. It is a wonder that agreement is ever reached!

Individualistic and interdependent ethoses

To apply and extend the Szalay model to the specific problem of intercultural negotiation between the United States and non-Western societies we have to establish a matrix of cross-cultural antinomies (contradictions) relevant to the diplomatic encounter. A good place to start is the fundamental antithesis hinted at in Szalay's discussion of corruption: that between the individualistic and collectivistic or interdependent ethoses. Geert Hofstede, in his encyclopedic study of the influence of national culture on management, provides considerable evidence to suggest that many aspects of organizational behavior can be grouped ("loaded") around the two poles.[2] Harry Triandis has also written extensively on the dichotomy, demonstrating its practical applicability in training and other contexts.[3]

(I readily admit that the following framework neglects the very considerable differences within the category of interdependent cultures. There is no suggestion that this rather stark, simplified classification has validity outside the context of this analysis. Obviously, in analyzing the various different cultures in their own right one would wish to present a much more variegated and complete picture, while inserting many reservations and glosses. But when American individualistic and non-Western collectivistic impulses confront each other across the negotiating table, there are sufficient recurrent and characteristic dissonances to suggest the existence of a gap about which it is possible and useful to generalize.)

The American stress on individualism is, as Edward Stewart points out, so deeply ingrained that Americans rarely question it.[4] But emphasis on the individual is an exceptional, rather than universally accepted, ethic. Individualism is grounded in the Protestant concept of predestination, which emerged in Northern Europe at the time of the Reformation and assures salvation to a predetermined elect that has been granted the gift of divine grace. Because salvation is assured and unconditional, there is no call for the intercessionary services of a priestly authority. Morally autonomous beings, the chosen individuals need resort only to their own consciences and their personal reading of the Holy Scriptures for guidance to the right and true path.

Individualistic cultures, of which the United States is a paradigm, hold freedom, the development of the individual personality, self-expression, and personal enterprise and achievement as supreme values. Individual rights, not duty to one's family or community, are paramount. Affiliation with a group or enterprise is based on personal choice. Typically, members of individualistic cultures belong to many different groups and associations, each catering to a different facet of life—professional, religious, and recreational. Personal relationships embrace all these areas of activity. Colleagues, friends, and coreligionists all have their separate place in the shifting mosaic of one's life. Mobility is highly prized, and if one social setting loses its enchantment, the individualistic citizen goes elsewhere.

Equality is the prevailing ethic in society and politics. Status is acquired, not inherited. Authority is a function of office and, although respected, may be freely questioned. Rights and duties are defined by law, not ascription. Contract, not custom, prescribes the individual's legal obligation to a given transaction, role, or course of action. Similarly, conflict is resolved through the courts rather than by group opinion or informal methods of conciliation. Litigation is frequent. The adversarial approach to debate, in which both sides plead their cases on an equal basis, marshaling their arguments in a logical and persuasive manner, is ubiquitous in politics, education, business, and indeed wherever opinions differ.

Of course individualism, particularly its encouragement of mobility and personal initiative, proved to be highly functional and adaptive for opening up and developing the United States. Its flexibility and openness also permitted the nation to absorb immigration in a way no collectivistic society, trammeled by hierarchy and tradition, could have. Finally, the economic and political dimensions of individualism (the free market and representative democracy), which were imported from Enlightenment Europe and which were so effective in unlocking the natural resources of the country, have become almost categorical ideological imperatives. Their demonstrable success has convinced Americans of the universal applicability of their way of life and their duty to spread its benefits around the world.

The interdependent ethos, exemplified by the non-Western states examined in this study, reflects quite different assumptions about the relationship between people and society. Its origins are to be sought in the historical predominance of the rural village community (and the need for partnership in harvesting crops or irrigating fields); the primacy of the extended family, clan, or caste; and rigid, stratified forms of social and religious organization. The concept of a personal, unmediated relationship between human being and deity is quite incomprehensible in this context. The collectivistic ethic has the welfare of the group and cooperative endeavor as its guiding themes, and it subordinates individual wishes and desires to that leitmotiv. Indeed, the individual is identified on the basis of group affiliation and individual needs defined in terms of communal interests.

Face (one's standing in the eyes of the group) must be preserved at all costs. Dishonor (the loss of a good name) is a fate worse than death. The honor of one's family has equivalent priority; the family name is sacrosanct. In the face-to-face society, where all transactions are personal and anonymity is not an option, no humiliation is ever forgotten. Because the social disruption caused by loss of face is likely to be severe—in some of these societies the feud is still endemic—elaborate mechanisms have evolved to protect not only one's own face, but also that of others.

Within this system individual freedom is constrained by duties to family and community. Group affiliation is acquired by birth and is not subject to personal preference. One's primary relationships and loyalties, therefore, are inherited, in-group, and often lifelong. The abstract concept of duty to the wider community, let alone government or state, is quite unfamiliar. Law, as some disembodied notion of justice, is meaningless. All decisions are personal decisions made on the basis of group affiliation and past favor. Transactions are conducted not within the protective framework of contract, but on a personal, face-to-face basis. "Frontality," the quality of unmediated contact with another person, is a word aptly applied (originally by the French) to this kind of relationship.

Within the family the authority of the father is unquestioned, and this model of superior-subordinate relations is replicated at all levels of society and politics. Roles are ascribed. Consequently, members of collectivistic societies accept hierarchy as part of the natural order of things and are strongly status conscious. Education fosters not individual autonomy, but respect for tradition and authority. Truth reposes in the traditions of the group and is not to be uncovered by lone intellectual inquiry or the give-and-take of debate. Wisdom and disputation, an essentially Western conjunction, are viewed as antithetical. Actions likely to disrupt group harmony are to be shunned and those that promote it, highly valued. Confrontation is anathema. Conflict is resolved not by resort to formal processes of law, but by mechanisms of communal conciliation, concerned less with abstract principles of absolute justice than with the requirements of continuing harmony.

The contrasting roles of language

The contrast in use of language by Americans and non-Westerners follows directly from the individualism-interdependence dichotomy and has far-reaching implications for intercultural communication. Basing her thesis on Edward T. Hall's famous dichotomy,[5] Stella Ting-Toomey sees interactions across the divide between *low-context* and *high-context* cultures as particularly prone to confusion.[6] While such a model involves simplifications and stark contrasts, it is nevertheless highly suggestive for an understanding of many of the problems that have emerged in U.S.–non-Western negotiations.

High-context communication is associated with key elements in the collectivistic ethic described above: the requirements of maintaining face and group harmony. A high-context culture communicates allusively rather than directly. As important as the explicit content of a message is the context in which it occurs, surrounding nonverbal cues, and hinted-at nuances of meaning. Communally minded persons are vitally concerned about how they will appear to others. There is no more powerful sanction than disapproval. Loss of face (humiliation before the group) is an excruciating penalty to be avoided at all costs. On the other hand, prohibitions tend not to be internalized and may well be evaded if nobody is watch-

ing. For this reason interdependent cultures may also be catego-
rized as shame oriented rather than guilt oriented.

Given the importance of face, the members of collectivistic cultures are highly sensitive to the effect of what they say on others.
Language is a social instrument—a device for preserving and pro-
moting social interests as much as a means for transmitting information. High-context speakers must weigh their words carefully.
They know that whatever they say will be scrutinized and taken to
heart. Face-to-face conversations contain many emollient expressions of respect and courtesy alongside a substantive element rich
in meaning and low in redundancy. Directness and especially contradiction are much disliked. It is hard for speakers in this kind of
culture to deliver a blunt "no." They wish to please their interlocutors, and they prefer inaccuracy and evasion to painful precision.
At the same time, the concern with social effect and not just the
transmission of information results in a propensity for rhetoric
and verbal posturing. Public discourse may be rich in invective, but
nothing personal is meant or perceived in the hyperbole.

It is hard for members of an interdependent culture to deal with
a stranger from outside their circle; great emphasis is placed on
the cultivation of a personal relationship before a frank interchange becomes possible. Timing is also important. Much probing
and small talk precede a request, because a rebuff causes great embarrassment. To an outsider, the high-context individual may appear insincere, suspicious, and devious, but these traits are simply
part of the veneer of courtesy and indirection essential to preserve
social harmony. Nor is mistrust a deviant characteristic but the
manifestation of an ingrained caution required for dealing with
members of other groups. In their own societies, interdependent
people are justifiably receptive to hidden meanings, always on the
alert for subtle hints known from experience to be potentially present in the tone of a conversation and the accompanying facial
expressions and gestures (body language) of their interlocutors.

The low-context culture, exemplified by the United States, reserves a quite different role for language. Very little meaning is
implicit in the context of an articulation. On the contrary, what has
to be said is stated explicitly. Indirection is much disliked.
"Straight-from-the-shoulder" talk is admired. "Get to the point" is
the heartfelt reaction to small talk and evasive formulations.
People have little time or patience for "beating around the bush,"
but wish to get down to business and move on to another problem.
Why waste time on social trivialities? Doing business should not

require the interlocutors to be bosom friends. Clearly, this propensity is associated with individualistic people's relative freedom from group constraints and niceties, and their ability to distinguish between professional and social role-playing.

Language, then, performs on the whole an informational rather than socially lubricative function. Accuracy (the "truth ethic") is the highest virtue. Politeness is obviously not precluded, but low-context culture hardly sees the need for contrived formulas and verbal embellishments. Contradiction is not felt to be offensive. The reverse is the case, because society flourishes on debate, persuasion, and the hard sell. Subtlety and allusiveness in speech, if grasped at all, serve little purpose. Nor does face possess the crucial importance it has for the high-context culture. An internalized sense of responsibility rather than a concern with outward appearances is the rule. Guilt, not shame, is the psychological price paid for misdemeanor. One is therefore less sensitive to what others say; little importance is attached to hint and allusion. Suspiciousness and an excessive preoccupation with hidden meanings are seen as morbid. Nonverbal gestures are paid little attention. In public discourse, although there are variant traditions, language remains factual and intended to inform, not impress. Content is taken seriously and rhetoric found tedious. Invective is less easily dismissed as so much hot air.

Monochronic versus polychronic concepts of time

Time is crucial in diplomacy. Major tactical and strategic judgments hang on assumptions about history, ripeness, timing, tempo, and duration. Preparing for a negotiation, one might ask such questions as these about the opponents: How heavy does historical grievance weigh on relationships? How important to them are short-range considerations versus long-range considerations? Indeed, to what extent do they plan for the future? Do they keep appointments diaries? Is punctuality important to them? What are their models of the future—better, more of the same, teleological, or cyclical? How do they perceive time—as a road stretching off purposefully into the future, or as an ocean lapping in on all sides, directionless? Is "time on their side"? Do they see it as a sequence or a confluence? At what point should a negotiation be initiated? When do they consider a dispute ripe for resolution? When do they think proposals should be made and at what tempo should concessions be offered, if at all? How patient are they? Can they postpone agreement, and if so, for how long? Do they consider the expeditious treatment of business desirable or undesirable? What do they believe is the optimal point at which to make their truly final offer? What, in fact, is the "end" for them—or the "beginning," for that matter?

Traditional societies have all the time in the world. The arbitrary divisions of the clock face have little saliency for cultures grounded in the cycle of the seasons, the invariant pattern of rural life, and the calendar of religious festivities. For peasants, work begins at sunup, when they walk out to their fields, and it continues until sundown, when they trudge their weary way home. Nature, not human will, determines their day; every task—plowing, sowing, reaping—has its due season. Timeliness is measured by days and weeks, not hours and minutes (let alone seconds). Personal encounters are not ruled by mechanical schedules; no conceivable activity could be more pressing or important than human contact. Steadiness, not haste, is the cardinal virtue. What has to be done will get done in the end. And in the overall scheme of things, where the individual counts for so little in the face of much greater, inexorable forces, what could be more futile than urgency?

In some areas of the United States this more leisurely approach to time can still be found, but in the modern metropolis quite different habits prevail. These days even industrialized agriculture demands as rigorous a production schedule as the factory. From the womb of individual freedom and endeavor has emerged a society governed by a ruthless taskmaster—the clock. The posttraditional, corporate person is at its service, his or her day segmented into tasks. The ticking of one's wristwatch regulates all work, play, family life, and social life. Even a meeting between friends is measured and limited by the imperatives of one's diary. "Time is money," a quantifiable commodity to be allotted with miserly pedantry. In an individualistic culture like the United States, grounded in personal fulfillment and the work ethic, "getting things done" is the prevailing value, and life is a treadmill of achievement.

Schedules and deadlines loom over everything. "Once set," Edward T. Hall writes about the American approach to time, "the schedule is almost sacred, so that not only is it wrong, according to the formal dictates of our culture, to be late, but it is a violation of the informal patterns to keep changing schedules or appointments or to deviate from the agenda." Enlarging on the latter point, Hall

suggests that American negotiators set particular stock by the arrangement of an agenda and are thrown off balance by a less meticulous negotiating partner.[7] He also contrasts the related American monochronic assumption that it is better to deal with one thing
and one person at a time, with the non-Western polychronic willingness to handle several tasks in parallel. Just as the latter habit
may be unnatural and annoying to Americans, the need to plan
everything ahead of time may appear very peculiar to the non-
Westerner.

Alongside this regimentation of the present, Hall draws attention to features of the American attitude to history that are quite
different from those found in collectivistic (and indeed almost all
other) cultures. The United States—to state the obvious—is not a
traditional society. Americans, as any visitor to Williamsburg dis-
cerns, take great pride in their past. But it is a past recreated com-
fortably, in the image of the present. The slave cabins are absent
from the spotless lanes of Williamsburg. It is an aesthetic past, not
a burning weight of bitterness. Traditions tend to be contemporary.
If the past obstructs progress, it is to be discarded. Tomorrow is
more important. Americans, Hall comments, "are oriented almost
entirely toward the future. We like new things and are preoccupied
with change. We want to know how to overcome resistance to
change."[8]

Americans, then, are mostly concerned with addressing immediate issues and moving on to new challenges, and they display
little interest in (and sometimes little knowledge of) history. The
idea that something that occurred hundreds of years ago might be
relevant to a pressing problem is almost incomprehensible. A sense
of history is in no way a qualification for public service. In marked
contrast, the representatives of non-Western societies possess a
pervasive sense of the past. They are likely to harbor long memories of their treatment at the hands of the United States and the
West in general. This preoccupation with history, deeply rooted in
the consciousness of traditional societies, cannot fail to influence
diplomacy. Past humiliations for these societies (which are highly
sensitive to any slight on their reputations) are not consigned to
the archives but continue to nourish present concerns. To anticipate one of my findings, American diplomats are often astonished
at what seems to be the inappropriate and irrelevant obsession of
others with "ancient" history. Mexicans, for example, never let
American diplomats forget Mexico's loss of its northern territories
in the nineteenth century, and subsequent cases of U.S. interven-

tion. Chinese, Egyptian, Indian, and Japanese negotiators are also highly conscious of the racist and imperialist outrages to which their countries were subject in the colonial era.

In American society, with its diaries and timetables, the business of government is a regimented affair. Monochronism reigns supreme. Despite the concern of the White House and Congress with public relations, there is often disregard for the messages time conveys. In 1989 the *New York Times* published a telling photograph showing President Mitterrand of France seated at a podium, having just finished reading a statement at the conclusion of a summit conference. At his side President Bush has just sprung to his feet and is anxiously eyeing his wristwatch.[9] Time beckons; on to the next capital. If it's Tuesday, it must be Bonn. A few extra moments would have made for a more graceful parting.

Low-context versus high-context negotiating styles

The cultural, linguistic, and temporal dichotomies described above can be seen to generate two quite different negotiating ethoses, both at the conceptual and practical levels: the low-context (individualistic) and the high-context (interdependent-collectivistic) styles. As I have argued at length, unhindered communication rests on the sender and receiver possessing matching assumptions. Exactly the same principle applies to unhindered negotiation: negotiation proposals are simply a special case of communicated messages.

Just what obstacles have actually hindered negotiation will be discussed in the following chapters. But first, it will help to point out the characteristic feature of the American approach to negotiating that most distinguishes it from others. Mushakoji Kinhide, a noted Japanese political scientist, believes that the basic incompatibility between American and Japanese negotiators (which he, like many other Japanese observers, takes to be virtually axiomatic) derives from a fundamental philosophical difference in views about the relationship between humans and their environment. The American *erabi* (roughly, "manipulative," can-do, or choosing) style, he argues, is grounded in the belief that "man can freely manipulate his environment for his own purposes. This view implies a behavioral sequence whereby a person sets his objective, develops a plan designed to reach that objective, and then acts to change the environment in accordance with that plan." Little attention is paid by the *erabi* negotiator, according to Kinhide, to the need to cultivate personal relationships or to special circumstances. Choices are "either-or" and are made on the basis of instrumental or ends-means criteria alone.[10]

In opposition to the can-do spirit stands the Japanese *awase* (roughly, "adaptive") style, which "rejects the idea that man can manipulate the environment and assumes instead that he adjusts himself to it." Oversimplified, dichotomous choices are eschewed. The world is seen as a complex, ambiguous place. Disembodied generalization bows to the imperatives of personal relationships. Subjective factors—the appeal to past obligation and request for present favor—may figure prominently. An *awase* negotiation, therefore, exemplifies the quality of frontality that we have seen to be such an important element of interdependent cultures. Social realities and concrete circumstances loom large. Negotiation is not an end in itself, to be treated in isolation, but simply one episode in an ongoing relationship. The implication is that short-term wisdom may be long-term folly.

Given that Kinhide was particularly addressing himself to U.S.-Japanese relations (and some features of Japan's negotiating behavior are peculiar to that country), the dichotomy he posits between the can-do and adaptive models may be generally applicable to the U.S.–non-Western negotiations examined here.

His characterization of the U.S. negotiating style is certainly consonant not only with the main features of American culture, but also with that ubiquitous pragmatism that Stanley Hoffmann found to be characteristic of U.S. foreign policy. Grounded in the pioneering experience of a young, expanding nation that had taken on and subdued the natural might of a continent, Americans saw every problem, material and social alike, as amenable to an engineering or technological solution. For a society supremely confident of its goals and values—indeed these were self-evident truths—means, not ends, became the focus of attention. In the foreign policy sphere, Hoffmann believes, "political issues tend, first, to be fragmented into components each of which will be susceptible to expert techniques and, second, to be reduced to a set of technical problems that will be handled by instruments which are equipped to deal with material obstacles but much less so to cope with social ones."[11]

Hoffmann's characterization of the American national style is exemplified by the theoretical literature on negotiation produced in the United States. An entire "how to negotiate" literature, the guiding principle of which is instrumental and manipulative, crowds the bookshelves. Howard Raiffa, whose *The Art and Science of Negotiation* is the best of its type, demonstrates how negotiators can break down a problem into its component parts, evaluate the relative costs and benefits of various negotiating options, and arrive at a solution that may maximize the payoffs to both sides.[12] Roger Fisher and William Ury, in their immensely successful *Getting to Yes*, propose a variety of "creative problem-solving" techniques intended to facilitate efficient and expeditious outcomes that will leave everybody better off.[13] Zartman and Berman, emphasizing the distinction central to the manipulative style (and alien to the adaptive approach), ask us to "remember that the problem, not the opponent, is the 'enemy' to be overcome. It is the problem that prevents good and beneficial relations and sours the other party's perception of things (including yourself), so the other party needs help to solve the problem, often against his own will and perception."[14]

Non-Western negotiators, I suspect, might seriously question the order of priorities in this latter contention. They would surely resent the patronizing attitude it reflects. In the following chapters the cross-cultural validity of the can-do, problem-solving paradigm will be put to the test. Is there, in short, a universally applicable model of international negotiation?

four

What Is Negotiable?

Before considering the mechanics of negotiation, it is worth pausing over those issues of status and sovereignty that have proved recalcitrant to diplomacy. The fact that such subjects are particularly loaded for collectivistic societies should come as no surprise in the light of the discussion so far. Inevitably, given American power, U.S. relations with China, Egypt, India, Japan, and Mexico have been marked by greater or lesser degrees of inequality. Although these nations are regionally dominant and possess great pride in their ancient civilizations, they would in many situations be cast in the role of supplicant or dependent. For status-conscious societies such a role possesses resonant implications. A Japan cast adrift by defeat may welcome the security of protection, recognizing in it the familiar and reassuring Japanese *amae* relationship of benefactor and dependent. But an India humiliated by British rule and governed by the elite Brahmin caste may find the prospect of subordination insufferable. Each case, in other words, has its own special features. What is common is the delicacy of the relationship; it requires on the part of the United States great sensitivity and insight. The substance of inequality can be acceptable only if it is disguised by the outward forms of equality.

But where, the reader may wonder, does cross-cultural dissonance enter the picture? Is the United States not equally sensitive to issues of pride and sovereignty? It is true that the United States has taken immense pride in being "number one" in the postwar

33

world and has displayed resentment at such perceived intrusions as Japanese real estate purchases. However, compared with the inordinate sensitivity of its collectivistic partners on these matters, the United States is relatively relaxed. It has attached great importance to military capability but not to the outward trappings of prestige for its own sake. No, the main source of dissonance lies elsewhere—in the American belief (to quote the title of a bestselling book on negotiation) that "you can negotiate anything." [1] The fact is that, in international relations, you cannot. To believe otherwise is a recipe for disappointment. McGeorge Bundy, a national security adviser in the 1960s, criticized President Johnson for precisely this culture-bound illusion. "Johnson treated Third World leaders like Senators," Bundy later observed. "He presumed that they were all reasonable men who could be persuaded to compromise on almost any issue if the right combination of threats and incentives was employed." [2]

Pride and status

The major obstacle to negotiation may lie, then, not in some vagary of the negotiating process, but in the inability of the parties to get to the bargaining table at all or, once there, to get down to serious negotiating. This inability may simply arise from a hard-nosed calculation that no benefit is to be gained from negotiation. On the other hand, in a number of cases investigated during this study, negotiations failed to get off the ground for more subjective reasons.

Indian pride, my sources agreed, has long hobbled relations with the United States. Time and again Indian diplomats and leaders took umbrage at real or imagined insults to their national dignity. On his visit to the United States in October 1949, Prime Minister Nehru of India found President Truman "indifferent and condescending." [3] Writing in November 1954, U.S. ambassador George Allen commented on the Indian "inferiority complex" as a hindrance to an air transport accord. [4] A similarly harsh judgment about the psychological difficulty some Indians have to this day in dealing with Americans was repeated to me by current U.S. Foreign Service officers. One suggested that Indians walk round with a "chip on their shoulder" and suffer from a melancholia derived from the thought that the world is looking down on them. Another identified a "Krishna Menon syndrome" (after the prickly Indian foreign and defense minister) compounded of a mixture of arrogance and hypersensitivity and found in certain quarters (by no means all) of the Indian foreign ministry from junior official to minister. A perceived imputation on their intellectual ability, any sign of arrogance or superiority, would produce an explosion.

None of the other relationships examined here reflected quite this intensity of psychological resentment, but a concern that the outer trappings of equality be meticulously respected was ubiquitous. When the United States intercepted an Egyptian airliner carrying suspected PLO (Palestine Liberation Organization) terrorists over the Mediterranean in October 1985, old sensitivities were stirred up. President Mubarak talked of an injury to "the pride of every single Egyptian." Memories of the British occupation flooded to the surface. "We are a nation of over 40 million, with 7,000 years of history behind us, not a bunch of 'coolies' to be pushed around by colonial masters," remarked an *Al Ahram* newspaper commentator to an Israeli journalist. "Don't think that because we are a poor country we are not a proud country. Even if we starve, our national pride will not be for sale."[5]

Since the restoration of diplomatic relations in 1974, American officials in Cairo have been well briefed on Egyptian sensitivities. It was not always so. After the 1967 Arab-Israeli war, prospects of negotiation hinged on the restoration of Egypt's shattered pride. Yet Mohamed Riad, who was Egyptian foreign minister at the time, recalls that Secretary of State Rogers cautioned one Egyptian diplomat not to "forget that you have lost the war and therefore have to pay the price."[6] In contrast, the breakthrough in U.S.-Egyptian relations following the 1973 October war was facilitated by Secretary of State Kissinger's grasp of the need to establish President Sadat's status as an equal. At their very first meeting Kissinger did so by first addressing Egypt's military achievements in the recent war. The Egyptian president, it was implied, "was not negotiating from weakness; he was not a supplicant; he had earned Egypt's right at the conference table; he had, in short, restored Egypt's honor and self respect."[7]

China has been quite explicit in its demand for equal treatment in relations with the United States, a desire fueled by recollections of the unequal treaties foisted on it during the nineteenth century and heightened by exclusion from a seat in the United Nations Security Council in the 1950s and 1960s. Pointing out this back-

ground, Kenneth Young rightly notes that "a century of humiliation at the hands of the Western powers, including Russia, has
made the 'Central Country' unusually sensitive to slighting and dis-
respectful treatment."[8] In 1954–55, U.S. acceptance of the "principle of equality and reciprocity" was a fundamental Chinese condition for the repatriation of American civilians held in China after
the revolution, even though Chinese citizens were free to leave the
United States at any time (most did not wish to).[9] In February 1970,
on the eve of the breakthrough in Sino-American relations after a
generation of dislocation, China made it known through the good
offices of Pakistan that it was prepared to accept a U.S. envoy. The
vital proviso was added that "they would, however, be upset if the
United States were to give the impression that Chinese overtures
derived from weakness or from fear." Kissinger immediately
passed on the desired assurance.[10]

The Mexican sense of pride and honor is rightly famed and
close to the surface in any dealing with the "colossus to the north."
In the case of Mexico, injuries to national pride are all placed at
the door of the United States. Old wars, interventions, and occu-
pations are recalled with ever-fresh bitterness. The upshot is that
virtually every negotiation becomes a test of national honor. Offended pride has prevented or aborted negotiations in the past:
postwar civil aviation negotiations failed for this reason. "We have
failed," wrote a high State Department official in 1950, "to appreciate and understand Mexico's desire to be treated on a basis of
equality."[11] However, although Mexican sensitivity remains, most
American diplomats are conscious of the problem. (Congressmen
and political appointees tend to be another matter—unless, that is,
they come from Texas!) Former ambassador John Jova (1974–77)
told me that he had always borne the need to avoid "humiliating
them" in mind. Any issue might trigger a sense of offended pride.
Public criticism was fatal.[12] Unfortunately, the press and Congress
pick on Mexico all too often as the whipping boy for the drug problem and illegal immigration. Nor did President Reagan's appointed
ambassador, John Gavin, endear himself to his hosts with his pro-
consular propensity to preach. Such criticism is not calculated to
elicit cooperation; quite the reverse, in fact.

Among the cases considered here, Japan's has quite unique features by virtue of its defeat and occupation at the hands of the
United States. Like other collectivistic cultures, Japan has viewed
the international community, by analogy with domestic society, in

hierarchical terms. Confirming this basic point, Kano Tsutomu perceives a national preoccupation with Japan's ranking in the world pecking order, which goes together with "hypersensitivity about international reputation and image." He argues that, as a consequence, the search for national identity has been a "traumatic experience." Shocked out of centuries of self-imposed international isolation by the arrival of Commodore Perry, uninvited, in the Bay of Yedo in 1853, Japan "became plagued with a strong sense of inferiority regarding the West." Once an unparalleled national effort at modernization had raised Japan to the ranks of the great powers, it then acquired a sense of superiority toward its Asian neighbors.[13]

After 1945 Japan, typically, *adapted* itself (a key cultural term) to defeat and "accepted the fact that they had been put into a secondary position in the world."[14] For years Japan was content to accept, at the international level, a relationship of guardian and ward vis-à-vis the United States (without necessarily agreeing on what this relationship implied). But the unequal provisions of the 1951 security treaty were rapidly overtaken by events as Japan recovered its economic strength and national self-confidence. Revision of the treaty so that it reflected, at least in form, an appearance of mutuality became vital to the preservation of the alliance. This revision was successfully carried out in 1960. Even then, unprecedented public emotion in Japan over the issue resulted in the last-minute cancellation of a visit by President Eisenhower and the resignation of the Japanese prime minister.[15]

Culturally grounded differences about the obligations imposed on the two sides by the partnership were at the root of another traumatic episode in postwar U.S.-Japanese relations, the notorious "Nixon shock" of 1971, when the decision of the American president to visit Beijing was announced without prior consultation with Japan. Observers believe that long-term damage was done to the relationship by this episode—which was, it should be stressed, one of form, not substance. Japan was unquestionably the major ally of the United States in the Far East; the implications of the American breakthrough to communist China would be momentous for Tokyo. But the worst feature of the American omission was its disregard for the outward form of the relationship. Was this the way to treat a partner? For Prime Minister Sato the episode was a public humiliation. Moreover, it could not fail to be interpreted "as evidence that the United States placed a low value on its relationship with Japan as a whole." It also made it more difficult politically for Japanese negotiators to make concessions in economic talks then in progress.[16]

Even Dr. Kissinger, in his memoirs, acknowledges the costly error:

> I believe in retrospect that we could have chosen a more sensitive method of informing the Japanese . . . It would have surely been more courteous and thoughtful, for example, to send one of my associates from the Peking trip to Tokyo to brief Sato a few hours before the official announcement. This would have combined secrecy with a demonstration of special consideration for a good and decent friend.[17]

Sovereignty

Culture is expressed not only in the way a society sets about ordering its existence, but also in the structuring of its priorities, that is, the goals or values it seeks to promote or defend. This structuring crucially determines what a society is or is not prepared to negotiate about. Each of the countries studied had its own area of inviolability—issues it was unhappy to discuss and which, if discussed, proved invariably contentious. For a culturally dominant power like the United States, whose movies are shown all over the world, Culture is not something to be protective about. Quite the reverse; Americans thirst for color and innovation. Not so for societies that fear that their traditional way of life is under attack from "modern" values (which are usually identified with the United States). An otherwise innocuous project may become the focus for acute controversy the moment it is branded an "instrument of American cultural imperialism."

Differing conceptions of history also have a profound effect on relations. Tainted by association with past episodes of perceived injustice, which still rankle for traditionalist societies, certain topics come to symbolize the national sense of wounded pride and resentment. It takes little to stir up such historical hornets' nests. For a future-oriented society like the United States, such preoccupation with the past seems irrational, even pathological.

Egypt's sore spot has been anything suggesting a restoration of a foreign military presence, with its evocations of the colonial experience. True, after the World Bank refusal in 1956 to finance the Aswan Dam project, and the Anglo-French-Israeli invasion, Egypt found itself drawn into a close military relationship with the Soviet Union, including hosting Soviet bases. It felt it had little choice, in the circumstances. But in the end the Soviet Union was to pay dearly for treating Egypt as a virtual colonial possession. At any rate, a series of attempts by the West in the early 1950s to bring Egypt into the Western alliance system was abortive. In 1951 Egypt was invited by Britain, the United States, France, and Turkey to participate in a Middle East command and to provide "facilities on her soil," a euphemism for base rights. Egypt rejected the proposal within two days.[18] Again in 1952 an Egyptian military mission visited Washington to discuss Egyptian arms requirements. The American proposal to link aid to an anti-Soviet Islamic military pact, the Middle East Defense Organization (which, among other things, would back a Moslem fifth column within the Soviet Union) shocked the Egyptians, and the talks ran aground. Conditions of another kind aborted military aid negotiations in 1954. The American requirement that U.S. arms be accompanied by a U.S. military assistance advisory group to ensure their proper use was quite unacceptable to Egypt. Prime Minister Nasser of Egypt spelled out his country's objections to American terms for assistance:

> Because of our history we have complexes in this country about some words—especially those that imply that we are being tied to another country. Words like "joint command," "joint pact," and "training missions" are not beloved in our country because we have suffered from them . . . I think your men who deal with this area should understand the psychology of the area. You send military aid, but if you send ten officers along with it, nobody will thank you for your aid but instead will turn it against you.[19]

By the 1980s circumstances had clearly changed and the rawness of the colonialist wound had somewhat eased. The fall of the Shah of Iran in 1979 and associated events rendered a military association with the United States more acceptable—provided it was based on the appearance of full equality and did not involve a massive, high-profile U.S. military presence. But old lessons had to be relearned in the Ras Banas affair. In the period of anxiety following the Soviet invasion of Afghanistan, the idea of a U.S. "facility" on a peninsula jutting into the Red Sea opposite Saudi Arabia was conceived of as a contribution to the rapid deployment force. The camp would have consisted of an airstrip, warehouses for the pre-positioning of materiel, and some residential quarters. Strangely enough, the initial suggestion came from President

Sadat, who was interested in cementing an anticommunist strategic alignment with the United States.

Accepted enthusiastically by Secretary of State Haig and the U.S. Air Force, the suggestion was viewed with foreboding by the State Department. Typically, Sadat had not thought through the details of his grand gesture, envisaging the camp not as a massive base coming under American control, but rather as something much less extensive and controversial, a more modest Egyptian depot or facility put at American disposal—ostensibly quite a different thing. A great deal hung on the terminology and on the way the camp could be presented to the Egyptian military and public opinion. A base would be unacceptable, evoking memories of the British, and then the Soviet, presence. A facility under Egyptian control would not be perceived as an intrusion on sovereignty. On the contrary, an arrangement of mutual benefit freely entered into would enhance, not detract from, Egyptian status.

Regrettably, the Pentagon either failed to grasp, or was insufficiently flexible to meet, Egyptian requirements. Much of the subsequent negotiation concerned such loaded issues as the U.S. military demands for uniformed Americans to be permanently stationed at the site, a transit facility at the port of Alexandria, and an extraterritorial road to Ras Banas. All these proposals were viewed with grave suspicion by the Egyptian Army. As the negotiations proceeded, obstacles piled up: although Egypt wished to handle construction and payments, funds appropriated by Congress for military construction purposes legally entailed the use of the U.S. Army Corps of Engineers; and even if the United States gave up its request for an American troop presence, a stockpile of degradable aviation fuel necessitated the presence of trained technicians.

Finally, after negotiations on the original scheme had ended in deadlock, agreement seemed to have been reached on a significantly scaled-back effort. There would have been an emergency "pass-through" facility involving minimal pre-positioning. But when a thick U.S. Army Corps of Engineers specifications manual asking for bids from contractors thudded on his desk, President Mubarak called it a day. To overcome national sensitivities demanded a lighter touch than this.[20]

For Japan the question of the Okinawa bases encapsulated two resonant themes: lost territories and nuclear weapons. The "particular potency," as Dr. Kissinger puts it, of the nuclear issue "in the land of Hiroshima and Nagasaki" need hardly be stressed.

Occupied by the United States long after the military administration of the main islands had ended, Okinawa was considered one of the most important American bases in Asia. It was also a storage site for nuclear weapons, although these were not permitted on U.S. bases in Japan proper.[21]

When the demand was raised in Japan in the mid-1960s for the reversion of Okinawa to Japanese sovereignty, all the ingredients seemed to be at hand for a first-rate diplomatic crisis. In Japan itself the issue became a focus of intense national sentiment. The first reaction of the Joint Chiefs of Staff was that conceding to Japanese requests would threaten vital American security interests. Fortunately, it was eventually realized in Washington that the basic issue was nonnegotiable and that U.S. obduracy would simply threaten the whole future of the alliance. Either Japanese wishes might be conceded with good grace or the United States could look forward to the unhappy prospect of a replay of the anti-American rioting that had forced the abandonment of the 1960 Eisenhower visit. President Nixon decided to bow to reality. By agreeing to restore Japanese rights over Okinawa and accepting "the particular sentiment of the Japanese people against nuclear weapons," he succeeded in preserving both the alliance and the bases.[22]

If a Japan chastened by defeat and ruin had made a virtue of necessity and fully aligned itself with the West in the postwar world, India—like Egypt of the 1950s and 1960s—resolutely set its face against such a course. The policy of nonalignment, defined as India's right to determine its foreign policy orientation freely and without duress, became sacrosanct. After all, Indian forces had fought and died in two world wars without even being consulted on the decision to go to war. Not only was alignment in the Cold War rejected, but fierce opposition was consistently expressed to anything that smacked of limiting Indian sovereignty. Even apparently secondary restrictions, such as conditions on the receipt and distribution of aid or the end use of U.S. technology, were taken as implying American trespass on Indian domestic prerogatives. However, in time of dire need India has overcome its distaste and displayed considerable pragmatism in negotiations. Growing interest in Western technology and a more market-oriented approach to economic development in the 1980s have also blunted the sharp edges of Indian concerns.

India's first crisis of conscience in relations with the United States came in 1951 at a time of famine in India and a desperate need for grain. From the beginning Nehru was far from "happy about accepting favors from the U.S." and "agreed to request food aid only because he could see no other way for India to surmount the crisis." Even so, he and his colleagues were distraught when the U.S. Congress conditioned assistance on the despatch of a mission to observe the distribution of the grain and to supervise the disbursement of counterpart funds (U.S. funds held in India in the local currency, to be spent in a way agreed upon by the two governments—in this particular case, Indian development projects). In a defiant speech Nehru rejected help with "political strings attached" as "unbecoming for a self-respecting nation." But in the end he found himself with no choice.[23]

What was to become a question of perennial concern, namely, the end use of materials and technology, first arose two years later when the U.S. government was upset to discover that India was selling thorium nitrate to the People's Republic of China. Under American law, a recipient of U.S. aid could not export this product, which has nuclear applications, to a communist country. Although this provision was not put in writing in 1951, the Indians had been officially informed of it. When Ambassador Allen brought the matter to the attention of the Indian minister of finance, the latter denied that India had ever requested U.S. aid. Then followed long and fruitless American attempts to persuade India to accept some kind of formal commitment to restrict its trade with communist countries if it were to continue to receive assistance. In an amazing scene, Allen asked Prime Minister Nehru whether the Indian government would be at least prepared to inform Washington in advance of future decisions to ship strategic commodities to barred areas. The prime minister wrapped himself in a proud and eloquent silence; he was not even prepared to answer the question. "Nehru," Allen reported home, "stared at the ceiling for a full minute, smiled, turned to Ambassador Donovan, who was present, and asked if he had ever been to Thailand before."[24]

During the 1962 emergency, with Indian and Chinese forces fighting along their common border, India had no alternative but to modify its nonalignment principles and accept military assistance from the West. It also agreed to American legal requirements for inspection of the use to which the arms were put. India went so far as to request U.S. transport aircraft with pilots and crews. But when Ambassador Galbraith decided to press the government of India "to promise a more cooperative role elsewhere" the effort failed. Sensing that they were being drawn into a "virtual alliance," the Indians retreated.[25]

In recent years the end use question has emerged as a central issue in U.S.-Indian diplomacy. Talks in 1981–82 on the supply of nuclear fuel to the Indian reactor at Tarapur were complicated by American demands for externally imposed constraints on the disposal of spent material. Looking back, Ambassador Goheen believed that American negotiators had been excessively optimistic about the possibility of the Indian government accepting the limitations of a safeguards regime (presumably nobody had bothered to look up the thorium nitrate case). President Carter was particularly slow to appreciate the intractability of the problem. Eventually, however, an agreement was concluded based on the supply of French, not American, nuclear fuel.[26] Moreover, in later negotiations for the supply of a U.S. supercomputer to India, the government of India, under pressure from its own scientific community, did concede more far-reaching safeguards on end use than ever before.

Despite—or perhaps because of—its propinquity to the United States and the enormous range of issues of mutual concern, Mexico has tenaciously sought to defend its sovereignty and independence from its great neighbor. It was the only Latin American country to refuse to sign a military assistance agreement with the United States. Washington's request in 1948 for permission to use Mexican territorial waters for defense purposes was turned down on the spot. More recently, Mexico has declined to allow U.S. Drug Enforcement Agency planes to overfly northern Mexico to spot landing strips used for drug sorties. Mexico has also rejected direct economic aid, for fear of becoming politically beholden. In 1978 it went so far as to rebuff a modest offer of aid for hurricane damage. Ambassador Patrick Lucey pleaded with the Mexican foreign minister to be allowed to help, but to no avail. Mexico has never even accepted Peace Corps volunteers under the Alliance for Progress. In all these and innumerable other cases, Mexico has refused to become involved in any arrangement that might be perceived to detract from its independence.[27]

On technical issues not perceived to touch on symbolic questions of sovereignty or evoke unfortunate historical associations, my sources were unanimous in praise of Mexican pragmatism. Indeed Mexico has sometimes preferred to keep issues at a technical rather than a political level, precisely in order to extract them from the emotive context of national pride. The trouble here is that Mexico and the United States have not always been able to agree on where the dividing line runs between politics and economics.

Whenever the United States has failed to grasp the highly political nature of what seemed to be simply a technical issue, it has faced frustration. Since 1938, when Mexico nationalized the oil industry and expropriated powerful U.S. companies in the process, oil has been a symbol of national pride and independence—part of the patrimony. Thus it was futile in the 1940s for the United States to make loans for the development of Mexican petroleum resources conditional on the return of private U.S. interests. "While the matter should be one of economics," a report for President Truman ruefully noted, "it has become primarily a political issue."[28] Time and again U.S. economic rationality has confronted a quite different Mexican logic.

Human rights

Where human rights are concerned, it may be American susceptibilities that are overlooked or underestimated by other cultures. It is not, one hastens to add, that only the West has discovered the Just and the Good; rather that the concept of human rights is taken by the United States to be synonymous with Western notions of individualism and legalism. Moreover, human rights activism (political action to affect human rights beyond national boundaries) is a particularly North American and North European preoccupation. Many other societies bitterly resent such activity both as interference in internal affairs and as reflecting a holier-than-thou attitude.

In a sustained critique of the International Bill of Human Rights, Surya Prakash Sinha excoriates it for ignoring "civilizational pluralism." As it stands, he argues, it reflects values and assumptions that simply do not apply universally. "Techniques of the West and even its life styles have been adopted by the world in varying degrees. Nevertheless, there continue to exist various value systems among various peoples of the world, manifesting different approaches to human emancipation."[29]

The bill, he continues, regards "the individual as the fundamental unit of society and the nuclear family as its fundamental group unit. This is an eloquent expression of individualism, which is fine. But the provisions stop there. They do not go any further in taking an adequate account of, say: the hierarchical family of China or Japan; the Hindu joint-family; or . . . African lineage and kinship systems . . ." For example, the bill defines the choice of marriage

partner in utterly culture-bound terms; its provision that marriage
be based on the consent of the partners can apply only in societies
where young men and women mix freely. It is meaningless in village communities, such as in India, where free association between
the sexes is deplored and marriage is arranged by the families.[30]
Sinha brings many other examples of this kind to demonstrate his
case. Other areas of the bill that reflect ethnocentric assumptions
are those dealing with social assertion, economic well-being, and
conflict resolution.

Different perspectives of human rights have particularly affected
U.S. relations with Egypt and the People's Republic of China. Hermann Eilts, ambassador to Egypt from 1974 to 1979, remarked
that Egyptians were "indifferent" to the issue of human rights.
"Given the life and death problem" of this sorely overpopulated
country, many of whose people live in a state of poverty, disease,
and undernourishment unknown in the West, there was a degree
of "callousness" about compassionate issues. For example, an Israeli request for the return of bodies of troops lost in the 1973 Yom
Kippur War, passed on by Ambassador Eilts to the Egyptian government, was turned down. The Egyptian government was not
motivated by "spite" but was simply "indifferent" to the issue.[31]

President Carter's emphasis on human rights was greeted with
open skepticism. Ismail Fahmy, former foreign minister of Egypt,
dismisses it contemptuously in his memoirs as "a pompous and
empty slogan."[32] This blatant incomprehension of a leading motif
of U.S. foreign policy, the true expression of the American view of
the world as a place to be perfected, not viewed with fatalism, could
hardly fail to lead to dissension. True enough, it can be seen to
underlie the 1985 *Achille Lauro* affair, which resulted in the worst
crisis in U.S.-Egyptian relations since their restoration in 1974. The
crisis came about when an Italian cruise ship, the *Achille Lauro,* was
seized in the Mediterranean by a group from the PLO, and an
elderly crippled man named Leon Klinghoffer was murdered and
thrown overboard. The PLO men handed themselves over to
Egypt, which then, rather than complicate relations with the Arab
world, put them on a plane for Tunis. President Mubarak claimed
ignorance of the murder and then added insult to injury by saying
to reporters: "Maybe the man [Klinghoffer] is in hiding or did not
board the ship at all." The United States, which had requested ex-
tradition of the murderers, ordered its fighters to intercept the
Egyptian airliner, which was escorted to an Italian air base, to the
chagrin of both the Egyptians and the Italians.[33]

A senior U.S. diplomat who played a key role in the affair mused (in a classic description of cross-cultural dissonance) that "the United States and Egypt looked at the same set of facts and came out with diametrically opposing judgments." Just as "corruption" means one thing for Koreans and quite another for Americans, "human rights" evokes quite incompatible meanings for Egyptians and Americans. The main Egyptian concern was to get the problem out of the way, precisely in order to restore relations with the United States and return to business as usual. Egypt never grasped the meaning for U.S. opinion of the death of an elderly, crippled American. Then, in an atmosphere of mutual recrimination, President Mubarak, reacting as the true son of a shame culture, "wrapped himself in Egypt's dignity," arguing that the PLO men had been guests of the Egyptian government. In this way, the United States was presented as violating Egypt's sacred Middle Eastern obligation of hospitality.

It is clear from the U.S. reaction and Chinese counter-reaction to the June 1989 suppression of the democracy movement in Beijing that nothing is calculated to sour relations between the parties more than a dispute over human rights, with America accusing China of inhumanity and China charging America with meddling in other people's business. The dispute has a strong element of inevitability, as if neither party can escape its deepest impulses. In the 1954–55 civilian repatriation negotiations the two sides had completely different views of the subject of the talks. The United States envisaged that its representative would meet with a Chinese delegate merely in order to work out the technical details of the release of American citizens. In document after document the State Department repeated the view that to "bargain" over the Americans would be "dubious morally and legally," tantamount to "bartering in human lives." China could not be permitted to obtain "political advantage" from the affair.

From the Chinese point of view, the handful of American citizens was of no inherent interest. China has been taking hostages for centuries. China's only concern was to extract an agreement that would establish China's symbolic equality of status and various other U.S. concessions. From the moment the issue was raised, the Chinese government made clear that any accord would have to be based on the principle of mutuality. When the formal talks started in Geneva in August 1955 the American representative, Alexis Johnson, found himself in an invidious position. His mission was "to get our people out," but without paying a price. Accordingly, his opening position was not a negotiating proposal in the usual sense but a call for the redress of a moral wrong. No negotiation can be conducted on this basis. This approach left the initiative in the talks to Chinese delegate Wang, who had every intention of bargaining for all he was worth and was able to set his own terms from the outset.

Only at the very end did it dawn on Johnson that the political hostage aspect did not shock the Chinese and that they regarded the release of the Americans as a "political act of grace and therefore directly related to other political factors in relations between the two countries."[34] China's adroit use of the American internees as a bargaining chip demonstrated an understanding of the value the United States placed on human rights. The cross-cultural error was that of the State Department, which failed to see that moral rectitude may not be enough. Nevertheless, the Chinese strategy ultimately backfired. Determined to wring every drop of advantage out of having the Americans in its hands, China declined to release them all at once and dribbled them out over the years, thereby providing a permanent irritant for public opinion and reinforcing its image of inhumanity, whereas a prompt release might have served it better.[35]

* * *

Relations between the United States and its non-Western interlocutors have often threatened to run aground on the twin rocks of pride and sovereignty. Status consciousness and historical grievance have produced an acute sensitivity on the part of these societies to any issue perceived to encroach on their sovereign rights and possessions. This sensitivity repeatedly influenced, and on occasion aborted, negotiations. With Mexico, territorial issues or questions of the national patrimony, such as oil and fish (believed to have been long exploited to U.S., rather than Mexican, benefit), were sure to be highly controversial. With Egypt it was anything that evoked associations with the hated British bases or the capitulations (extraterritorial legal rights for foreigners). In the case of India, nonalignment was a touchy issue. For China, a nineteenth- and twentieth-century victim of aggression and occupation, the issue of Taiwan released deep emotions, and legal prerogatives were to be jealously guarded. In Japan's relationship with the United States, an ominous strain of historical resentment has sometimes appeared. American disregard for the protocol of alliance has been damaging, but on the other hand, Japan's conditioning by *amae* has given it a lopsided view of the obligations of partnership. Territorial integrity and freedom from nuclear weapons have also been tender spots.

Preoccupation with sovereignty and independence have produced an acute ambivalence at the heart of these nations' relations with the United States. On the one hand each of them has felt the need at some time for American aid of one kind or another. In time of famine, grain has been a dire necessity. As developing nations for at least part of their history, they have also sought the benefits of American technology and investment. Yet this sometimes inescapable requirement for assistance has clashed with their no less powerful drive for autonomy and freedom from dependence on the West, rendered doubly heartfelt by their ever-present concern with matters of national pride and status. The end result has been recurring friction, resentment of help rather than gratitude for it, and consequent deep American frustration.

Collectivistic cultures attach to the issues of sovereignty and national pride the same importance that they associate with questions of honor and status at the individual level. Similarly, form may overshadow substance. Finally, all of the nations discussed here have undergone wrenching changes and severe soul-searching in their common effort to modernize and catch up with the West. They have been forced to ask painful questions about the validity of traditional beliefs and seen cherished values threatened by a seemingly irresistible tide of westernization. In these circumstances any perception of an American intrusion into the jealously guarded realm of sovereign prerogative—the formal right and responsibility of a state to manage its own affairs without outside interference—may seem to endanger their very identity and self-respect as human beings.

five

Setting Out the Pieces
Prenegotiation

In the following chapters I shall examine the effect of cross-cultural differences on the process of negotiation, drawing on examples from the recent history of American diplomatic exchanges with China, Egypt, India, Japan, and Mexico. Various schemes have been suggested for breaking the negotiating process down into its component parts. One of the most original is that of Zartman and Berman, who talk of diagnostic, formula, and detail phases.[1] Another imaginative model is that of Daniel Druckman, who sees turning points and crises taking negotiators over a series of negotiating thresholds.[2] With due respect to these valuable contributions, it is doubtful whether they can be considered free of culturally grounded assumptions and therefore universally applicable. Although my objection should become clearer during the course of this book, suffice it to say at this point that Japanese analysts of negotiation would find it difficult to agree on the constructive function of either general formulas or crises. On the contrary, the instinct of the Japanese is to make every effort to sidestep confrontation and crisis, and to avoid what they see as the peculiarly American propensity to formulate general rules to cover specific cases.[3]

The framework to be used here (in order to avoid as much as possible the more blatant kind of cultural bias) divides negotiation into four rough-and-ready phases: preparation, beginning, middle, and end. This division is not intended to make any analytical point about negotiating but merely to act as an organizing device. (The reader will discover that even the concepts "beginning" and "end" are not culture free. Nevertheless, the Japanese are certainly aware of the meanings Western negotiators attach to those terms.[4])

The first phase to be discussed is the preparatory one. In recent years the concept of prenegotiation has attracted growing interest. The latest work on the subject, *Getting to the Table,* defines it as the phase beginning "when one or more parties considers negotiation as a policy option and communicates this intention to other parties. It ends when the parties agree to formal negotiation . . ."[5] The main problem with this definition is that it covers everything and nothing. States may propose negotiation over some issue, yet their suggestion may not be taken up for years. It does not seem useful to include within a theory of negotiation any activities, however important, that are more properly thought of as belonging under the rubric of decision making, conflict resolution, tension reduction, reconciliation, and attitude change. If everything in the evolution of a relationship can be included in the prenegotiation phase, then the concept loses all analytical focus. To avoid this drawback I propose, therefore, to restrict my attention to the preliminary contacts, direct or indirect, initiated to prepare for a negotiation that the parties have already agreed to undertake.

Recognizing the disadvantage of assimilating prenegotiation in conflict resolution, Brian Tomlin examines the prelude to the negotiation of the U.S.-Canadian Free Trade Agreement. His analysis of the episode provides a very clear expression of the North American *erabi* (instrumental) approach to negotiation. Preparation for the negotiation, according to Tomlin, was very much a problem-solving exercise, a search for "joint solutions."[6] It involved "inventing and choosing among alternative definitions of the problem, inventing and choosing among alternative ways of handling the problem so defined, and setting the themes and limits—parameters and perimeters—that are necessary to guide a solution."[7]

Now it is clear that this approach is excellent in clearing the way for a U.S.-Canadian negotiation. The question is whether it is equally applicable in negotiations involving the representatives of high-context cultures. On the basis of admittedly partial and preliminary evidence, the answer is probably no. All negotiations involve a problem-solving element and a relationship element. But if individualistic, low-context negotiators can be described as primarily problem oriented and have the definition of the problem and the clarification of alternative solutions uppermost in their thoughts, high-context negotiators are seen to be predominantly relationship oriented. For them, negotiation is less about solving problems (although, obviously, this aspect cannot be dismissed) than about attending to a relationship. For interdependent cultures it is not a conflict that is resolved but a relationship that is mended. And when a problem does arise—a trade dispute, a financial crisis, the threat of famine—it cannot be solved in isolation, like a crossword puzzle, but only within the context of the given relationship. In international relations the consequence is concern both with the international relationship and with the personal ties between the interlocutors.

Establishing a personal relationship

For high-context negotiators, then, the initial concern is to exchange the sterility of the business files that are tossed on their desks for a tangible sense of the humanity of the other side. One of the threads running through the negotiating practice of interdependent cultures is a discomfort with purely technical, "let's not waste time but get right down to business" attitudes. Frontality, not anonymity, is the dominant ethic. For the smooth conduct of affairs in these societies, partners need to establish warm, personal ties. Raised in a setting where the intimacy of the extended family or peer group is the norm, high-context persons do not compartmentalize their relationships. They cannot relate successfully to cold and faceless partners. Thriving on personal attention as a plant thrives on sunshine, they are uncomfortable without it and unable to relate to the issue at hand. The consequences of this need for affiliation are felt at every stage of the negotiating process. It should therefore be immediately clear that a priority of the prenegotiation phase is to create an affinity between the negotiating partners. This affinity, better than anything else, will facilitate the later conduct of business.

Mushakoji Kinhide, in his study of Japanese diplomacy, is in no doubt that "the first order of business in Japan is the establishment of a personal relationship between the parties which will allow them to speak frankly and to give and receive favors."[8] For a low-context individual it is hardly customary to view negotiation as an exercise in ingratiation. In the cases of negotiation studied here, it is difficult to assess the consequences of American negotiators neglecting personal ties in the prenegotiation phase. What is clear is that success in negotiation was invariably assisted by careful attention to just this factor.

The 1971 U.S.-Japan monetary crisis was the result of a rising imbalance in trade between the two countries and a large U.S. balance-of-payments deficit, matched by burgeoning Japanese foreign currency reserves. Among the various measures called for by the Nixon administration was an upward revaluation of the Japanese currency, the yen. An adjustment in exchange rates, it was hoped, would stimulate American exports to Japan and dampen Japanese imports to the United States. Japan was far from enthusiastic at this prospect, favoring the existing state of affairs. In November 1971, Secretary of the Treasury John Connally arrived in Tokyo. Japanese ministers, who had awaited the outspoken former governor of Texas with some trepidation, "were treated to a generous serving of Texas charm." From the moment of his arrival at the airport, Connally set out to impress his hosts. Finance Minister Mizuta was complimented on his legislative skill and took away an abiding impression of the Texan's "courtly manners." Other concerned members of the Japanese cabinet were considerately visited in their own offices (rather than being invited to come to meet Connally).

Wisely, Connally made no attempt on this visit to negotiate, let alone put pressure on his hosts, but insisted that his aim was to exchange opinions and, picking up a phrase used by Japanese diplomats, "to improve mutual understanding." In private he set out American needs—not demands—for monetary adjustments and trade liberalization. This low-key, relationship-oriented approach was precisely the right strategy to adopt. The Japanese do not react kindly to pressure, *faits accomplis,* or heavy-handed attempts at bludgeoning them into submission. They do need a great deal of time to achieve their famous domestic consensus. Summing up the achievement of Connally's prenegotiating visit to Tokyo, Robert Angel writes: "He left his negotiating counterparts in the [Ministry of Finance] and the [Liberal Democratic Party] in a better position to compromise with American demands than they had been before he arrived—perhaps his primary objective."[9]

Connally's behavior was, unfortunately, all too exceptional. During 1984 negotiations over reforms in Japan's financial markets, the abrupt manner of U.S. negotiators is thought to have affronted

many Japanese and been self-defeating. Treasury Secretary Donald Regan, his Japanese counterparts complained, behaved as if he
were cutting a deal on Wall Street, rather than engaging in delicate
diplomatic negotiations with the representatives of a sovereign
state "known to need gentle persuasion."[10]

Observers of Chinese negotiating behavior emphasize a similar
attention to the long-term dimension of relationships rather than
just short-term issues. Richard Solomon argues that

> the most fundamental characteristic of dealings with the Chinese is
> their attempt to identify foreign officials who are sympathetic to their
> cause, to cultivate a sense of friendship and obligation in their official
> counterparts, and then to pursue their objectives through a variety of
> stratagems designed to manipulate feelings of friendship, obligation,
> guilt or dependence. This reflects the workings of a culture that has
> developed to a high level the management of interpersonal relations
> (*guanxi*); a society that stresses interdependence rather than individu-
> ality; and a political system that sees politics as the interplay between
> superior and dependent and the rivalry of factions rather than the as-
> sociation of equals.[11]

Solomon notes that on several occasions Chinese officials have
implied that unless the United States showed flexibility in negotiations, its friends in the Chinese government would be harmed. In
1972, when normalization was being discussed, Zhou Enlai's standing was suggested to be on the line. In 1981–82 Deng Xiaoping
repeatedly told American visitors that he would be in trouble if the
question of U.S. arms sales to Taiwan was not satisfactorily resolved. The Chinese government has also been skillful in giving
privileged access to, or lobbying, officials known to be sympathetic
to their cause, avoiding those who were felt to be more critical.[12] In
1978, for example, during the normalization negotiations, Chai
Zemin, the head of the liaison office of the People's Republic of
China in Washington, met with National Security Adviser Zbigniew
Brzezinski, an enthusiastic and vociferous proponent of U.S.-
Chinese strategic cooperation, and told him: "The U.S. bears the
major role in reaching a successful conclusion," meaning that U.S.
concessions were required.[13] Ogura Kazuo, in an insightful study
of Sino-Japanese negotiations, agrees that the creation of and
appeal to "friendly circles" is a recurrent tactic of Chinese
diplomacy.[14]

The personal touch is equally important in preparing the
ground for negotiations with Mexico. Glen Fisher points out that

the various ongoing commissions within which American and Mexican officials tackle common problems provide ideal frameworks for productive cooperation. Such commissions include the U.S.-Mexico Commission for Border Development and Friendship and the International Boundary and Water Commission. "By being continuing bodies with members working with each other over time, an essential personal rapport can be generated, and a familiarity with the other side's decision-making process can be gained and appreciated."[15] In the 1962–63 resolution of the Chamizal boundary dispute, the long-standing friendship of the two principals, Ambassador Mann for the United States and Ambassador Tello for Mexico, proved invaluable. At the technical level, sterling work was also performed in the commission. Over the years U.S. officials such as Boundary Commissioner Joseph Friedkin had established close ties with their counterparts that facilitated the solution, outside the limelight, of many problems.[16]

As for U.S.-Egyptian relations, Ambassador Hermann Eilts believes that personal relations are of the essence throughout the Arab world and that the success of his Cairo embassy was related to his ability to establish close personal ties with key Egyptian leaders. Without a strong basis in convergent relations, however, these personal ties would not have helped. As valuable as more formal representations, he added in an interview, were the hours spent in informal conversation with his counterparts. Not only was this time well spent from the point of view of cultivating contacts, but information acquired on such occasions might also come in useful in the future. ("Look here, don't you remember saying to me . . .")[17] A predecessor of Eilts, John Badeau, agreed that the way to get along best in Egypt was "to practice a fairly personal diplomatic stance." He made a point of seeing Nasser regularly, fostering a mutuality of interests.[18] The personal approach to Egyptian leaders became the hallmark of the Kissinger period of Middle East diplomacy, was inherited by President Carter, and was passed on to Secretary of State George Schultz in the 1980s. Former senior State Department official Joseph Sisco believes that Americans have a special gift for friendship with Egyptians, derived from the egalitarian tradition of U.S. culture, which contrasts, in Egyptian eyes, with the arrogance remembered from the old days of British imperialism.[19]

One cannot exaggerate, in my view, the benefits U.S. diplomacy derived from the remarkably warm relationships cultivated by Kissinger and Carter with President Sadat. In her essay on the role of prenegotiation in the American mediation of the 1978 Camp David Accords, Janice Stein quotes the following significant extract from President Carter's memoirs: "In my private visits with Sadat he emphasized again and again that his main concern was about me . . . It was imperative to him that the United States and Egypt stand together."[20] Stein convincingly demonstrates the use made of prenegotiation by the United States to define the problem, delimit the agenda, select participants, and shape a negotiating strategy. She pays rather less attention to Israeli and Egyptian preparations (which did not fit this pattern). But surely the single most noteworthy feature of the Camp David conference of September 1978 was Sadat's willingness to place his own fate and that of his nation in the hands of the leader of a foreign power—President Carter. Having gone to Jerusalem and stated his case before the Knesset, Sadat was at a complete loss as to what to do next. Apart from characteristic, face-to-face attempts to woo such Israeli politicians as Defense Minister Ezer Weizman and Leader of the Opposition Shimon Peres, Sadat's main tactic was simply to rely on "my friend Jimmy Carter." Rarely can a patron-client relationship have achieved such pronounced expression.

From the first, Sadat's negotiating strategy for achieving a settlement of the Egyptian-Israeli dispute (a conflict that had been pursued in five wars) was to put himself completely into American hands, displaying utter trust in American fair-mindedness. It was a remarkable conception, unintelligible unless the networks of mutual obligation that prevail in Egypt as in other interdependent societies are taken into account. Patron-client relationships are based on long-lasting, affective ties between a powerful protector and a loyal ward. Under Sadat the circle of friends, or *shilla*, became a key instrument in the exercise of power in the face of the "hydra-headed" Egyptian bureaucracy.[21] For a man who was notorious for personalizing the conduct of international affairs (as Foreign Ministers Ismail Fahmy and Mohamed Kamel confirm),[22] it was quite natural to project assumptions about the value of client status onto his relationship with the United States.

The first strands in the fabric of friendship were woven by Sadat in the aftermath of the 1973 Yom Kippur War. He told Secretary of State Kissinger, in Cairo to consolidate the cease-fire, that "he was determined to end Nasser's legacy. He would reestablish relations with the United States as quickly as possible and, once that was accomplished, he would move to friendship." Sadat did not quibble over details but concentrated on essentials: establishing a

personal relationship. Astonishingly, he left it up to the secretary
of state to decide how best to deal with Jerusalem.[23]

Sadat, Kissinger recalls, "had an uncanny psychological discern-
ment," handling each American president he knew with skill, gain-
ing the confidence of each. "He worked at identifying Egypt's interest with America's own. He repeatedly challenged us to enter
the negotiations not as mediator but as participant, or else he offered to accept what we put forward."[24] Sadat's trusting and open-
hearted manner greatly appealed to President Carter, who writes
in his memoirs: "There was an easy and natural friendship between us from the first moment I knew Anwar Sadat. We trusted
each other. Each of us began to learn about the other's family members, hometown, earlier life, and private plans and ambitions, as
though we were tying ourselves together for a lifetime."[25] Observing the bonding between the two men, Secretary of State Cyrus
Vance confirms that they achieved a "sincere and real" rapport. He
adds: "Because Sadat trusted Carter, he was repeatedly willing to
take Carter's word that a given step was necessary . . ."[26] Later, at
Camp David, Carter put this trust to excellent use, although not
quite in the way Sadat may have expected. The U.S. president, it
turned out, was better able to separate business from friendship
than the Egyptian leader.

Preventing surprises

High-context cultures are also shame cultures. Standing, reputation, and honor are paramount. Outward appearances are to be
maintained at all costs. Thus the high-context negotiator has an
abiding nightmare: loss of face. Face may be lost as a result of
many developments: a premature or overeager overture that is re-
buffed by one's opponent; exposure to personal insult, in the form
of either a hurtful remark or disregard for one's status; being
forced to give up a cherished value or to make a concession that
will be viewed by the domestic audience as unnecessary; a snub;
failure to achieve predetermined goals; the revelation of personal
inadequacy; damage to a valued relationship. The list is endless,
for in the give-and-take of a complicated negotiation on a loaded
subject, anything can happen.

The high-context negotiator seeks, insofar as possible, to ensure
that "anything" will *not* happen. The more uncertainty, abrasion,
the risk of the unexpected, and the shadow of failure can be

removed from the impending encounter, the better. An ideal negotiation would be one in which every move was foreseen and cho-
reographed in advance. Contrast this aversion to risk with the propensity for crisis of the low-context, American negotiator. Far from
deploring the unforeseen and the abrasive, the latter relishes the
prospect of cut-and-thrust, the exploitation of an unexpected opportunity, the pressure-cooker atmosphere of short time and taut
nerves in which innovative solutions unexpectedly emerge. What
matter if egos are bruised? The main thing is to solve the problem.
Glen Fisher recalls a State Department official who was accused by
his staff "of being prepared to create crises when none existed
because he so enjoyed meeting crises."[27] The general truth of
this observation will be apparent not only to the observer of
American politics but also to the student of American political
science. The discipline has developed an entire subfield of crisis
studies.

High-context cultures have evolved a variety of prenegotiation
stratagems intended to head off just such crises, with their unwelcome potential for loss of face. The Japanese style is to engage in
lengthy and cautious efforts to gather information about the other
side's needs and perceptions through informal soundings. While
learning as much as possible about the opponent's likely position
in the forthcoming talks, the Japanese instinctively avoid striking a
premature posture. In the *awase* tradition Japanese negotiators
adapt to reality rather than pit themselves against it. At the same
time, consideration for the opponent can be built into the meticulous process of consensus building, both within and between agencies, that characterizes decision making in Japan.[28]

A typical example of Japanese prenegotiation can be found in
the instructions sent to the Japanese delegate to the Versailles conference following World War I: "Before presenting our already
established demands to the Allied Powers," Foreign Minister
Uchida Yasuya wrote, "we should first exchange views with them,
altering our demands somewhat by deleting or abbreviating sec-
tions, while we continue to work on those policies as yet not completely decided upon."[29]

Whereas the Japanese prefer to determine the position of their
adversary in advance of the actual negotiation, the Chinese tend to
adopt the reverse technique: they establish ahead of time a number of irreducible principles that are their own preconditions for
entering talks. These principles may be insisted on for years. Once
the other party agrees to negotiate, it will have implicitly conceded

the essentials of the Chinese position from the outset. Although the Japanese and Chinese styles are apparently contradictory, I argue that they perform the same purpose: to avoid the intimidating uncertainty of a leap into the unknown.

Long before the United States entered into negotiations with the People's Republic of China in 1978 for the normalization of relations, it was aware of three Chinese conditions: cessation of diplomatic relations with Taipei, withdrawal of U.S. military forces and installations from Taiwan, and abrogation of the U.S.-Taiwan defense treaty. Under the circumstances Washington did not challenge the principles directly, probably correctly viewing any such effort as an exercise in futility, but sought to modify them to suit the special relationship between the United States and Taiwan after normalization.[30]

A favorite technique to avoid possible future embarrassment is to use informal or unofficial contacts at the preparatory stage in order to extract prenegotiation assurances, commitments, or other forms of guarantee against failure in the impending negotiations. "For Japan," Michael Blaker argues, "efforts to secure opposing commitments through understandings (*ryokai*), consultations (*uchiawase*), and preconditions (*senketsu joken*) are central to its prebargaining approach."[31] Thus at the preparatory stage of the U.S.-Japanese textiles negotiations, Prime Minister Sato ("in good Japanese fashion," as Dr. Kissinger wryly records) sent ahead a mutual friend to reach agreement on "basic issues of principle" with President Nixon's national security adviser. Without official standing in the Japanese government, the intermediary "could easily be disavowed" if necessary.[32]

One of the great diplomatic achievements in U.S.-Mexican relations was the 1963 settlement of the Chamizal boundary dispute. The dispute arose in the mid-nineteenth century when the Rio Grande changed its course and a small parcel of land shifted from the Mexican to the U.S. side of the border in the area of El Paso–Ciudad Juarez. The United States rejected an arbitration award made in 1911, and since then the issue had festered, impeding the settlement of other nonrelated boundary problems. Prenegotiation was probably decisive in the 1963 success. It was an irreducible matter of pride to Mexico that the Chamizal be transferred from El Paso to Ciudad Juarez in conformity with the 1911 award. The Mexicans believed it was their rightful property and they wanted it back.

Before entering into detailed negotiations, therefore, the Mexi-

can government insisted on prior assurance of satisfaction and received it at two levels. At the actual negotiating level Mexico could
be reassured by the known position of the U.S. ambassador to Mexico—and chief negotiator—Thomas Mann. He and his Mexican
counterpart, Ambassador Tello, had been friends for years. Indeed, their involvement with the Chamizal dispute went back to
the early 1950s when Mann actually worked with Tello unofficially
on the problem. All told, Mann made five trips at that time to El
Paso and several to Mexico City. He did not conceal his personal
view, which became the basis of the final accord, that the United
States would have to honor the 1911 award and that one possibility
was to reroute the course of the river. (This idea was to form the
basis of the final, ingenious technical solution.) At that time, political circumstances were unpropitious, and these unofficial soundings never acquired an official character. However, they did play a
role in preparing the ground for the successful 1962–63 talks.[33]

But Mexico's principal guarantee against embarrassment came
at the U.S.-Mexican summit of June 1962 between Presidents John
F. Kennedy and Lopez Mateos. The Mexican delegation insisted
that reference to the Chamizal in the final communiqué contain
words to the effect that the whole area would revert to Mexico.
Given Texan opinion, this insistence was domestically very difficult
for the United States. One meeting between Ambassador Mann
and the Mexican foreign minister broke up on just this point. The
solution came in the classic diplomatic shape of an ambiguous formula. Both presidents agreed to "instruct their executive agencies
to recommend a complete solution to this problem."[34] This instruction was taken by Mexico to mean that Mexico would get all the
Chamizal back, and by the United States to mean that difficulties
"on the ground" would be taken into account. But the decisive consideration was that there had been a commitment of political will
at the highest level, and that Mexico had good reason to think that
it would not be disappointed.

Another important dispute between the United States and Mexico in which prenegotiation proved its worth was over the pollution
of the Colorado River. The actual negotiations, which took place
in 1973, are described in greater detail in chapter 6. Of interest at
this point is the prenegotiation strategy that was adopted to facilitate the forthcoming formal talks. The two preparatory moves exactly paralleled those made in the case of the Chamizal. First, at a
meeting of the presidents of the two countries a solemn commitment was made "to find a definitive, equitable, and just solution to

this problem at the earliest possible time." Second, President Nixon designated a special representative for the negotiations, former attorney general Herbert Brownell, who engaged in extensive preparatory contacts with all interested parties in Mexico City and on the spot, in the Mexicali valley.[35]

Neglecting prenegotiation is a tried and tested method for ensuring negotiation failure. Besides being well advised to consult meticulously with Mexico in advance of a formal negotiation, the United States has to take care that any initiative appear to come from the Mexican side and not be an American imposition. Most important, there must be no surprises. Infringement of any of these rules may prove fatal. Their importance was stressed by several sources, including Steve Lande, chief U.S. trade negotiator with Mexico from 1976 to 1982.[36] In the American system of government, negotiating positions have to evolve from a painstaking process of interagency consultation to be acceptable to concerned domestic players. This practice may foster an unfortunate propensity on the part of U.S. delegations to view an opening proposal as an end in itself—while leaving the other side out of the equation.

Time and again American negotiators have indeed displayed this tendency. In 1946 U.S.-Mexican negotiations on an air transport agreement ran aground on this very reef. "Shortly after the beginning of the negotiations," Ambassador Thurston reported, "it became increasingly apparent that the Mexican delegation felt that the United States had not come to Mexico to negotiate, but to implement the decisions previously arrived at by the U.S. Civil Aeronautics Board" authorizing five American airlines to operate into Mexico. He had no doubt about the Mexicans' patent resentment and "feeling of imposition." In the circumstances "it was agreed that no purpose would be served by further discussions at the present time." Thurston concluded that there was a substantive dispute between the two sides (Mexico demanded a prior division of the traffic, the United States favored free competition). Nevertheless, he was "particularly struck by the need for evolving some method for preventing the wounding of Latin American sensibilities by prior decisions of the Civil Aeronautics Board in cases involving routes which are to be the subject of later negotiations with them."[37]

There have been other virtually identical cases over the years. In June 1969 U.S. and Mexican representatives met in Mexico City to discuss the drug problem. A rumor that Washington was considering a passport requirement for Americans traveling to Mexico

did not create an atmosphere of trust and confidence. The head
of the U.S. delegation, Attorney General Richard Kleindienst, put
his foot in it from the start. Stressing the need for greater cooperation between the two countries, he confronted the Mexicans with
a set of formal proposals earlier recommended by a presidential
task force. Attorney General Julio Sanchez Vargas of Mexico was
taken aback. One American suggestion for the direct aerial application of herbicides on Mexican territory produced the polite but
tart rejoinder that they be tested first in the United States. At the
end of the talks, which were supposedly informal, no agreement
whatever had been reached on new means to intensify the Mexican
antidrug campaign. Moreover, a big and highly publicized American drive against drugs—Operation Intercept, spearheaded by la-
borious, disruptive (and fruitless) searches at the border—was a
complete debacle because the United States had failed to ensure
prior Mexican cooperation.[38]

During Patrick Lucey's term as ambassador (1977–79), exactly
the same error was repeated. The United States proposed a twelve-
point program on immigration. There had been no advance consultation with the Mexicans, and the foreign minister was "livid."
At a meeting Lucey agreed to change a couple of minor points of
the program, but this step was insufficient to placate his colleague.[39] Strictly speaking, the issue was a domestic American one
and not dependent on Mexican consent. Still, Mexican cooperation
was essential in a wider sense if progress on the problem was to be
made. During Lucey's incumbency Robert Wilcox served as science
counsellor in the Mexico City embassy. He was adamant that initiatives, to get anywhere, had to be "fronted as their own" by the
Mexican government, and negotiating strategies had to take this
need into account. Thus American proposals on the development
of solar energy got nowhere. The only projects adopted were those
submitted by the Mexicans.[40]

* * *

As recent research suggests, prenegotiation may contribute to the
success of negotiations. By the same token, neglecting it may
impede success. However, consistent with the American tendency
to view negotiation as primarily a problem-solving exercise, the literature tends to pay insufficient attention to the interpersonal side
of the activity. When negotiations involving the United States and
high-context, interdependent nations are examined, the impor-

tance of cultivating relationships in the preparatory phase clearly emerges. It is not, one hastens to add, that high-context negotiators ignore the problem at issue; rather that they decline to disentangle it from the wider, long-term framework of affective relationships within which it is lodged.

A similar difference in focus can be discerned in the way the issues at stake are addressed. Janice Stein, summing up the findings of *Getting to the Table,* concludes that "in every case, prenegotiation framed the problem and set the limits of the negotiation to follow. Without an analysis of the process of getting to the table, we cannot explain the shape of the table, who gets there and who doesn't, what is on the table and, equally important, what is kept off."[41] To that summary I would add the need for face-salient, shame cultures to set perimeters, not so much on the process of negotiation as on the configuration of the final outcome. In the Anglo-Saxon tradition great stress is laid on creating the conditions for an equitable contest. A whole vocabulary, redolent with approval, exists to describe this state of affairs: fair play, level playing field, rules of the game, due process, and so on. Face-salient cultures, in contrast, are less enthusiastic about competition, with its potential for affront and painful confrontation, than about ensuring a result that will protect their cherished dignity.

six

Let the Contest Commence
Opening Moves

With the formal opening of negotiations the contrasts and contradictions between the individualistic and the interdependent models of negotiation begin to take practical effect. Dichotomies appear
at the levels of philosophy, procedure, and tactics. At a general
level, the U.S. emphasis on immediate issues rather than long-term
relationships, already observed in the prenegotiation phase, continues. And in the American tradition of egalitarianism (whatever
the power discrepancy between the parties), interlocutors are
treated as equals, deserving no more and no less respect than is
due all men and women. Due process and not personal preference
is what counts. For a negotiated settlement to be valid it is expected
that it will be arrived at in conformity with certain objective rules
of equity and fair play. The concept of reciprocity has a prominent
place in this design. Mutual benefit is a value very much at the
heart of the contract-based, individual-oriented, commercial culture that exists in the United States.

Tactically, American negotiators assume that each side will start
out by presenting its proposals to the other, so that a process of
give-and-take will get under way. Concerned more with practical
expedients than with grand conceptual schemes, they are interested in getting down to discussing detail—the "nitty-gritty"—as
soon as possible. They expect discussion to be businesslike and to

the point; ad hominem appeals, moral suasion, and rhetorical discourse are viewed as suitable for the hustings and the theater, but not for the negotiating table. As to the bargaining itself, typically, American negotiators are aware of the inevitable gap between opening bid and minimal acceptable outcome, and of the desirability of leaving themselves some room for maneuver. Although they may have a fallback position ready in anticipation of maneuvering, they are unlikely to envisage an immoderate retreat. To put in an excessive opening bid would conflict with the ingrained American sense of proportion. In the negotiation to follow, they suppose, both sides will make incremental concessions until a mutually satisfactory solution is arrived at, in the nature of a reasonable compromise. The Americans may be surprised to discover that not all these anticipations are shared by the other side, for they are grounded in a particular, and far from universal, approach to negotiation.

Who goes first?

For the low-context negotiator it seems natural for the parties to a negotiation to commence the contest by setting out their opening positions as clearly as possible. The resemblance between this procedure and that of a court of law or a high school debate will not have escaped the reader: it is rooted in that adversarial style on which American law and politics are posited. However, as we have already observed, the dislike of confrontation found in interdependent, face-salient cultures (together with certain features of domestic decision making) may prescribe a rather different procedure, namely, to postpone showing one's hand for as long as possible. In this case the American side is likely to find itself right away at a severe tactical disadvantage.

China and Japan were found to be particularly prone to hold their fire in the first round of talks. In a comparison of American and Japanese negotiating styles, Leo Moser, a veteran diplomat and Asia specialist, observes the discord produced from the outset:

> When the Americans state their position, the Japanese tendency is to listen quite carefully, to ask for additional details, and to say nothing at all committal. This lack of response is likely to frustrate the American side, which wants a counter-proposal put on the table "so that give-and-take can begin." To the Japanese, this approach may appear overly

aggressive, embarrassing, even impolite. They may also consider it un-
wise to expect the two delegation leaders to make initial, clear statements of their negotiating position; wouldn't it be wiser to let them
speak only after the two sides had worked out a mutually acceptable
position at the working level? To Americans the Japanese response is
liable to seem standoffish, dilatory, even "inscrutable."[1]

This analysis is well exemplified by the first round of the U.S.-
Japan air service negotiations of the early 1980s. Both sides sought
expanded passenger and cargo access to each other's markets, beyond traffic rights, as well as the redress of certain grievances. (The
American delegation to the talks was chaired by a State Department official and also included two representatives from the Department of Transportation and three from the Civil Aeronautics
Board. In other words it was a fairly typical interagency team, most
of whose members were not professional diplomats.) In preparation for the opening round in Honolulu in January 1981, the U.S.
delegation developed a detailed set of proposals that offered substantial incentives to Japan in return for appropriate concessions.
As is common in American practice, the offer did not represent an
exaggerated bargaining position that could be whittled down in a
subsequent haggle, but what was considered to be a fair and bal-
anced package. In a sense, the United States had already reached
a compromise—with itself.

In Honolulu, negotiations immediately settled into the mode described by Moser. With the unveiling of the American package, the
Japanese delegation was able to probe away to its heart's content
rather than present a proposal of its own. It was utterly predictable
that the Japanese would prefer to learn as much as they could
about their rival's position before embarking on the painstaking
task of domestic consultation and consensus building that marks
their own decision-making process. Moreover, they had acquired a
considerable tactical advantage, for without making a single concession of their own or even revealing any of their cards, they now
knew what minimum gains they could expect from any agreement.

It was only at the second round of the talks in April that Japan
tabled its own counterproposal. "It satisfied," in the censorious
words of one of the American delegates, "virtually all of Japan's
objectives and none of the aims of the United States." Unwisely
taking umbrage, the United States rejected it as "counterproductive and self-serving." By round three in May, it had dawned on the
Americans (to their annoyance) that their adversaries were going

to eke out their concessions belatedly and in small amounts.[2] Unfortunately, having offered its own carrot right at the beginning, the United States had left itself minimal leverage. The opening package may have offered an equitable solution to the problem in American eyes, but it quite ignored the fundamental fact that negotiation involves an interaction between at least two parties who may not be playing by the same rules.

Chinese negotiators, like the Japanese, are slow to present their opening position. But once they do, Paul Kreisberg (a veteran Asia hand) told me, they are immovable. Their position is viewed as a matter of principle and they "virtually never withdraw."[3] The logic of Chinese strategy is explained by another China watcher as enabling them "to conceal their cards while forcing the other side to reveal its hand. By letting the other side speak first, they can also point out contradictory aspects of its position and make full use of them."[4]

In preparation for the 1978 U.S.-China normalization negotiations, the Carter administration had carefully planned a "dance of the four veils" strategy, which envisaged the American delegate presenting his government's proposal on each of the major issues separately and in sequence ("seriatim" is the technical term for this approach). He would move from one item to the next only after testing "the Chinese reaction on each sensitive issue."[5] At least that is what was supposed to happen, but China had a different game plan in mind.

It is worth pausing for a point about the administrative arrangements for the talks. Leonard Woodcock, the head of the U.S. Liaison Mission in Beijing and U.S. negotiator, was not a career diplomat but did have years of negotiating experience as a labor union leader. Typically, for a negotiation of such extraordinary importance, Woodcock's freedom of action—and therefore the input of personality—was strictly circumscribed. Using the White House communications system for direct contact rather than the State Department's, National Security Adviser Zbigniew Brzezinski and his staff regularly provided Woodcock "with systematic and extraordinarily detailed instructions."[6] In short, this performance was not a solo, but a negotiation meticulously orchestrated by the government apparatuses of China and the United States.

The first meeting between Ambassador Woodcock and his Chinese counterpart, Foreign Minister Huang Hua, took place on July 5, 1978. As agreed by President Carter and his principal foreign policy advisers, Woodcock proposed an agenda of four items to be tackled in turn. On July 14 China responded "by suggesting that the United States first make a comprehensive presentation on all the major issues, obviously wanting," Brzezinski remarks in his memoirs, "to smoke out the American position."[7] Keeping strictly to his instructions, Ambassador Woodcock ignored the Chinese request and proceeded according to plan with the first item on the agenda. The Chinese side declined to respond. Sticking to his guns, Woodcock proceeded unilaterally with the agenda. Doing so did not help at all in the face of Chinese persistence; Beijing had taken the measure of its opponent. Eventually, as Woodcock himself reports, the entire U.S. position was laid out in its entirety in five meetings held from July to mid-September. Then and only then did the Chinese answer. In the words of Deputy Secretary of State Warren Christopher, they "had not responded sequentially; they responded to the overall presentation and then Vice Premier Deng came into this matter." Meanwhile, enjoying the luxury of going second, "the Chinese listened to Woodcock's presentations, finding fault with the American proposals and raising many 'nit-picking' questions, but moving very slowly and cautiously."[8]

Given the Chinese refusal to play the game by American rules it is remarkable that Brzezinski and his team at the White House did not see fit to rethink their strategy. That they did not, but galloped on into Chinese fire, is rather reminiscent of the Charge of the Light Brigade. It was magnificent, but it was not war—or give-and-take, for that matter.

Adoption of a supplicant posture

American assumptions of equality in negotiation may fare no better than those of reciprocity. For hierarchical cultures, as we have observed, it is natural to transfer preoccupation with status from the domestic into the international arena. And in negotiations on most issues involving the United States, the single most salient feature is the colossal preponderance of American power. It is impossible for a high-context negotiator to overlook this fact of international life, however down-to-earth and unaffected the U.S. interlocutor. Ironically, although a patronizing attitude would be deeply resented, several of the nations examined here were not adverse to turning their relative weakness vis-à-vis the United States to bargaining advantage by adopting a supplicant posture at the outset of negotiations.

The appeal to weakness is particularly associated with Japan. Many observers, including some Japanese, have noticed Japan's tendency to take on the role of supplicant in negotiations with the superpowers. In so doing, Japan is instinctively projecting onto its foreign relations the characteristic psychological orientation of dependency found throughout its society. *Amae,* as it is called, is the inferior partner's expectation of the stronger party's benevolence in a hierarchical relationship. In return for protection and consideration the weaker party need offer only gratitude and a sense of indebtedness. He or she is not committed to any specific act of reciprocity. *Amae* imposes an onerous burden of lifelong responsibility and is possible only in a highly stratified society that attaches a supreme value to the fulfillment of well-defined roles and duties. It contrasts with the Judeo-Christian ethic, "Love thy neighbor as thyself," in which behavior toward others is grounded in one's personal self-esteem. Interdependent cultures reverse the causality: one's self-esteem is derived from others' approbation.

Numerous examples of the Japanese appeal to weakness, grounded in *amae,* can be detected in Japanese-American relations. In the 1971 monetary crisis Japan countered pressure to revalue the yen by throwing itself on U.S. benevolence. Japan, it argued, "is a small nation, poor in natural resources, and therefore dependent upon foreign trade . . ."[9] In a 1977 fishing dispute, *Asahi Shimbun* appealed in an editorial for American understanding of the misery of Japanese fishermen: "We do hope that President Carter will not disappoint the Japanese, who are allied with America and have profound trust and friendly feeling toward the American people."[10] In the Nixon-Sato textile negotiations, it has been argued, the root of the damaging and drawn-out wrangle lay in a clash of cross-cultural expectations. As the weaker partner, Sato is said to have expected his powerful American patron to sympathize with the domestic difficulties he faced from the powerful Japanese textiles lobby. Nixon, on the other hand, who had been forthcoming in the Okinawa bases negotiations, had equally good reason to hope that Japan would reciprocate with "voluntary" quotas on textile exports. When both sides found their expectations disappointed, an essentially secondary disagreement escalated into a major crisis in relations.[11]

There is an element of paradox in the use of *amae* tactics outside the special case of a Japanese-American negotiation. Since the Second World War, Japan and the United States have arguably had a sort of *amae* relationship. But in almost any other case one could mention, the necessary feature of mutual obligation, of protection in return for loyalty, is absent. Indeed, Third World powers are more likely to resent dependency than to cultivate it. Egypt and Mexico have been proud and vigorous in defending their independence against real or imagined Western encroachments. Yet, as we have already noted, in occasions of dire need the only argument that the weaker state can use may be the appeal to the *amae* responsibility of the stronger.

Glen Fisher, observing the Mexican penchant for playing the weaker partner in negotiations with the United States on occasion, was unsure whether it was a calculated tactic or a sincerely felt position.[12] Whatever the case, the situation has occurred regularly. In 1943 Mexico and the United States were engaged in important negotiations for sharing the waters of the great Colorado River, which, after running most of its course through American territory, enters Mexico for a short distance before reaching the Gulf of California. The construction of the Hoover Dam and U.S. irrigation projects meant that by the time the Colorado River reached the Mexican farmers of the Mexicali valley, little water was left over for their needs. The negotiation was aimed at agreeing on a guaranteed allocation.

In an unexpected demarche the U.S. ambassador was called into the Mexican foreign ministry to be greeted by a delegation including the foreign minister, the minister of agriculture, and other cabinet officers. Their message was dramatic: an unusually dry season had aggravated the water shortage, and the inhabitants of the Mexicali valley and their crops "were in immediate danger of catastrophe." The matter was of "urgent and immediate importance" and the ambassador was urged to take the matter up directly with President Roosevelt. In Ambassador Messersmith's judgment, "they were not staging a show for me." Subsequent inquiry, however, cast their claim in doubt. The day after the meeting a U.S. inspector measured more water passing into Mexican territory than its farmers could use. What had happened? The under secretary of state believed that it was a "scare tactic." Officials concerned with the Colorado River talks concluded that it was indeed so: "that certain Mexicans may be trying to induce us to set the precedent of assuring the delivery of a greater amount of water than we now contemplate allocating by treaty."[13]

Years later the problem reemerged. The 1944 treaty dividing the waters of the Colorado had fixed the quantity, but not the quality, of the water. Both sides had different assumptions on the matter.

The completion in 1961 of a drainage channel in Arizona, running into the river, meant that Mexican farmers now received unusable runoff irrigation water, heavily polluted by fertilizer salts. The United States was accused of violating the 1944 treaty. In a classic gesture combining both magnanimity and patronage, it accepted without quibbling its responsibility for the quality of the water. (That this kind of behavior is far from axiomatic was brought home to me by a State Department official with long service in India. Faced by a similar appeal from Bangladesh for a more generous water allocation, the government of India sent the supplicant packing. "Magnanimity," I was told, "is not a word in their vocabulary.")

From 1962 to 1972 a series of interim measures was undertaken to dilute the Colorado's saline content. In 1972 it was decided to seek a permanent solution. When the two sides entered the formal stage of the negotiation in June 1973, Foreign Minister Emilio Rabasa of Mexico adopted a classic *amae* posture, otherwise surprising from a conventional negotiating perspective: he had no proposal to make; any solution would have to come from U.S. negotiator Herbert Brownell and his team. "They wanted help from the United States, period," Mr. Brownell remarked. They got it. Under the terms of the final agreement the American government committed itself to the unprecedented step of constructing, at enormous cost, a desalination plant to supply Mexico with water of acceptable quality.[14]

A further example of the Mexican appeal from weakness occurred in the Mexican debt crisis of 1982. After Mexico had accumulated debts of approximately $80 billion during the fat years of rising oil prices, the bubble burst in 1982. In June, the Bank of America failed to syndicate a $2.5 billion loan for Mexico. On August 13, 1982, Mexico's foreign reserves stood at just $200 million while the net outflow through the central bank of Mexico was running at $100 million a day; trading in U.S. dollars was suspended. The same day Finance Minister Silva Herzog of Mexico flew to Washington. Like Rabasa, he had no specific plan or proposal.[15] That was up to the United States.

Peter Wallison, one of the Treasury Department officials who participated in the negotiation, commented on the almost suicidal element in the Mexican approach: unless an American rescue package was forthcoming, Mexico would default on its massive debt with, it was believed, catastrophic consequences for the international financial system. Ambassador Gavin colorfully characterized the Mexican approach as follows: "We'll slash ourselves and bleed to death on your carpet." Here was *amae* as moral blackmail. In the event, the Mexican ploy proved effective. The U.S. team (ably led by Tim McNamar, deputy secretary of the Treasury) in a tour de force over a hectic weekend, succeeded in putting together a rescue package including a $2 billion loan. There was no Mexican default.[16]

The Egyptian-American version of *amae* had its remarkable epitome in the relationships President Anwar Sadat cultivated with U.S. leaders. At the Camp David conference of September 1978, at which the framework of an Egyptian-Israeli peace was negotiated through the good offices of the United States, *amae* was the essence of the Egyptian president's strategy. On the second day of the summit, Sadat disclosed to President Carter in advance a series of concessions to be used at appropriate moments in the negotiations.[17] This extraordinary gesture of trust only makes sense within the context of an *amae* relationship in which the client relies on the munificence of his patron. Carter got nothing like it from the ultra-low-context Israelis, who kept him at arm's length. In the judgment of Hermann Eilts, who was present at the talks, the end result was that Sadat went far beyond the limit of the concessions he had intended to make. In return for agreement to freeze the settlements, Israel achieved a string of concessions on the Palestinian autonomy issue.[18] Sadat's approach, which cost Egypt dear at Camp David, rested on the assumption that the client, in return for love and trust, can expect to receive special favors from the patron. Unfortunately for Sadat, Carter (coming from a different cultural tradition) was not inclined to confuse friendship with substance. In the crunch he predictably leaned on the more pliable party.

Two states that have not adopted a supplicant posture are India and China. The contradiction between the drive for autonomy and the appeal for special treatment has already been pointed out. China and India were not ready to compromise their independent credentials in the cases examined. Although circumstances might force them to accept help, they would not acknowledge any reciprocal obligation.

In the case of China, ideology and the Cold War prevented the development of an aid relationship. Not so in the case of democratic India, which was offered, and received, U.S. assistance in diverse forms over the years. With an acute sense of national pride, India evolved a unique strategy for saving face: it would accept needed assistance, but it would not say please or thank you. The style was established during the 1951 famine, when Prime Minister Nehru grudgingly accepted American grain shipments. At the end of his report on a key meeting with Nehru on the subject, Ambassador Henderson describes the following significant scene: "For the first time the Prime Minister talked with me about the Indian need for foodgrain. His questions indicated that he had an active interest in the matter and would like to see the proposed legislation enacted. He did not, however, express any hopes on the subject or any appreciation of the efforts on India's behalf of the United States Government."[19]

In later years the government of Mrs. Gandhi replaced absence of gratitude with what the Johnson administration perceived as deliberate ingratitude. At a time when American grain ships were unloading at Indian ports, Mrs. Gandhi went so far as to send a warm birthday greeting to Ho Chi Minh, the leader of North Vietnam, a country then at war with the United States. President Johnson's reaction was violent, and cables to the Delhi embassy (according to Ambassador Chester Bowles) "burned with comments about 'those ungrateful Indians.' " Bowles's analysis of Indian behavior was perceptive. "Indian officials," he writes, "seemed almost to be searching for ways to prove that India's integrity as a sovereign nation could never be bought with American wheat."[20] Mrs. Gandhi adopted a neo-Marxist thesis to explain why gratitude was not only inappropriate but would actually be perverse. It was India that was owed a debt by the rich Western nations, which had achieved their own success and prosperity by exploiting the "riches and labour of the colonised countries."[21]

Why has India been unwilling to exploit the appeal to weakness when others have swallowed their pride and done so where necessary? After all, India is no less familiar with habits of patronage and mutual obligation than Egypt, Japan, or Mexico. Indeed it is the paradigm case of the rigidly stratified society, its caste system binding its citizens into a bewildering lattice of rights and duties. Perhaps the answer is to be found in the unique pattern of obligations created by the Hindu ethic. *Dharma* (duty) defined two categories of recipients to whom one was under a mandatory obligation to give alms: those with a religious vocation and the lowest of the low, the untouchable and deformed. Thus men of status most certainly do not ask for charity. Moreover, in the charitable transaction both parties are simply acting out metaphysically predetermined roles. Gratitude in these circumstances is irrelevant.[22] The other point to note is the limitations placed by caste on the giving and receiving of food. In Bernard Cohn's explanation of the phenomenon: "High status is symbolized by being able to take the rarest kinds of food from the fewest people. It is much better to give and have one's food taken than it is to receive. A Brahman theoretically can take only uncooked food from anyone of lower status than himself; hence, at a feast, a Brahman should cook his own food." [23] If one remembers that the Indian political elite are mostly high-caste Hindus, it becomes possible to understand better why the request for assistance in the international sphere should be so odious. Moreover, the prospect of laboring under a burden of obligation is simply intolerable.

Assuming the moral high ground

A corollary of *amae* is to present oneself at the outset as the morally injured party, deserving of redress. Mostly devoid of the conventional advantages of economic and military power in negotiations with the United States, Third World states have learned that the Northern European Protestant conscience, inherited by the United States (and Canada), provides them with an effective lever of influence. From the high ground of moral superiority, they can direct their rhetorical fire at Washington's exposed moral positions. Because the United States, like some of its other Western partners (most notably the Netherlands, Britain, and the Nordic countries), does acknowledge a vocation to act as a moral arbiter, spreading justice and aid to the developing world, such arguments find great resonance in public opinion.

India, therefore, although reluctant to play the role of supplicant, is never loath to attack supposed American moral shortcomings. American negotiators tend to be intensely irritated by Indian moralism, the assumption that India is somehow the repository of righteousness and objective truth in the world. Of course they are irritated; many Americans perceive that select role for themselves. Making this point, Paul Kreisberg, who served in India in both the 1950s and the 1970s, comments wittily that negotiating with Indians is intensely frustrating because it is "like negotiating with yourself!" [24]

Another serving U.S. diplomat with long experience of India suggests that the Indian preoccupation with status makes it imperative for the Indian diplomat to establish his superiority in the negotiation at the earliest possible moment. This practice grates against the instinctive American desire to establish the equality of the interlocutors. Such a concept of equality is viewed by one's Indian counterpart as an eccentric and "unacceptable notion." Hence, at the outset of talks Indian negotiators tend to parade "a litany of all your past failures, abuses of them, sins," while India's record is presented as one of "great principle and universal approbation." Faced by this barrage, flustered American negotiators may either rebut their interlocutors' charges point by point—a fruitless exercise—or, if they have any sense, thank them for their helpful explanation and then get on with the business at hand. In parenthesis, my source noted that Japanese negotiators are utterly shocked and mortified by such offensiveness in negotiation and may even withdraw from future meetings altogether.

Perceptive Indian commentators complement this highly unusual picture by pointing out the American contribution to the "dialogue of the deaf." R. V. R. Chandrasekhara Rao writes that "self-righteous attitudes on both sides" have hindered the U.S.-Indian relationship:

> America's anti-colonial tradition, its rise to economic primacy through hard work and initiative, made the Americans tend to exhibit moral superiority. With this has gone a natural tendency to react with indignation when chinks in their moral armour are exposed. India has its own holier-than-thou mentality traceable to its consciousness of an immemorial cultural heritage and reinforced by the manifest ethical content of the Mahatma Gandhi-Nehru tradition. When rivals contend in terms of moral attitudes not only does compromise become difficult but, more important, exposure of lapses leads to a loss of credibility.[25]

Moral indignation and mutual recriminations dominated the tone of U.S.-Indian relations at various periods, including the Dulles-Nehru period of the 1950s, the Mrs. Gandhi-Johnson period in the 1960s, and the Mrs. Gandhi-Nixon and Mrs. Gandhi-Carter periods of the 1970s. In this kind of atmosphere it was difficult to cooperate on matters of common concern. On the other hand, objective factors should not be ignored: American arms supplies to Pakistan, India's mortal enemy, exerted an invariably harmful influence on relations (although they have not affected the U.S.-Indian rapprochement since 1982).

India's dash for the moral high ground is demonstrated by its position in 1981–82 negotiations over the question of the supply of nuclear fuel for the Tarapur nuclear facility. Under the terms of the 1963 contract to build an atomic power plant outside Bombay, the United States agreed to supply enriched uranium for the 30-year life of the agreement. In return India agreed to use only American-supplied fuel. Following India's "peaceful nuclear explosion" in 1974, there was an outburst of moral indignation in the United States. Demands were made for India to adhere to the Nuclear Nonproliferation Treaty. It was only with great reluctance that further uranium shipments were made. The plot thickened in 1978 when the U.S. Congress passed the Nuclear Nonproliferation Act. The United States now claimed that India was obliged to accept new restrictions on the end use of nuclear fuel.

In 1981 the government of India decided to bring the matter to a head. A delegation of Indian experts arrived in Washington determined to hold the American government to the letter of the 1963 contract: the fuel should be supplied with no added restrictions on its use. For its part the United States was caught in a bind. True, it had entered a commitment to supply nuclear fuel. But Congress absolutely required new safeguards. Negotiations, then, had acquired a moral dimension that obscured their apparently technical nature. India relished its posture of the injured party; it would not let the United States off the hook. It was not interested in the American suggestion that India turn to other suppliers, of which there was no lack. Ambassador Goheen, President Carter's appointee to the Delhi embassy, felt that India sought the moral high ground in two ways: first, by insisting that the United States honor its original commitment, even though it could not in the changed circumstances; and second, by insisting that it was unfair and hypocritical to criticize India's nuclear program—specifically, to insist that India adhere to the nonproliferation treaty—before the superpowers did something about their own nuclear stockpiles. In the end, the problem was resolved not at the technical level but at the highest political level. Mrs. Gandhi decided to turn a new leaf in relations with the United States—whether under pressure from the Indian business community or because of the Afghanistan war is a subject of conjecture. Given the political will, a simple solution was found: France would now supply the fuel.

Striking an accusatory posture is also a typical Chinese tactic. Ogura Kazuo notes its use in negotiations with Japan. To put the Japanese on the defensive, Chinese negotiators assiduously dredge up past "faults" and "errors" that have damaged relations. Demonstrating his point with a convincing list of examples, the author argues that it reflects a Chinese wish "to rectify the views of the other side." China's position must not only prevail but must also be acknowledged to be morally superior.[26] Richard Solomon observes the same tactic in Sino-American negotiations. He cites the 1975 meeting of Henry Kissinger with Deng Xiaoping, when the Chinese leader repeatedly asserted that "the U.S. owes China a debt" on normalization because of the intention expressed by President Nixon in 1972 to establish diplomatic relations by the end of his second term.[27] Presumably, the intervening events in Washington between 1972 and 1975 had somehow escaped Deng's attention.

By the time of Cyrus Vance's first visit as secretary of state to China in August 1977, Deng was claiming that Kissinger had "agreed that the United States owed a debt to China and that normalization would be in conformity with Chinese conditions." It would be interesting to know how Kissinger had indicated his "agreement"! The Chinese leader also alleged that in a December 1975 discussion President Ford had promised to normalize relations after the 1976 elections. But here Deng was caught out in an incomplete truth, because he omitted to state that Ford had qualified his statement with an "if." All would depend on the working-out of the Taiwan issue.[28]

China also based its opening position in the 1983 textile trade negotiations on its supposed role as the injured party. Although there had been a dramatic growth in Chinese textile exports to the United States (73 percent by volume in 1981), and unemployment in the U.S. textile industry reached 15.5 percent in 1982, the Chinese negotiators skillfully argued that they were at a disadvantage in the larger context of Sino-U.S. trade. They pointed to a 1981 overall trade deficit of $2.9 billion and a "textile trade deficit" of $450 million. Finally, they held that threatened protection of the U.S. textile industry would hurt China more than the status quo hurt the United States, because textiles accounted for more than one-third of their total national exports. But these arguments cut little ice with the American delegation.[29] U.S. trade negotiators are less concerned with questions of moral philosophy than are their diplomatic colleagues.

In contrast to seeking the moral high ground by adopting an accusatory posture, China has also shown itself skilled at using unilateral "goodwill" gestures to establish American "indebtedness." In 1955, for example, Beijing released a group of eleven American airmen on the day before the opening of the civilian repatriation talks. And in 1969–72 the Chinese implemented a whole series of unsolicited concessions. These included the release of prisoners, the famous invitation to the U.S. ping-pong team, and the gift of panda bears. All these signals were shrewdly directed at public opinion, did not need to be reciprocated (and hence evaded possible snubs), and put China in the best possible light. They also ensured that the United States, not China, was put under a moral obligation for favors already received. Shenkar and Ronen have observed that if there is one thing that disturbs Chinese negotiators, it is to be placed under a burden of moral indebtedness. A debt "must eventually be repaid, perhaps at a higher cost."[30] Better by far that one's bargaining partner be beholden.

A moralistic tone can be frequently detected in Mexican-U.S. negotiations. Doris Meisner, an immigration expert who served on the U.S.-Mexican Commission on Migration, recalled that every meeting started off with a litany of Mexican grievances at U.S. conduct over the years. This recitation was extremely unpleasant for the American delegation. "I really just cringed . . . it bothered me a great deal . . . being berated like that." It never occurred to the American delegates to defend their country's record or, conversely, to point out the shortcomings in Mexico's conduct toward the United States over the years. And even if it had, Meisner admitted that they had no historical knowledge upon which to draw. Another issue frequently raised by the Mexican delegation and calculated to create defensiveness on the American side concerned the "violation of the rights of Mexican nationals" by agents of the U.S. Immigration and Naturalization Service.[31]

A similar story was related by Timothy Bennett, deputy assistant trade representative for Mexico from 1985 to 1988. In 1986 a U.S. delegation went to Mexico to discuss Mexico's accession to the General Agreement on Tariffs and Trade. The delegation was flabbergasted by the Mexican opening statement, which ran through Mexican grudges against the United States going back to the nineteenth century. Bennett's reaction was that it was all a ploy "to set us up . . . put a guilt complex on us."[32]

The most notorious example of Mexican hectoring came during President Carter's February 1979 visit to Mexico City, at a time of deadlock in negotiations over the supply of Mexican gas to the United States. In his public opening remarks President Lopez Portillo of Mexico launched an extraordinary assault on his astonished guest. "Among permanent, not casual, neighbors," Portillo lectured, "surprise moves and sudden deceit or abuse are poisonous fruits that sooner or later have a reverse effect. Consequently, we must take a long-range view of ourselves. No injustice can prevail without affronting decency and dignity. It is difficult, particularly among neighbors, to maintain cordial and mutually advantageous relations in an atmosphere of mistrust or open hostility." How this broadside was supposed to promote trust and amity was left unclear.[33] In private, Lopez Portillo was even more offensive. A member of Carter's entourage described the Mexican leader as using "stiff, harsh language, blaming the United States for everything that had gone wrong since the beginning of man." The U.S. president, who was eager "to find practical solutions to bilateral problems, found the Mexican's accusatory monologues unwarranted and irritating."[34]

Principles before detail?

At the opening stage of talks negotiators must decide how to present their case in the most convincing and tactically advantageous light. Edmund Glenn, a former State Department interpreter (and a source of inspiration for researchers in the field of intercultural communication), argued from practical experience that culture and language were formative in the choice of approach. Three basic styles of persuasion, he believed, are available. One, the "factual-inductive," draws conclusions on the basis of factual evidence; eschewing grand philosophical debate, it plunges straight into discussion of concrete detail. This style is in the Anglo-Saxon, pragmatic tradition of the common law, which has had such a formative influence on philosophy, science, and politics. The second, the "axiomatic-deductive" style, argues from general principles to particular applications; it seeks a principled underpinning for every practical derivation. It is usually associated with the Roman law tradition and other axiomatic systems. The third, the "affective-intuitive" style, makes its pitch on the grounds of emotion, aiming not at the head of the audience but at its heart.[35] Elements of the two latter styles have already been observed in the appeals to weakness, moral indebtedness, and friendship of high-context negotiators. In this section we shall examine the tendency of some (but not all) of these same negotiators to appeal to general principles before turning to particular cases, and consider the impact of this tendency on negotiations with representatives of the Anglo-Saxon school.

From the evidence of this study it is clear that American negotiators do rely overwhelmingly on the "factual-inductive" approach. This style is the one used by the State Department and by other domestic agencies to prepare their negotiating briefs. It is also consonant with the legal training that so many American public officials have received. Finally, and perhaps most important, concrete specificity is the form invariably required by the Congress of the United States. Imprecision in legal documents is anathema to the nation's legislators. Open-ended, vague, or ambiguous commitments fly in the face of all their instincts, and a treaty not couched in appropriate language is given short shrift.

The appeal to principle, however, is utterly characteristic of the Chinese negotiating style. Writers on the subject are unanimous on this point. At the first stage of negotiations Chinese negotiators tend to avoid detail and instead seek to reach agreement on broad, apparently philosophical, principles that are to govern any ensuing contract. "A Chinese official," Richard Solomon concludes, "can be expected to initiate a negotiation either by pressing his foreign counterpart to agree to certain general principles, or by invoking past agreements of a general nature with the foreigner's predecessors which he is expected to accept and abide by."[36] Only when there has been a meeting of minds on the principles governing the negotiation does the Chinese official wish to move to specifics. This style is almost the exact opposite of the American approach, in the view of Lucian Pye. Americans assume, he suggests, "that progress in negotiations is usually best facilitated by adhering to concrete and specific details, avoiding debates about generalities, which can easily become entangled in political or philosophical differences." However, Pye warns that it would be a serious error for American negotiators to concede seemingly vague general principles on the grounds that they are "up in the air," without specific application. Later in the negotiation their Chinese counterparts will present them with a philosophical promissory note, to be repaid in practical coin.[37]

According to Pye, the U.S. propensity for concrete discussions and the Chinese attachment to general principles seriously hindered any improvement in relations in the 1950s and 1960s. He cites just such disabling dissonance in the Korean truce talks and the drawn-out ambassadorial talks. The U.S. strategy of proposing limited agreements on concrete issues such as the exchange of journalists collided with the Chinese insistence on general principles implying the abandonment of Taiwan. Such conditions were quite unacceptable to the United States. A renewed attempt under President Kennedy to improve relations fell foul of the same problem.[38]

Pye's argument is certainly borne out by the evidence of the

abortive talks held between the two sides on the Taiwan question
in 1958. The Chinese position was that any agreement should rest
on a general renunciation of the use of force. Because this demand
entailed recognition of the Beijing government by Washington, it
was quite out of the question at the time. Secretary of State Dulles
suggested that it would be constructive to move away from arguing
over issues of abstract principle to the pressing, practical problems
involved in the mechanics of a cessation of hostilities. But a cease-
fire was "totally impermissible" in the opinion of the People's Republic of China. A secure cease-fire without an overall renunciation of force would leave the U.S. right to engage in "individual or
collective self defense" in the Taiwan area intact, while depriving
China of its right to resort to force to liberate Taiwan.[39]

It was not until 1972 that Beijing and Washington put their joint
signatures to an agreement establishing the framework of their relationship (the Shanghai communiqué). This document (a radical
departure in its form from established U.S. diplomatic practice)
entailed, in effect, American adoption of the Chinese reliance on
general principles. (The international circumstances were very different from those of 1958, of course.) It stated, inter alia, the
agreement of the two sides

> that countries, regardless of their social systems, should conduct their
> relations on the principles of respect for the sovereignty and territorial
> integrity of all states, non-aggression against other states, non-
> interference in the internal affairs of other states, equality and mutual
> benefit, and peaceful coexistence. International disputes should be
> settled on this basis, without resorting to the use or threat of force. The
> United States and the People's Republic of China are prepared to apply
> these principles to their mutual relations.[40]

How was it possible for the United States to transcend its familiar insistence on specificity in both the conduct and the outcome of
negotiations? The answer seems to be in the acceptance by National Security Adviser Henry Kissinger (the principal negotiator
in all these contacts) of the need to adopt the Chinese approach at
this time if the two sides were to get anywhere. At his first meeting
with Zhou Enlai in July 1971 Kissinger eschewed the "conventional
wisdom," which would have "counseled the removal of specific
causes of tension." One of those problems, Taiwan, "permitted no
rapid solution, while the others were too trivial to provide the basis
of an enduring relationship. The answer was to discuss fundamen-
tals . . . Precisely because there was little practical business to be

done, the element of confidence had to emerge from conceptual discussions. Zhou and I spent hours together essentially giving shape to intangibles of mutual understanding."[41]

It is hard to escape the thought that the conceptual, rather than empirical, approach came easier to Kissinger—Harvard intellectual, nuclear strategist, and student of Metternich and Talleyrand—than it would have to the average State Department official. Kissinger was also well prepared, then, when confronted by Egypt's penchant for general principles. This preference had confused Americans in the past. President Johnson was puzzled when the only message delivered him from President Nasser on the occasion of a visit by Vice President Sadat in 1966 was the enigmatic "All we want is understanding." Egypt wanted neither wheat nor aid. "What we want, and we think it is the key to everything, is understanding."[42] Nasser surely meant that it was useless for the two countries to address details without broader agreement on the basic nature of the relationship: Was Egyptian nonalignment between the superpowers to be tolerated? Was the relationship to be one of mutual respect? Were Egyptian concerns and Israeli concerns to be given equal weight?

Henry Kissinger was first confronted by Egypt's tendency to anchor agreements in general principles before the 1973 war. In February 1973 he met with President Sadat's adviser Hafez Ismail in New York. Ismail proposed that the two sides work to achieve "an agreement on fundamental principles ('heads of agreement')." He did not clearly explain what he meant by that proposal, although he did insist on one absolute precondition for Egypt's joining a negotiating process with Israel: Israel's prior agreement to return to its 1967 borders with all its neighbors.[43] After the 1973 Arab-Israeli war Kissinger entered into direct negotiations with President Sadat for a disengagement agreement to separate the armies of Israel and Egypt in the Sinai. Sadat's first move in the talks was to take Kissinger to one side, away from the experts, and tell him, "We first have to agree, you and I, on the principles on which they will work." Having reached a broad understanding on purposes in a remarkably short time, Sadat left it to his military experts to translate "the general agreement to practical form."[44]

With the Shanghai communiqué under its belt, and with some insight now into Sadat's work methods, the Nixon administration agreed to formulate the basis of its relationship with Egypt in terms of a general text. Under the heading "Principles of Relations and Cooperation Between Egypt and the United States," the two states set themselves a whole series of "tasks" to occupy them in the years ahead. Here was broadbrush diplomacy with a vengeance. They would "intensify consultations at all levels," "continue their active cooperation and their energetic pursuit of peace in the Middle East," "develop their mutual relations in a spirit of esteem, respect and mutual advantage," and so on, in an ambitious agenda of cooperative endeavors.[45] It was bold, it was sweeping—and it was very un-American. U.S. diplomacy, Ambassador Eilts acknowledges, tends to prefer more specific agreements. He himself was uncomfortable with the open-ended commitments that the United States had signed. The promise, for instance, that "the United States will make the maximum feasible contribution, in accordance with Congressional authorization, to Egypt's economic development," was liable to create unfulfillable expectations.[46]

In the consultations between the Egyptian and American governments both before and after President Sadat's November 1977 trip to Jerusalem, the aim was also "to produce some prior understanding on basic principles, some frame of reference." Once this understanding had been achieved, Egyptian-Israeli negotiations would concentrate on working out the details.[47] The search for such a framework continued through 1977 and 1978 and was eventually realized in the Camp David Accords of September 1978. It is clear that, despite its usual bent, American diplomacy, as in the China case, had successfully accommodated itself to the deductive approach favored by its interlocutor.

Mexico, too, tends to argue in terms of axioms, but it also displays a willingness to address problems in a pragmatic spirit. This "principled pragmatism" was evident in the Chamizal boundary negotiations. Ambassador Tello, the Mexican delegate, did not conceal his conviction that it was all a matter of principle. But Ambassador Mann grasped "that the psychological line of the boundary was far more important than the actual physical line." In other words, once the United States conceded the 1911 award in principle, Mexico would be flexible in practice.[48] And so it proved. Mexico had no interest in actually demarcating a boundary running through the center of an El Paso school. This distinction between the ideal and the achievable underpinned the final agreement. Of the 437.18 acres estimated to have been awarded to Mexico in 1911, the government of Mexico agreed to accept 71.18 acres from an area of El Paso slightly downstream from the Chamizal zone.

In the 1979 U.S.-Mexican gas talks the ultimate solution hinged on a similar distinction. The apparently straightforward focus of the talks was the price to be paid Mexico for the supply of natural gas. But energy is an emotive subject for the Mexicans, and the danger that they would be accused of selling out their patrimony to the United States was foremost in the minds of Mexican negotiators. Their opening position, therefore, was to insist on pegging the price of their gas to the heat equivalent of number two fuel oil delivered in New York Harbor—a roughly comparable energy source. The attraction of this proposal to Mexico was that the United States would not be acquiring an unfair bargain and exploiting the Mexican people. Unfortunately, the offer was unacceptable to the Carter administration (and particularly to Secretary of Energy Schlesinger), which proposed to pay U.S. domestic suppliers only two-thirds that price.

The first sessions of talks were unproductive. Julius Katz, the joint leader of the U.S. delegation, recalls the Mexicans appealing to many principles, including justice and equity. The Americans proposed an alternative pricing formula, but with no success. The Mexicans, terrified of appearing to have sold out, "clung like bulldogs" to their position. Price, as another American official realized, had become "a matter of national honor." On August 3 Ambassador Lucey met with President Lopez Portillo, at Katz's urging, to determine whether there was any genuine interest in an agreement. Portillo is reported to have said that his problem was "not with prices but with principles."[49] Lucey took this statement to mean that the Mexican president was signaling acceptance of the current American offer, but it turned out that Portillo actually intended just the opposite.

The key to the negotiation proved to be a switch in the American approach, away from discussing pricing formulas based on some energy equivalent to discussing specific prices. As long as the negotiations were conducted at a theoretical level no progress was made: the delegations were transfixed by principled disagreement. It was only when the "carpet trading" started that convergence became possible. Katz had been tipped off by Diaz Serrano, the director general of PEMEX (Petroleos Mexicanos, the Mexican national oil conglomerate), that this was the way to go: "This is just like buying a used car." In Katz's opinion there was a true ambivalence in the Mexican position between insistence on honor and willingness to haggle. But in the final analysis the Mexicans were ready to climb down from the high tree of principle in order to cut a deal, as long as it could be justified before public opinion.[50]

Unlike China, Egypt, and Mexico, India and Japan demonstrate no propensity for the deductive style of presentation. Japan, indeed, is said to have the same sort of resistance to it as the United States. Kinhide argues that the *"awase* style places emphasis on the special circumstances that distinguish each concrete case and work to make general principles inapplicable."[51] So we may conclude that the axiomatic approach is not to be considered an invariant component of high-context negotiation.

* * *

The contrast between egalitarian and hierarchical cultural expectations was one theme of this chapter. Another was the contradiction between low- and high-context approaches to compromise. Americans tend naturally to assume a give-and-take model of negotiation in which reciprocal concession leads to eventual compromise. This model may, however, be confronted by a quite different one, which does not take reciprocity or compromise for granted but is quite happy to demand one-sided concessions in payment of a supposed moral debt or as the duty of the stronger party.

It was observed that the U.S. delegation's premature disclosure of its position might result in serious disadvantage in the face of a less confiding opponent. Finally, the pragmatic American preference for treating specifics was found to run up against a high-context leaning to achieve agreement first on axioms and philosophical principles. One way to reconcile this contradiction is to combine the two: to agree on practical steps under a canopy of general principles that meet the other side's psychological needs.

seven

On Tactics and Players
Middle Game I

The concept of a middle game in negotiation is admittedly an artificial one. There is not much, for instance, in Japanese or Chinese behavior to distinguish this stage from the preceding one. Japanese reticence, first detected in the opening phase, may simply continue; Chinese negotiators may persist throughout in a holding and probing mode until a critical point is reached, when they jump straight to their final offer. Nevertheless, the distinction is still useful. For one thing, it permits an orderly presentation of the evidence for the working of cross-cultural dissonance. In the long haul between the inception and termination of the negotiation, differences in the use of language and contrasting understanding of such key concepts as time, authority, and negotiation itself come into focus.

But the main justification for the distinction is that the baseline culture for this investigation—that of the United States—does suppose a separate function for the intermediate stage of talks. American negotiators tend to assume that a certain process of give-and-take, governed by identifiable rules of the game, is appropriate in the period between the presentation of one's opening proposal and the final, intense resolution of the contest. Whether shared by other cultures or not, this psychological fact is in itself relevant, tending to affect the course and outcome of talks. Indeed, if the thesis of this study is correct, disagreement on the significance of this phase is precisely one cause of confusion.

What, then, are American expectations for the middle game? The most intuitively plausible model for Americans is the one known as "concession-convergence," according to which the parties start out from different positions and approach each other in a series of concessions until they arrive at a compromise. In its crudest version, concession-convergence portrays negotiators as inching toward each other incrementally along a continuum. This notion more or less corresponds to Americans' day-to-day experience of bargaining over a car or a house. A more sophisticated version of the model, intended better to capture the essence of international negotiation, has participants not inching but "jumping," and not haggling over a deal, but engaged in a "joint search" for a "formula."[1] In practice this version is less radical than it appears at first sight, because a joint search under conditions of perceived competition necessarily implies concessions offered and received. Moreover, although the term "formula" has the advantage of emphasizing the conceptual dimension rather than the quantitative dimension of international problems, it is still expected that the contending positions of the parties will be reconciled through a compromise.

Bidding

High-context negotiators do not necessarily share American assumptions about give-and-take. At this point readers may object—from their experience of holidays in Cairo, Hong Kong, or Guadalajara—that the give-and-take of bargaining is hardly alien to those places. To clarify the matter it will be helpful to adopt a distinction between two paradigmatic types of negotiation observed by William Quandt in the Middle East.[2]

One is the *suq* (Arab market) model. Bargaining is preceded by elaborate ritual, much drinking of coffee or tea, and the exchange of social courtesies in order to establish a personal relationship. The bidding itself starts off with the seller asking a price that is much higher than he expects to receive. The buyer, in turn, is expected to make an offer that will also leave him considerable leeway for adjustment. After haggling for some time—and patience and imperturbability are of the essence—the bids of the parties will progressively converge until they arrive at an agreed figure. When they do shake hands on the deal, both sides must feel that they have gained something. An unhappy customer will not come back. This is the model that is familiar to the tourist in the Third World.

But not everybody is expected to haggle, nor is everything a fit object of haggling. There is a time and a place for it. One of the peculiarities of the etiquette of bargaining is that it shifts with the social status of the bargainer. "Men of honor and prestige in the Middle East do not bargain," argues Lebanese anthropologist Fuad Khuri, "even when they realize that the goods they have bought have been overpriced. This is because bargaining, like pennypinching, does not go with prestige."[3]

A similar proviso is attached to the scope of haggling. Business transactions obviously provide a suitable occasion for the activity. Matters concerning the honor of the group most certainly do not. Here a quite different mode of operation takes effect, involving the resort to mediation, gestures of conciliation, and face saving. Quandt refers to this pattern of behavior (not very aptly) as the *bedouin* model. Although he makes his distinction with particular respect to Egypt, it can also be seen to hold for all the face-salient, high-context societies examined here. Whenever a problem arises touching on the "sacred" values of sovereignty and identity, the "profane" give-and-take mode, which has its quintessential expression in the marketplace, must be discarded or concealed.

As could be predicted, in transactions involving prices and quantities the *suq* model seemed to be generally applicable in the cases examined. Bidding followed predictable lines in questions such as the 1983 textile negotiations with China, the 1942–43 talks with Mexico over distribution of the waters of the Colorado River, the 1953 thorium nitrate purchase from India, and negotiations between the U.S. Department of Defense and the Egyptian War Ministry over the cost of using Egyptian range facilities. It would be worth investigating further examples of this mode (and comparison with Western cases might also be of interest), but the pattern was clear. Just how good U.S. negotiators are at haggling is not resolvable on the basis of a limited sample. My impression is that trade negotiators haggle better than technical experts, although most Americans tend to be uncomfortable with the exaggerated posturing of the *suq*.

The validity of Khuri's observation that "carpet trading" is not engaged in by notables or in matters of honor is also borne out. Kissinger observes that Zhou Enlai "never bargained to score petty points. I soon found that the best way to deal with him was to

present a reasonable position, explain it meticulously, and then
stick to it." At one point in the negotiations over the 1972 Shanghai
communiqué Zhou assured Kissinger: "You do not have to trade;
all you have to do is to convince me why our language is embarrassing."[4] (This style of negotiation—adopting a reasonable opening position, then sticking to it—known as Boulwarism, has been
used as a strategy of wage negotiation in the United States. However, it has never really caught on because, significantly enough, it
tends to antagonize one's interlocutor.[5])

Kissinger had a similar experience in dealing with Anwar Sadat.
The Egyptian president, Kissinger writes in his memoirs, "generally did not haggle; like Zhou Enlai . . . he started with his real
position and rarely moved from it." In the January 1974 disengagement talks Kissinger asked the Egyptian leader how many battalions of troops he wanted in the limited force zone (separating
the two armies). Sadat wanted "as near ten as possible" and settled
for eight, which was as high as the Israelis would go. The Israeli
negotiators had pressed Kissinger to try for a lower figure with
Sadat before finally agreeing, but Kissinger declined. "I thought I
knew my man; it would backfire if we started haggling."[6]

Between the extremes of the *suq* and *bedouin* models—"carpet
trading" and an austere refusal to bargain at all on matters of
honor or high principle—there is what we may call "normal" diplomatic bargaining for the reconciliation of contending positions.
Much international negotiation comes into this third category,
which contains elements of both prototypes. This mix is doubly
confusing, for one can never be absolutely certain which mode is
prevailing at a given time. Nor is it certain that the non-Westerners
themselves, given the psychological difficulties they sometimes
have in dealing with the United States, always know.

The most salient cross-cultural antinomy in the middle phase is
a disagreement between high-context and low-context negotiators
on the value of compromise. Faced by opponents who adopt tough
opening positions that they are ready to modify only slowly and
grudgingly (if at all), and who are not irresistibly pulled toward a
"reasonable compromise," Americans may find themselves at a tactical disadvantage. It is here that Glen Fisher detects the principal
difference between American and Mexican approaches to negotiation: whereas American negotiators "are among the most enthusiastic proponents of compromise," Mexicans perceive no inherent
virtue in accommodating their adversaries.[7] In practical terms this
difference implies that Mexican negotiators maintain their posi-

tions more tenaciously than do their American counterparts. One American diplomat, with experience of dealing with the Mexican government on drug-related issues, felt that the "lion's share" of concessions was invariably made by the American side. "We gave in 75 percent of the time, the Mexicans 25 percent of the time."

Of course, it could be argued that the United States is in an inherently weaker position on the drug issue because it is more eager for cooperation. However, Timothy Bennett, who dealt with trade issues, observed the same phenomenon. His explanation was that American negotiators are generally more anxious for agreements because "they are always in a hurry" and basically "problem-solving oriented." In other words, they place a high value on resolving an issue quickly. Their catchphrase might be, "Some solution is better than no solution." An interagency team would be put together, fly to Mexico City, and try to get down to the job at once. Having clarified the points at issue, they would seek a solution and move on to tomorrow's problem. Impatience led to a willingness to concede more than they should have in order to get a deal. With a more leisurely view of time, the Mexican delegation had an advantageous position from the outset.[8]

American willingness to concede, however, would not be important were it not confronted by a much greater tenacity on the part of the Mexicans. Adolfo Aguilar accounted for the stubbornness of Mexican negotiators in negotiations with the United States by referring to the burden of history and his compatriots' consciousness of the tremendous difference in size and power between the two countries. They are obliged to exercise great caution in making concessions by the sense that any agreement with the United States "carries a high risk of surrendering important national interests."[9]

The confrontation of these contrasting styles is exemplified by the negotiation of the 1957 U.S.-Mexico air transport agreement. Having dragged on through several inconclusive rounds over more than a decade, negotiations resumed in May 1955. Ambassador White, the chief U.S. negotiator, became almost distraught with the intransigence of his Mexican counterpart, Minister of Communications Buchanan. In a meeting with President Ruiz Cortines of Mexico in March 1956, White complained bitterly about his treatment:

> Buchanan had been a stumbling block for a long time. I said that Buchanan had stated, among other things, that all the concessions have been made on the Mexican side. But this is just not borne out by the

facts. The facts are that we have made countless concessions over the years, each one of which has been accepted by the Mexicans and then they have gone on to make further demands and to raise fictitious issues . . . When we permitted CMA in 1947 unlimited flights between Mexico City and Los Angeles it was on the understanding that it would lead to a bilateral agreement and so far it hasn't and, similarly, in 1951 when we permitted Aerovias Guest to fly from Mexico City to Miami we were given the same assurance but we still have no bilateral agreement. I said that Buchanan had tried these tactics again several times . . . [10]

White's intercession with Cortines did not alter the situation one whit. Clearly the problem was not Buchanan the individual. Only when the United States resorted in September 1956 to the ultimate threat to terminate all services by Mexican airlines into the United States was Mexico finally convinced that it had extracted every last possible concession.

The final agreement was highly favorable from the Mexicans' point of view. As they had demanded, it was done as an exchange of notes, not in the form of the standard U.S. air transport agreement (which was attached as an appendix). The contract was for one year only, not, as the United States had requested, of indefinite duration. On the most important point—whether there would be a division of traffic (to protect the weaker Mexican airlines) or free competition, as the United States had long insisted—the agreement substantially met Mexican concerns: Mexico was given exclusive rights on three routes, whereas on three others the parties would run only one airline each; that is, there would be some competition, but it would be strictly limited.[11]

In a laboratory study it was found that Indians—like Mexicans—are more competitive bargainers and are prepared to bargain longer than Americans.[12] These differences were displayed in the 1953 thorium nitrate affair. After India, a U.S. aid recipient, supplied thorium nitrate (a prohibited commodity under the terms of the Battle Act) to the People's Republic of China, the U.S. government insisted on a formal Indian commitment "not to do it again." Otherwise the aid program would have to be canceled. As far as India was concerned, the U.S. demand was unacceptable and flew in the face of the untrammeled exercise of Indian sovereignty—a matter of national honor on which no concession was possible. Nehru preferred no aid to aid with strings.

The initial American proposal came on August 13 in the shape of a detailed legal document, which, it was suggested, should form the basis of an exchange of notes. In the proposed document the U.S. government would recognize the Indian right to trade with whom it pleased, while the government of India would equally accept the American right to grant or withhold financial assistance to India if strategic materials were sold to enemies of the United States. Accordingly the Indian government would agree to desist from future shipments of restricted items. This proposal was turned down by Under Secretary Pillai at the Indian foreign ministry on the grounds that Prime Minister Nehru "might make a rash decision if confronted with the draft, leaving no room for negotiation."[13]

Accordingly the United States shifted its position. On September 18 Ambassador Allen proposed a simplified oral statement meeting U.S. concerns. He wished to be assured that although the government of India did not accept the Battle Act as binding, it (a) had "no intent" to ship listed commodities to prohibited destinations and (b) would inform the ambassador of "any change in the situation." Although Pillai did not reject this form of commitment in principle, he did object to its specific content—a fine distinction. "He urged that we not press GOI too strongly on this issue in order not to weaken his hand and the hands of other GOI officials genuinely working for a solution of this matter." By now, Allen was eager to get the issue out of the way and had concluded that no general declaration or commitment would be forthcoming.[14]

And so it continued. The U.S. government balked at the alternative of cutting off aid and decided to solve the problem in another way—by purchasing the total Indian production of thorium nitrate. On January 16, 1954, Secretary of State Dulles pronounced himself content with the "thorough airing" the problem of restricted commodities had received. In this situation, he concluded, the United States might well attain its objective by putting the matter squarely in the hands of the Indian government with the implication that it had a "moral responsibility" to control the export of Battle Act items.[15] And there the matter rested. It had been a counterproductive exercise and an inelegant withdrawal.

Of all the cultures discussed here, the Japanese has been the most closely scrutinized in recent years. Experts are in general agreement that few societies find give-and-take more distasteful. Instead of step-by-step concession, Thayer and Weiss observe, Japanese negotiators "call for consideration of their situation and reiterate their initial position." They "may have little leeway to do otherwise, because of the difficulty they have had in reaching consensus within their own ranks."[16] Leo Moser adds that they are likely to be unresponsive to "trial balloons" and suggestions for compromise, much to the surprise of Americans. Americans "may then see their Japanese counterparts as simply unwilling to compromise or as uninterested in keeping the negotiation process alive."[17]

Apparent Japanese immobility in the middle game has indeed been a recurrent and disconcerting feature of U.S.-Japanese negotiations. In the textile negotiations in 1970 Japanese Foreign Ministry officials were unable to get representatives of their own textile industry to agree to a modification of a formula that had proved quite unacceptable to the Nixon administration. Rather than appear empty-handed at the resumed talks, Japanese negotiators presented a "position paper" that was in fact no more than a summary of the current state of internal Japanese consultations. U.S. negotiator Peter Flanigan was "taken aback" and "expressed extreme unhappiness with the failure of the Japanese government to take a clear stance." Nor was this case an isolated one; the Japanese persistently failed to come up with counterproposals.[18]

To American taste, the Japanese make concessions "slowly and grudgingly," in the words of Michael Blaker. Initial positions are abandoned only after painful soul-searching and the prolonged evolution of a new domestic consensus.[19] This pattern certainly held up in the 1981 air service negotiations. It also characterized the 1985–86 semiconductor negotiations over U.S. allegations that the Japanese were dumping microchips on the American market. The U.S. position was that a major trade dispute would be triggered unless Japanese industry cut overcapacity, raised semiconductor prices (which were artificially low), and permitted improved U.S. access to the Japanese market. At informal meetings in July 1985, Japanese trade officials agreed to encourage increased purchases of U.S. microchips but declined to alter prices. While preparations for an antidumping suit went ahead, the United States demanded more far-reaching concessions. On August 23 there were further talks on the subject, but little progress was made because the Japanese side would not move from its earlier stance. It was not until November that the Japanese made an improved (but still unsatisfactory) offer on both prices and access. In December, negotiations had reached an impasse and were broken off. When they were resumed in January 1986 Japan, in typical fashion, repeated its previous proposal without modification.[20]

Different notions of time are clearly also a prominent factor in the frustration that seems such a frequent accompaniment of U.S.-Japanese negotiation. All too often the two sides find their rates of concession utterly unsynchronized. Of course, the frustration cuts both ways. Whereas Americans find Japanese negotiators painfully deliberate, the Japanese view American negotiators as alarmingly precipitous. Haste, one observer has remarked, evokes "a sense of confusion and chaos" in Japanese minds. Their instinctive response is to dig in their heels.[21] In the semiconductor affair, U.S. Department of Commerce initiation of an antidumping suit in the middle of talks shocked Japanese officials, conditioned by domestic practices to expect a protracted process of consultation and negotiation.[22]

In the case of the People's Republic of China, the intermediate stage between the opening moves of a negotiation, when initial proposals are put on the table, and the end game, when the final terms of the agreement are hammered out, is recognized to possess unusual features. Richard Solomon argues that the Chinese do not view negotiation "as a highly technical process of haggling over details in which the two sides initially table maximum positions and then seek to move to a point of convergence through incremental compromises. Indeed, they disparage haggling and can show remarkable flexibility in making concrete arrangements once they have decided it is in their interest to conclude an agreement."[23] It has been suggested by some scholars that the Chinese are not comfortable with the concept of reciprocal bidding—mutual and serial concessions—because of a culturally derived reluctance to incur an obligation to anyone from outside their primary kinship group.[24]

Thus, rather than engage in a protracted exchange of bids, they prefer to spend the middle game in a meticulous and patient probing of the firmness of their opponent's position in order to gauge the real nature of its bottom line. Having established to their own satisfaction their opponent's absolutely irreducible minimum, they then jump to a final position intended to reconcile contending principles. This philosophy of negotiation clearly flies in the face of many American assumptions, for example, that one's opening position must have some "give" in it, that concessions are made and reciprocated at discrete intervals throughout the middle game, and that the outcome will be a compromise somewhere in the middle. To a rival negotiator mainly concerned with discovering the American bottom line, flexibility, by indicating the softness of the U.S. position, may impede and not facilitate agreement.

In his study of U.S.-Chinese negotiating in the ambassadorial talks of the 1950s and 1960s, Kenneth Young warns that "Americans tend to put too much material between what can be conceded away and what cannot be given up under any circumstances."[25] Despite some experience—and considerable study—of negotiating with the People's Republic of China, precisely this approach was taken by the Carter administration in the 1977–78 normalization talks. Secretary of State Vance acknowledges that he intended to start out with "a maximum position" on the Taiwan issue: U.S. government personnel would have to remain on Taiwan after normalization (Beijing would not tolerate an official presence, only a nonofficial presence through an ostensibly private organization). "I did not expect the Chinese to accept our proposal, but I felt it wise to make it, even though we might eventually have to abandon it." Confusing matters even further, Vance then made, alongside this "soft" position, a major unreciprocated concession at his first meeting with Foreign Minister Huang Hua of China: the U.S. defense treaty with Taiwan would "lapse" and the withdrawal of military forces and installations from the island be completed. When, the following day, Huang Hua reiterated the Chinese position and noted that normalization would be further delayed, Vance hastened to add that the U.S. position was merely "a starting point for discussion."[26] Playing their hand closer to the chest, the Chinese kept back one crucial trump from the final normalization agreement. Three years later they used it to extract yet more U.S. concessions in a quite separate game.

In the 1955 talks for the repatriation of American citizens kept in China against their will, the same characteristic pattern of early, unreciprocated concession by the United States is found. At the second session of the talks on August 2, Chinese delegate Wang seized the initiative and put forward a series of demands, among which he called on the United States to supply a list of names of Chinese who had been issued exit visas and proposed that third-party countries take charge of both the American and the Chinese nationals. At the next session on August 4, Ambassador Johnson spent the whole time responding to the Chinese position and handed Wang the requested list of seventy-six names. Far from thanking him, Wang "expressed dissatisfaction" and demanded a complete list of names of Chinese nationals in the United States. Other unreciprocated U.S. concessions followed in subsequent sessions, including the major one of agreeing to third-party representation (pp. 9, 14).[27]

By August 23 the negotiation had stuck on the Chinese refusal to agree to release all Americans at once. In an appeal to Wang's sense of fair play, Ambassador Johnson implicitly admitted the failure of his approach. Johnson "carefully outlined [the] successive concessions we had made to obtain agreement and repeatedly stressed 'we could go no further.'" He poignantly added, "'We did not even have a definite promise, much less [the] performance we expected.'" Wang continued to fight tenaciously to avoid an explicit commitment. On September 6 there was a final battle over how to characterize the exercise by expatriates of their right to return home. Johnson made a stand on including the word "now." Wang refused point-blank, insisting on the (vague) term "expeditious." Johnson admitted that "although I used to [the] maximum my very strong negotiating position [I] was entirely unable to shake him" (pp. 76–77). Reasoned persuasion, it transpired, was not enough against patient tenacity.

Even at this late stage Johnson still had one final card to play. The agenda of the talks, agreed to on August 1, contained two items: the civilian repatriation issue and "other practical matters at issue between the two sides" (implying the U.S. economic blockade of China and the confrontation over Taiwan). It was this second item that the Chinese were really interested in, not the handful of unfortunate American civilians. Item one was simply the entry price for item two. However, Wang never revealed his interest by the merest hint and ignored Johnson's statement that he would not proceed to anything else until item one was settled (pp. 52, 59). Deciding that an imperfect agreement was better than no agreement, the United States conceded the Chinese position. This concession was a damaging comedown hardly calculated to help U.S. credibility. In simultaneous "agreed announcements" issued on September 10 the "right to return" was acknowledged, but there was no explicit determination of when (pp. 85, 86). The U.S. State Department was to regret this omission for years afterward.

Habits of authority

The crucial influence of culture on political norms and conduct should have been clear at least since the publication in 1940 of Fortes and Evans-Pritchard's classic anthropological study, *African Political Systems*. For reasons of academic parochialism, however, political scientists largely ignored the insights of anthropology.

The "political culture" school did, admittedly, use the term "culture," but in a narrow, specialized sense, and it was more concerned with the study of national institutions and attitudes than with investigating the organic link between political behavior and culture as it is understood by anthropologists. Only in recent years have political scientists begun to realize, alongside their colleagues in management studies, that behavior in both public and private organizations is simply one facet of the overall culture.[28] The logical conclusion is that intercultural communication problems can affect international relationships involving foreign ministries, departments of commerce, and defense ministries just as much as business corporations.

In any negotiation the actual interaction between the delegations represents the tip of an iceberg of internal governmental consultation and decision making. Negotiators are not free agents but representatives of departments and interests. They are therefore obliged to make continual judgments—whether consciously or not is immaterial—about one another's political and administrative processes. How constrained are one's opposite numbers by domestic political factors? Do they have the discretion to make binding decisions? If they do not, who does? Are decisions made on the basis of some conception of the national interest, or are they influenced by sectorial and even private considerations? Whom, in short, do one's counterparts speak for?

National bureaucratic operating procedures and traditions are of the essence here. Any tendency to project one's own culture-bound expectations onto others is bound to confuse and complicate the issue. However, the most unfortunate and least avoidable dissonance may arise not from any cognitive misjudgment but from the institutional encounter between incompatible and invariant administrative procedures. Havoc may be wrought not by the ill will of individuals, but by the preprogrammed working of their respective systems.

The United States and its non-Western partners have quite different political traditions and habits of authority that may interact to affect the chemistry of negotiation. Behind the formal constitutional facades lie habits of governance that are deeply rooted in the respective national cultures. The origins of Chinese and Egyptian bureaucratic procedures are lost in antiquity. Collectivistic societies tend to be paternalistic and hierarchical, and they take the relationship of dominating father and compliant children as their paradigm of leadership. In the individualistic culture of the United States, power is divided and dispersed precisely to avoid the emergence of an absolute and centralized authority, which is viewed with deep suspicion as a threat to individual liberties. Whereas it would be hard for Egyptian or Mexican officials to question a presidential decision directly, American officials would feel it their duty to make their views known, hardly seeing such an action as a challenge to duly constituted authority.

The American system of checks and balances—of rivalry between executive and legislature, and of the supremacy of due process of law—can be particularly confusing for those used to more paternalistic habits. That the American president should be hemmed in by rival sources of power and unable to make decisions without question or appeal is indeed puzzling. Nasser believed that Lyndon Johnson could "do anything" he liked when he became president of the United States.[29] With the renewal of diplomatic relations between Cairo and Washington in 1974, the Egyptian government received firsthand instruction from Secretary of State Kissinger on such matters as the power of the Congress to block appropriations, and the divergent views of the State Department, the Department of Defense, and the Treasury. Nevertheless, despite this growing insight, the Egyptian government still tended to underestimate the limits on presidential power.[30] Even at the height of the Watergate crisis Foreign Minister Fahmy believed that Nixon's "authority was strongly felt by everybody . . . it was clear that he ran the show single-handedly on behalf of the United States." (This view would not be universally shared.) When facing a delegation led by Kissinger, Fahmy projected this same perception of omnipotence onto the secretary of state.[31] Later, Fahmy was deeply disillusioned when Carter admitted that he "could not simply impose his own views" on Congress and public opinion.[32] Unfamiliarity with truly representative government, and the possibility that factors external to the bureaucracy might have an input into decision making, inclined Fahmy to exaggerate his American interlocutors' freedom of action.

It is strange to find that Mexicans, too, despite their proximity to the United States and long experience, overestimate U.S. presidential authority. They assume, Alan Riding comments, "that not only the executive branch but Congress, the judiciary, the state governments and even municipal authorities in the United States are all subservient to the President."[33] Because the many agencies that deal with Mexican-related issues in the vast Washington bureaucracy do so in a relatively autonomous (and all too often uncoordinated) manner, the impression is given of either extraordinary deviousness or confusion over priorities.

A graphic illustration of Mexico's misperception of U.S. presidential authority came in 1977, during talks concerning the supply of Mexican gas to the United States. The initial round of negotiations was conducted between PEMEX (Petroleos Mexicanos) and a consortium of U.S. oil companies and crystallized into a memorandum of intent signed in August 1977. Because of opposition to the deal in the Congress and from Secretary of Energy Schlesinger, the original agreement eventually fell through. The Mexicans had been warned by U.S. officials that any agreement was subject to ratification by federal regulatory agencies as early as April of the same year, but they failed to fathom the administrative process. Accustomed to the dominant role of the chief executive in their own country, they assumed (in the words of a key U.S. official) "that Carter could wave a magic wand and the deal would go through." [34]

The converse of an American president's hampered exercise of power is the ability of a Third World (but not Japanese!) leader to make clear-cut decisions. There were many examples of this phenomenon in the cases examined: Mrs. Gandhi's decision in 1982 to cut through the thicket of debate and agree to settle the nuclear fuel issue; Sadat's extraordinary virtuoso performance in the peace process with Israel mediated by the United States; the on-again, off-again decision making of President Lopez Portillo of Mexico in the gas talks and 1982 debt negotiations. To the extent that it is easier both to comprehend and to deal with a centralized system of decision making, there is little evidence that U.S. negotiators were hampered by this factor. In fact, the danger in dealing with a personalized system of government is the possibility of underestimating the power of bureaucracy. On matters that do not come to the personal attention of the chief executive, the bureaucracy still plays the dominant role.

A 1988 study of Indian bureaucratic morality by two Indian academics strikingly exemplifies the incongruence of American and Third World (but, again, not Japanese) administrative procedures and norms, external features notwithstanding. The authors' point of departure is their insistence that "an understanding of the Indian bureaucracy must include its symbolic relationship with the Indian culture." Officials are bound to conform to "culture-bound" behavior or risk "social disapproval." Despite the formative British influence on the Indian civil service, formal patterns are overridden by informal practices. Rigid hierarchy, "mutual suspicion," and an authoritarianism "destructive of any team spirit" are the norm. The evasion of responsibility is rife. "When confronted with a difficult decision, the Indian bureaucrat seldom makes any attempt to tackle the problem with initiative and imagination. Instead, he will refer the matter to another department to make a series of unnecessary references to subordinates to gain time."[35]

Foreign Service officers with experience of Delhi strongly corroborate this portrait. Indian officials are described as being eager to shuffle responsibility onto someone else and reluctant to exercise personal judgment or make decisions. They are more likely to find reasons for inaction than for action, and they are very subservient to their ranking superiors. An experienced State Department official observed that the caution of the Indian bureaucrat had a very direct impact on negotiations: all successful negotiations, he argued, have a momentum of their own. But there was inevitably a point when the engaged officials, having arrived at an agreement to their own satisfaction, had to be prepared to sell it to their superiors. Indian negotiators were reluctant to do so.

Another State Department official, who served for four years in a senior position in the Delhi embassy, observed that Indian negotiators thought of two things: (a) how they were perceived by their superiors and (b) how the public would react. The higher the negotiators ranked in the bureaucracy, the greater their sensitivity to these points. Point b was more important even than point a. If an official felt that he could not defend a position before public opinion—parliament and the press—he would subvert it, whatever the wishes of his minister. But if he felt that a position was defensible and he had a directive from on high, then he was likely to be cooperative. By and large, then, my source continued, the Indian bureaucrat was "exceptionally cautious" and "unwilling to expose himself." He found little difficulty in slowing things down or sabotaging the process altogether. Influenced by opposing interests, local officials negotiating with Pepsi Cola to set up an Indian subsidiary were able to drag the negotiation out for years.

My sources were uncertain about the helpfulness of establishing contact with officials at a high level in the Indian hierarchy. One view was that doing so might facilitate a negotiation in the sense that high-level approval would filter down and favorably influence the negotiators directly involved. On the other hand, a minister might give his apparent consent to an idea and promise to intervene, but nothing would follow. "You get this kind of runaround for months on end," said one of my sources. It is significant that N. Ram, an Indian, decries precisely the practice of bypassing the appropriate official. He notes that in the nuclear fuel talks the

Indians strongly resented the penchant of the leader of the U.S. delegation, Assistant Secretary of State James Malone, for going over the head of his opposite number—an atomic energy expert— to discuss the issues privately or informally with the Indian External Affairs Ministry official. Malone's perception that his diplomatic colleague might be more receptive was misguided. "The approach did not seem to enhance confidence in the U.S. negotiating position." [36] Highly "sensitive to the rank of the person negotiating with them," Paul Kreisberg adds, senior Indian officials also resent having to negotiate with someone of a lower status. [37]

Many of the features of the Indian bureaucracy are reproduced across the Indian Ocean in Egypt. Negotiating in Cairo can be a nightmare for American diplomats, for they find themselves entangled in a congeries of disorganized, inefficient, and overlapping ministries. Officials are unwilling to accept responsibility and are, on the whole, unfamiliar with Western concepts of planning and administration. America's aid program in Egypt has been hindered by these factors from the beginning. Once Congress had voted Egypt an aggregate sum of $250 million (in December 1974), the U.S. embassy in Cairo then had to negotiate with the various ministries how this money was to be spent. The experience was chastening—and typical. The Ministry of Development demonstrated an inability to plan properly or to determine its priorities, the minister simply presenting the embassy with wish lists. When Ambassador Eilts turned to the prime minister for guidance, he was told, "You decide." Short ministerial incumbency was an added complication. On agricultural matters, talks began with one minister and continued with another, who put in a new and fanciful request for, of all things, an agricultural museum. [38]

The General Motors negotiation provides a classic case study in the problems of negotiating with the Egyptian bureaucracy. General Motors, which already had a truck plant in Egypt and was pleased with the productivity of Egyptian workers, entered into talks with the Egyptian government in 1984 to set up an automobile spare parts industry. A deal would have been of great mutual benefit. The Egyptian plant would have provided spares for the large home market and would have been well placed to export to Europe, Saudi Arabia, and the Persian Gulf. It would have provided thousands of jobs, both saved and earned foreign currency, and provided the nucleus for the development of ancillary industries. What should have been a six-month negotiation dragged out for years. In the first place a cautious President Mubarak declined to give a lead but left the matter in the hands of the manifold ministries and interests involved. A senior diplomat described him as "the ultimate creator of consensus in this ultimate bureaucratic system." Leaders in paternalistic systems are not necessarily autocrats.

Many other bureaucratic obstacles hindered progress. A bureaucracy embedded in the socialist, statist dogmas of the Nasserist period found the General Motors wish to build upon private enterprise deeply distasteful. Officials, sometimes benefiting financially from vested interests, proved obstructive. Procrastination was the order of the day. Negotiations were not always conducted in a spirit of candor. In the end the deal fell through over the refusal of the Egyptian customs agency to grant General Motors exemptions from import duties. "It could not," I was told by a senior Egyptian source with unconscious irony, "allow for any exceptions."

Chinese and Japanese bureaucracies present rather different and special features compared to those of Egypt and India. Collectivism and hierarchy have taken a different turn in the Far East. Dealing with the Chinese, Henry Kissinger has written, is like being "engaged in one endless conversation with an organism that recalled everything, seemingly motivated by a single intelligence." Each remark by a Chinese official was part of a purposeful overall design.[39] Other American negotiators have talked of an "unfolding dialogue" as they moved rung by rung up the ladder of the Chinese hierarchy. By keeping interlocutors at arm's length at first, and only gradually permitting them access to the higher echelons of the bureaucracy, the Chinese are able to assess at leisure their negotiating position and reserve the denouement for the moment of ripeness.[40]

For individualistic Americans, then, to negotiate with the Chinese is to be pitted against something beyond the realm of everyday experience. How could Alexis Johnson, having helped to write his own negotiating instructions in 1955, do other than assume that his Chinese counterpart had some similar leeway for discretion? But, as we have seen, Johnson's most eloquent powers of persuasion were futile in the face of someone whose role and training obliged him to reiterate undeviatingly the line determined in Beijing. The first stage of wisdom in negotiating with the Chinese is to grasp that one is confronted with the world's oldest bureaucracy.

Since the Nixon-Kissinger period the United States has obviously gained considerable direct experience of doing business with the People's Republic of China. The very peculiarity of the

Chinese system in Western eyes has alerted the State Department
to the need to modify work methods in dealing with Beijing. Cyrus
Vance, secretary of state under Carter, indicates that he was well
aware of the pitfalls of jet-age diplomacy. In the 1978 normalization talks it was decided to have a resident negotiator in Beijing,
not a special envoy. "The Chinese decision-making process," he observes, "is a methodical, careful one, which requires extensive consultations among the leadership after each proposal. Trips by
senior American officials, bathed in the glare of publicity, would
not have left the Chinese enough time to go through the difficult
process of adjusting their positions."[41]

Such insight into Chinese decision making has not always been
matched by equal appreciation of Japanese requirements. A recurrent cause of confusion in U.S.-Japanese negotiations has been the
American failure to appreciate the essentially consensual style of
Japanese decision making and, hence, to make allowances for the
very limited ability of Japan's political leadership to impose its
views on the bureaucracy. In the Japanese system of government,
as has been frequently pointed out, initiatives originate from below
and not from above. Through the painstaking process of decision
making known as *ringisei*, a draft (*ringisho*) circulates among all
concerned middle-ranking officials to be appraised and discussed.
By the time the document reaches the highest echelon it represents
a consensus of opinion that is highly resistant to modification.
Leaders, seen as being above the detailed day-to-day management
of affairs and playing a largely moral and representative role, are
expected to have absolute confidence in subordinates and to approve the document without change.[42]

Japanese ministers, therefore, do not perform an intrusive, ini-
tiatory executive function, as in the American tradition. Former
Foreign Service officer Thomas P. Rohlen comments that Japanese
managers are simply not as busy as their American counterparts
but adopt a calmer and more detached attitude. "When I worked
in the State Department," Rohlen observes, "the Secretary of State
was very much involved with daily events. He was not sitting back
watching how the State Department worked. Kissinger hired others to do that for him." In Japan this would not be the case.[43]

In negotiation after negotiation American decision makers have
been disappointed by the failure of Japanese leaders to fulfill
American expectations. In 1955 Foreign Minister Shigemitsu of
Japan was obliged, at the insistence of Secretary of State John Foster Dulles, to sign a joint communiqué committing Japan to a

greater contribution to regional defense. But the Japanese government was actually interested at the time in a revision of the lopsided 1951 security treaty, and in the face of domestic necessities Shigemitsu was forced to retreat from the commitment contained in the Washington communiqué.[44] Again in 1969 Prime Minister Sato was browbeaten at his summit with President Nixon into endorsing a formula on textile imports that went well beyond the limits of the Japanese domestic consensus. Back home, lower-level Japanese officials rejected the agreement reached by their own prime minister. Unable to deliver on his assurances, Sato was embarrassed, and the Nixon administration was outraged. Extraordinarily enough, the same pattern repeated itself a few months later. What Sato accepted in Washington was repudiated by his negotiators in Tokyo.[45] The most recent occasion on which American misapprehension about the working of the Japanese system caused distress was in 1987, during negotiations to improve access to Japanese construction projects for U.S. firms. At a Reagan-Nakasone summit, American officials believed that the Japanese prime minister had promised to open the door to public works projects. When detailed negotiations resumed at the level of experts, Japanese officials were perceived to have reneged on Nakasone's summit "pledge."[46]

* * *

An unmistakable tendency to intercultural confusion can be seen in these examples. But dissonance was mutual. Used to dealing with leaders who lead, American statesmen found it natural to meet with their Japanese opposite numbers at a critical juncture in the negotiations in order to break the deadlock at the highest level. The possibility that the locus of practical authority lay elsewhere, that Japanese decision-making procedures could not be bypassed, and that the personal pledge of a minister (with the best possible intentions) might not be redeemable did not occur to them. For their part, Japanese ministers were quite unable to say no. They preferred to take the line of least resistance rather than lose face by admitting that they could not meet American anticipations. Had their own intercultural communication skills been sharper they would have realized that Americans do not take kindly to broken promises.

eight

Sounds, Signals, Silence
Middle Game II

In the Anglo-Saxon adversarial legal and negotiating tradition, a central role is reserved for the exercise of persuasion. Civilized people of goodwill, it is firmly believed, are amenable to reasoned argument. Like advocates in a court of law, negotiators are expected to make a logical case for their point of view. Out of the interplay of opposing arguments a formula will emerge that is satisfactory to both sides. In the problem-solving, *erabi* paradigm, therefore, reason is seen as the vehicle of progress. Otherwise, negotiation would be reduced to a crude contest of power, a state of affairs profoundly antithetical to the enlightened Westerner. But is this assumption generally shared across cultures? If not, what levers of influence are likely to work best with high-context negotiators?

It may seem obvious that negotiators should seek to persuade each other. But a moment's reflection from a cross-cultural perspective serves to caution one that nothing should be taken for granted. For a start, different cultures, as Edmund Glenn warns, reason in different ways—some inductively, some deductively, some emotionally. Japanese writer Abe Yoshio goes so far as to argue that his countrymen eschew logic altogether, intuiting a conclusion with no intervening steps. He contrasts the Western employment of "logical thinking to convince the other person" with

the reluctance of the Japanese to attempt to persuade their interlocutors, "even if they are certain they are correct." In these circumstances dialogue performs no purpose in negotiation: "No
matter how much one negotiates there is no concrete result, no
agreement on the basis of a thorough statement from both sides as
to where their differences lie."[1]

The Japanese view debate as unwelcome, a threat to communal
harmony. In a study comparing American and Japanese subjects,
a wide, cross-cultural gap was found in attitudes toward the notion
of due process. Explicitly accounting for the difference in terms of
the individualism-collectivism dichotomy, the author concluded
that the "adversarial, bargaining style of conflict resolution" chosen by Americans was not congenial to the Japanese. The Japanese
expected the parties to a dispute simply "to do the 'right' thing," in
other words, to conform to behavior determined by the pattern of
obligation implicit in the relationship.[2] This idea is difficult to comprehend for someone not brought up in the Confucian tradition,
with its intricate lattice of roles and duties.

Means of influence

In the middle phase of negotiations, then, the distinction between
the American, problem-oriented approach versus the non-
Western, relationship-oriented approach toward negotiation reas-
serts itself. Interdependent cultures, declining to isolate a problem
from its interpersonal or intergroup context, are less impressed
than their American interlocutors by solely instrumental considerations. The major asset in this setting, it transpires, is the ability
not to marshal a conclusive argument, but to apply the personal
touch in one's dealings, appealing to an affinity that transcends the
immediate business transaction. Before it is possible to engage in a
frank and productive exchange with the members of high-context
cultures one must gain their confidence and trust. The implication
is that a good negotiator will possess outstanding social skills as well
as technical competence.

"So much is personal" in dealing with Mexicans, I was told by an
old Mexico hand. It all boiled down to "me and you," not "my government and your government," and so friendship and personal
rapport had to be carefully cultivated. (Indeed, the Mexicans
sometimes overstepped the bounds of propriety in their wish to
ensure a favorable atmosphere between negotiators.) Before busi-

ness could be done, one had to know one's partner reasonably well. Long lunches, sometimes even more than formal negotiating sessions, were the occasion for progress. Joseph Friedkin, who served for many years on the U.S.-Mexican Boundary and Water Commission, recalls that in the Chamizal negotiations the commission met formally only "when we sat down to sign something." Most of their work was "very informal, usually two on two or one on one."[3] Herbert Brownell, chief U.S. negotiator to the Colorado River salinity talks, made his decisive breakthrough on a walk with Foreign Minister Rabasa (reminiscent of the famous Paul Nitze "walk in the woods" accord with a Soviet arms control negotiator). Fortunately, the two men enjoyed good personal relations.[4]

Ellsworth Bunker, one of the most experienced American roving ambassadors and negotiators in the postwar era, mediated an agreement between Egypt and Saudi Arabia in 1963. Among the techniques of negotiation that he found most effective in working with Arabs, John Badeau (ambassador to Egypt at the time) recalled, was the use of a "personal as opposed to official argumentative presentation." Whether as a result of intuition or sound briefing, Bunker grasped the strongly personal element in inter-Arab rivalries. As a *wasit* (intermediary) passing between the disputants, he knew that the person-to-person element was of the essence. He would say to Nasser, " 'I've got to have something in my hand to go back with. You can give me this,' rather than arguing on the higher level of disembodied Egyptian-U.S. interests. He could do this charmingly, but very, very firmly."[5]

It does seem that the quality of the personal relationship at the highest executive level has also had substantive implications. President Kennedy, for instance, appreciated that it was helpful to maintain a personal correspondence with President Nasser. His letters were businesslike and straightforward, but they were carefully drafted to contain a warm, personal element. In addition to regular notes, Kennedy also made a point of keeping Nasser informed through other channels of anything that might impinge on their relations. By notifying Nasser in advance of the sale of Hawk antiaircraft missiles to Israel, Kennedy managed to soften the blow. On other occasions the Egyptian president had been angered by less. U.S.-Egyptian relations greatly improved during this period.[6] In contrast, Nasser developed an antipathy for President Johnson. Although they never met, Nasser studied Kennedy's successor carefully in word and picture. An undignified photograph showing Johnson displaying his famous operation scar in public shocked

Egyptians as unbefitting the leader of a great nation. Then President Johnson abandoned the practice of writing personally to the Egyptian leader. Whether this action was the cause or the effect of a deterioration in state-to-state ties is a moot point. It had the practical effect of closing a useful channel of communication when it was most needed—in the Middle East crisis of May-June 1967.[7]

President Johnson did at first achieve a striking personal rapport with Prime Minister Indira Gandhi of India, however. In January 1966 Mrs. Gandhi visited the United States for eleven days. Behaving toward her with "Texan chivalry," Johnson addressed her as "little lady." Strange as it may seem, Mrs. Gandhi blossomed at this display of flirtatiousness and attention. The trip was productive politically, and the two sides succeeded in putting together a package of reforms of the Indian economy to be accompanied by U.S. assistance.[8] American officials had long realized the need to cultivate personal ties with the proud and sensitive Indian leaders, ever since an unsuccessful visit by Jawaharlal Nehru—Mrs. Gandhi's father—to the United States in October 1949, marked by disappointing meetings with President Truman and Secretary of State Acheson.[9] Chester Bowles (ambassador to India 1951–53 and 1963–69) determined to cultivate Nehru and as wide a circle of Indians as possible on arrival, succeeded superlatively, and became one of the most popular U.S. ambassadors ever to serve in Delhi.[10]

President Eisenhower reached the conclusion that Nehru was "often more swayed by personality than logical argument. He seems to be intensely personal in his whole approach . . ." Accordingly, he suggested that Secretary of State Dulles "urge our new Ambassador there to do everything possible to win the personal confidence and friendship of Nehru."[11] Ironically, Eisenhower's vice president, Richard Nixon, established a very poor personal relationship with Mrs. Gandhi, who viewed him, in the words of a State Department official, as a "slippery, untrustworthy" customer. They met in 1969 when Nixon visited India, and in November 1971 on the eve of the India-Pakistan war. Their mutual dislike was palpable. Nixon loathed what he perceived as Mrs. Gandhi's condescending and self-righteous manner. Mrs. Gandhi clearly found no common language with this personally least engaging of presidents.

What arguments worked best in negotiations? No consistent pattern emerges on this question. It is easier to point to those that have proved ineffective. As one would expect in dealing with high-context, face-salient societies that place such emphasis on group harmony and the avoidance of personal friction, confrontation is not an acceptable mode of behavior in negotiation and is likely to be counterproductive. "Table thumping" was out of the question in dealing with the Egyptian government, Ambassador Eilts emphasized. Former ambassador to Mexico Jova (1974–77) stressed the need to avoid ultimatums. He always tried to "get the message across in a softer, more indirect way." Above all, one had to avoid "humiliating them," giving the appearance that the Mexicans were "taking orders from Washington." He believed that public criticism of the Mexican government was "fatal." [12]

One of Jova's successors, John Gavin, deliberately ignored this caveat and found his effectiveness in Mexico City curtailed, and some pressure created for his removal. Appearing before a Senate subcommittee in 1986, Gavin strongly defended his outspoken style. The Mexican "dread of [U.S.] intervention" should not deter the pursuit of "a frank, an open, and a respectful dialogue." His view was well received by critics of Mexico in the Senate. Senator Peter Wilson (R-Calif.), for instance, thought that the time for undue sensitivity on the part of the United States was "really past if we are going to deal with the monumental problems that are afflicting both nations . . . the United States cannot engage in politeness." Why Mexico should be more responsive to strident criticism was not explained. State Department professionals learned long ago that rhetoric—"Mexico bashing"—might be popular back home but was not calculated to elicit Mexican cooperation. "Denunciation is counterproductive," points out William D. Rogers, a former assistant secretary of state for inter-American relations. "Quiet diplomacy, a sense of our long and troubled history together, a sensitivity to the very special psychology of our coexistence, these are the essence of the relationship." [13]

Corroborating Rogers's view, Christopher Dickey of the *Washington Post* observed among Mexicans an "almost oriental obsession with saving face." He concluded that "the fastest way to reach a dead end in any kind of negotiation is to force an issue." According to Dickey, the difficulties faced by the United States in the 1979 gas talks were largely a result of the pugnacious approach adopted by the U.S. Department of Energy. [14] It is quite true that Mexican negotiators found Secretary Schlesinger abrupt and arrogant. By all accounts he behaved in a rude and offhand manner. He later became a peculiar butt of their displeasure. There was, however, a substantive and not simply subjective disagreement, namely, the secretary's view that the Mexican asking price was far too high. In the end, the price achieved by the United States was better in real terms after Schlesinger's brutal veto than it would have been otherwise. Although his manner may have offended the Mexican government, it did not cause the breakdown of talks.

Hectoring apart, the United States appears to have substantial, tangible assets to bring to bear in a negotiation, especially with Third World countries (the balance of advantage with respect to Japan is clearly different). Yet experience indicates that here, too, the attempt to condition the supply of a particular benefit such as financial aid, military assistance, or food relief on the other side's compliant behavior is likely to be counterproductive. Egypt's point-blank refusal to have any truck with Western alliance schemes in the 1950s has already been mentioned. If the supply of American arms was to be contingent on foreign policy concessions, Nasser preferred to turn to the Soviet Union. Failure to recognize the futility of crude pressure in dealing with Egypt (or India for that matter) was to cost the United States dearly.

After the announcement of the so-called Czech arms deal between Egypt and the Soviet Union in September 1955, paid for by the mortgaging of the Egyptian cotton crop, Secretary of State Dulles concluded that Egypt was unlikely to be left with sufficient foreign exchange to service loans then under negotiation with the World Bank to build a dam at Aswan. He was also determined to give the Egyptians a short, sharp lesson for their association with the Soviet Union. In a dramatic gesture, Dulles baldly informed the Egyptian ambassador of the rejection of the loan application. The Egyptians were humiliated and infuriated. Far from becoming more compliant with American wishes, Nasser was even more alienated from the Western world and driven deeper into the Soviet camp. Within twenty-four hours of Dulles's snub he decided to nationalize the Suez Canal.[15]

Later attempts by the United States, particularly the Congress, to use food aid as explicit levers of influence were also a resounding failure. To some senators it appeared self-evident that because Egypt was receiving one-third of all its grain from the United States it should be compliant with American wishes, for example, on the need to make peace with Israel. But as Ambassador Badeau argues, Egyptians would not concede a deeply felt principle "for greed or for money." The mere suspicion, he writes, that food was being used for political ends robbed it "of much of its diplomatic usefulness."[16] In the mid-1960s, following a series of unpleasant incidents in U.S.-Egyptian relations, Ambassador Lucius Battle informed the Egyptian minister of provision that he thought the time was inappropriate to press President Johnson about the supply of wheat (under the Public Law 480 program). The message reached Nasser in garbled form, although its purport was clear enough. In a speech that day at Port Said, Nasser launched a vitriolic personal attack on President Johnson: "The American Ambassador," he stormed, "says that our behavior is not acceptable. Well let us tell them that those who do not accept our behavior can go and drink . . . from the sea . . . we are not going to accept gangsterism by cowboys."[17]

Much the same pattern can be found in U.S.-Indian relations in the 1950s and 1960s. The 1951 negotiations for a loan with which to purchase two million tons of American wheat after the failure of the monsoon rains were conducted under the shadow of congressional demands for an Indian quid pro quo in the area of foreign policy. It appeared to Nehru that the United States was "taking advantage of India's food shortage to drive a hard bargain."[18] He certainly was not going to abandon nonalignment in exchange for aid. If used with tact, aid can create goodwill; mishandled, it may only feed resentment.

The futility of pressure, even under apparently auspicious circumstances, was again demonstrated in the aftermath of the 1962 Sino-Indian border war. Initially, the United States gained enormous credit in India for coming so promptly to its assistance at a difficult time. The temptation to capitalize on this fund of goodwill to achieve other foreign policy goals proved irresistible for the Kennedy administration and particularly its envoy Ambassador John Kenneth Galbraith. In cooperation with the United Kingdom, the United States began a process of mediation between India and Pakistan to resolve the Kashmir dispute. Overriding the doubts of Under Secretary of State Chester Bowles, Galbraith unwisely seized on India's acute need for military supplies to force concessions on it. In a letter to President Kennedy, Galbraith outlined how pressure was to be judiciously exercised: "We are urging the importance of a settlement as a prime goal of Indian foreign policy, for that makes our military aid both possible and effective."[19]

In the immediate aftermath of the war, Nehru was content to play along with the mediation initiative, unwilling to antagonize the United States and Britain while continued Western support and military supplies were needed. Given Nehru's views on Pakistan and Kashmir there was no chance that he would agree to meaningful concessions. The talks dragged on. Finally, Galbraith decided to confront Nehru. "If I did not press hard," he writes in his diary, "the failure would be blamed on me . . . So I made the best of a bad situation and tried too hard." He saw Nehru on two occasions to bring his "careful buildup of persuasion here in India to a climax." Nehru turned him down flat both times and the initiative petered out.[20] Unfortunately, the end result was to dissipate most of the capital that the United States had acquired as a result of helping during the emergency. Gratitude was converted into resentment. Indians concluded that the United States had taken advantage of their moment of weakness to force on them an unacceptable course of action.

The pattern repeated itself in 1965 on an issue not of security but of development. Difficult and drawn-out negotiations between a U.S. consortium and the Indian government for the development of the Indian fertilizer industry were hindered, rather than helped, by the intervention of Averell Harriman, the U.S. roving ambassador. Harriman had been involved in the 1962–63 Kashmir mediation effort and it is therefore extraordinary that he should have duplicated Galbraith's error. At a "most stormy meeting" with the Indian finance minister, Harriman threatened drastic cuts in aid unless India created appropriate conditions for investment by American business (that is, the fertilizer consortium). The meeting was utterly counterproductive. Indian officials became convinced that pressure was being exerted on India to approve a project about which they had serious doubts. Finance Minister Krishnamachari was so incensed by the episode that he advocated terminating the negotiations. After pondering the matter the Indian government decided that an abrupt move on its part would be inexpedient and would have negative effects on India's relations with the United States and the World Bank. Negotiations continued, but Harriman's rough treatment of Krishnamachari certainly contributed, together with certain other factors, to the demise of a project that had appeared promising at first.[21]

The reluctance to say no

The contrasting uses of language by Americans and their non-Western negotiating partners have provided fertile grounds for misunderstanding. In the straightforward style of American culture, language has primarily the instrumental function of transmitting information. For the members of face-salient societies, however, it performs the important role of social lubricant, easing and harmonizing personal relations. High-context individuals are unable to subordinate the personal impact of a message to its semantic accuracy. A painful and disruptive truth is no virtue to those who measure all actions, verbal and nonverbal, in terms of social consequences.

A striking feature of collectivistic, high-context speakers consistently remarked upon by American diplomats is their dislike of the negative; a direct contradiction is invariably avoided. This is a particularly remarked feature of Japanese discourse. I have noted its appearance in U.S.-Japanese relations in the previous chapter. One episode in particular has entered the annals of intercultural misunderstanding. On Prime Minister Sato's 1969 trip to Washington, President Nixon insisted that Japan exercise export restraint. Mr. Sato's classic reply, delivered with a heavenward glance, was, "*Zensho shimasu.*" Literally translated as, "I will do my best," the expression really means, "No way." Nixon naturally understood it to mean that he had his guest's agreement. When there was no practical follow-up, he denounced Sato as a liar. But unlike Americans, who expect yes or no answers, Japanese are quite happy with the gray areas. "They hate 'no,' and they hate 'yes,'" as an American official put it.[22] Expressions such as "*taihen muzukashii*" ("very difficult") are quite translucent ways of saying no, but without the unpleasantness the Japanese associate with a blunt rejection.[23]

Masao Kunihiro, a Japanese anthropologist, goes so far as to pick out this feature "as the most important characteristic of the Japanese language and the cognitive behavior of the Japanese people." The reluctance to say yes or no, to agree or disagree, is rooted, he argues, in a deep-seated aversion to either-or, dichotomous thinking. The Japanese instinct, unlike that of Westerners, is not to categorize or differentiate, but to combine and reconcile. He points to this factor as a powerful "source of gaps in intercultural communication."[24]

The first lesson to learn in Egypt, one eminent diplomat remarked, is that "Egyptians hate to turn you down; they never say no." A colleague with long service in Mexico City noted that the Mexican habit was "not to say no, just never to say yes." In other words, a negotiation might continue indefinitely and indeterminately. How, then, was one to know whether consent was genuine or feigned? If one's antennae were sufficiently attuned to accompanying verbal and nonverbal signals, it might be possible to read between the lines. Otherwise, the true message became clear only in retrospect. If nothing happened, then one had been the victim of the "social affirmative."

An amusing instance of Egyptian politeness being mistaken for agreement occurred at the beginning of presidential envoy Robert Anderson's secret mission to try to mediate between Nasser and Prime Minister Ben Gurion of Israel in January 1956. Anderson presented his proposals in a strong Texan drawl and was encouraged by Nasser's nodding and smiling in apparent agreement. After Anderson returned to his hotel, his colleague Kermit Roosevelt stayed behind for a few minutes at Nasser's request. "What," Nasser wanted to know, "was Mr. Anderson talking about?" Neither he nor his vice president had understood a word. Roosevelt rushed off to intercept an upbeat cable Anderson was dictating for Secretary Dulles.[25]

Because persistence (not taking no for an answer) is a fairly familiar American trait, Egyptians' reluctance to disappoint their interlocutor may set the scene for mutual disappointment and frustration. William Quandt argues that drawn-out negotiations of this kind are a sure "sign that the Egyptian side is not ready for a deal but does not want to bear the onus for breaking off negotiations."[26]

This inconclusive pattern of behavior has repeated itself on several occasions in recent years, often in negotiations involving the U.S. Department of Defense. One negotiation that dragged on for almost a decade concerned the passage of nuclear-powered warships of the U.S. Sixth Fleet through the Suez Canal. The Egyptian government was genuinely sensitive to the environmental risks, real or imagined, of nuclear power and of its possible effect on navigation through the canal. Ambassador Eilts first raised the issue in the mid-1970s with Sadat, who sent him on to Defense Minister Gamasy. The latter noted in turn that his authority did not extend to running the waterway and shuffled him off onto the bureaucracy. And so it continued, all the while the U.S. Defense Department failing to take the point. Some years later, President Mubarak was persuaded to agree, and in 1984 a nuclear-powered warship went through the canal for the first time. But it was a pyrrhic victory that used up excessive credit. When National Security Adviser John Poindexter tactlessly leaked news of the ship's passage, the agreement, which Egypt had entered into reluctantly and against its better judgment, was immediately called off by the embarrassed Egyptians.[27]

Much the same pattern was repeated in negotiations initiated by the Department of Defense for a privileges and immunities agreement to cover the naval and military medical research unit staff in Cairo. Defense Minister Kamal Hassan Ali gave his good-humored assent, although in fact Egyptians resented American personnel being granted extraterritorial status in a manner all too reminiscent of the hated capitulations. (Incidentally, the unit had already functioned for years without such an agreement.[28]) Yet another example of Defense Department legalism and rigidity was the case of the ill-fated negotiations for an American facility at Ras Banas on the Gulf of Suez. Inherited by a reluctant Mubarak from Sadat, the negotiations ran into insuperable difficulties. Unwilling to meet American conditions and unhappy about the prospect of a base reminiscent of the Soviet (and before that the British) experience, the Egyptian government was caught in a bind. Although agreement was out of the question, it was loath to offend the United States by a blunt refusal. Negotiations might have continued indefinitely had the American side not forced the issue.[29]

For high-context individuals it is always easier to agree than to disagree. Confronted by a persistent and undesirable request, they find the "social affirmative" the best way out of an uncomfortable situation. The fault is not theirs but that of their obtuse interlocutor, who has failed to draw the correct conclusions from the hesitancy and unenthusiastic nature of the reply. Not even a sophisticated and cosmopolitan ambassador like John Kenneth Galbraith was immune to this solecism. The occasion was the first days of the 1962 Sino-Indian border war. The State Department (looking ahead to the postwar period and a possible resolution of the Kashmir dispute) decided that it would be helpful if Nehru requested, through U.S. good offices, Pakistani assurances of nonintervention. Galbraith describes in painful detail his insensitive importuning of the Indian prime minister.

Nehru, whose forces were being pushed back by seemingly irresistible Chinese pressure, appeared (according to Galbraith's own account) frail, old, and desperately tired. Galbraith asked him if the United States could inform Ayub Khan, the Pakistani leader, that India would welcome Pakistani assurances. Nehru replied lukewarmly that "he would have no objection to our saying so." This was not good enough for the ambassador. Galbraith then "moved in very hard." Would Nehru say that he would *warmly accept* such assurances? Looking "a little stunned"—as well he might—Nehru consented, adding that such a gesture might be helpful for the future. Galbraith resolved to press home his advantage. Could Nehru *assure* him that he would respond to such assurances? Yes, "on some appropriate occasion he would," Nehru responded with telltale discomfort. Galbraith moved in for the kill. "This was a time for generosity and he should be *immediately forthcoming.*" Pressed to the wall, Nehru agreed.[30] It was a ruthless performance by Galbraith, and an empty triumph. Of course Nehru, under extreme duress, had no choice but to give his unwilling consent. To beg a favor of Pakistan, a sectarian state that in Indian eyes stood for the antithesis of everything secular India represented, was excruciating. It was a bad beginning to a doomed mediation.

In the case of Mexico, identical inhibitions on the expression of a blunt refusal can be readily observed. The three days of talks that preceded Operation Intercept, the largest drug enforcement effort ever launched on the U.S.-Mexican border, were marked by Mexican disenchantment with American proposals. Mexico had not been consulted in the formulation of those proposals and yet was being required to comply with far-reaching measures that were likely to be extremely disruptive. It was impossible in a single round of negotiations to secure the far-reaching cooperation and coordination required to make the operation a success.

Unable to express their wholehearted consent, yet unwilling to reject American proposals out of hand, the Mexicans predictably opted for polite and emollient expressions of goodwill and encouragement. They agreed to nothing concrete. At the conclusion of the conference the two delegations jointly declared their firm resolve to use all available resources "to strengthen further the cooperative efforts" against drug manufacture and shipping. This essentially vacuous formula was apparently sufficient to convince U.S. attorney general Kleindienst that he had obtained the support of the Mexican government for his plan and that he could look forward to its cooperation in a drive against the sources of marijuana. Both judgments proved utterly ill founded.[31]

Directness versus indirectness

To the dislike of confrontation and contradiction high-context cultures add a related, characteristic propensity for indirect and understated formulations. In both cases there is a similar underlying motive: the wish to avoid an abrupt and abrasive presentation, to maintain harmony, to save the face of the interlocutor. Meaning is better imparted by nuances that permit a dignified retreat. More-over, relatively homogeneous, traditional societies are able to take much more for granted in their discourse than highly mobile, so-cially fluid cultures like that of the United States. The Japanese particularly take pride in their familial skill at reading between the lines, at intuiting the intention behind an elliptical hint. They even have a term for it: *haragei*—communicating from the belly, that is, reading the other's mind, or talking around an issue until a consen-sus emerges.

In view of the American preference for straight talking, how-ever, Americans may take subtlety and opacity for evasiveness and insincerity. Clearly, to do so is to judge from a culture-bound per-spective. Protecting the feelings of one's interlocutor and relying on shared meanings are very far from a lack of frankness, let alone deliberate falsehood. At this point the reader may object that surely no U.S. officials worth their salt could be misled by circum-locution? And non-American diplomats surely realize by now that Americans need things spelled out? No, for all their experience, many diplomats on both sides of the cultural divide have fallen into the trap of assuming that members of other cultures always mean what they appear to say.

On the eve of the departure of Prime Minister Sato of Japan for a crucial summit with President Nixon in 1970, Sato released the following remarkable statement to the press: "Since Mr. Nixon and I are old friends, the negotiations will be three parts talk and seven parts *haragei*." Nothing could have been more natural for Japan's prime minister than to assume that he could have a heart-to-heart talk with the leader of his country's closest ally, a man he consid-ered a personal friend.[32] Sadly, his faith was misplaced. Nixon de-clined to intuit Sato's domestic difficulties and insisted he agree to an explicit five-point proposal as the basis for a settlement. Simi-larly, in the more recent construction industry talks the Japanese Ministry of Foreign Affairs has been accused of communicating in such a circumspect fashion that the American side had real diffi-culty in ascertaining its true position.[33]

Egyptian articulations have also been a source of puzzlement. In December 1968, during the interregnum between the Johnson and Nixon administrations, Secretary of State Dean Rusk presented a seven-point proposal to Foreign Minister Riad of Egypt at the United Nations. He had been encouraged to do so by Ashraf Ghor-bal, head of the Egyptian interests section in Washington. After some delay, the Egyptian response came back from Cairo. It turned out to be "legalistic, nit-picking." The State Department viewed this less than enthusiastic reply as a rejection. "When somebody accepts something, they give you a clear answer," is Richard Parker's common-sense explanation of this judgment. But is American common sense the same as Egyptian? Ashraf Ghorbal insisted that it was "not a rejection, an acceptance."[34] Was it so, or was an embarrassed Ghorbal defending his earlier advocacy? Even today it is hard to penetrate the double layer of obscurity. The likeliest conclusion is that the Egyptian foreign ministry was reluctant to commit itself on the eve of Nixon's inauguration, yet was equally loath to rule out a rather helpful American initiative. In the event, the proposal died of neglect.[35]

On the eve of Sadat's November 1977 Jerusalem visit, which so surprised the Carter administration, American diplomacy quite failed to grasp the Egyptian president's position and intentions. As William Quandt points out, "From their very first meeting Sadat had indicated his skepticism about [the] Geneva [international conference] as a forum for actual negotiations." But Sadat's repeated, albeit elliptical, hints fell on deaf ears. In August he told Secretary Vance that "there was no rush with respect to Geneva. It could be later in the year or 'whenever we are really ready.' " Foreign Minister Fahmy repeated precisely this formulation—"Egypt was not in a hurry for Geneva"—in September.[36] Sadat wanted substantive talks with Israel before Geneva—without a Syrian veto, Soviet interference, and the complicating presence of the PLO. On October 1, Sadat made a final, unsuccessful effort to convey his views to Carter, urging "a phase of preparatory talks before going on to Geneva to complete the details."[37]

As a result of continued administration support for reconvening the Geneva conference, Sadat became convinced of the need to travel directly to Jerusalem. As we now know, the Sadat visit paved the way for an Egyptian-Israeli peace. At the time, however, it astonished the U.S. government. When I asked Harold Saunders, a central figure in the negotiations, about this period, he acknowledged that he and his colleagues had failed to perceive Sadat's unhappiness. Why, Saunders wondered, did Fahmy not come out and tell his American counterparts that Sadat was not interested in Geneva? Perhaps, he mused, they did not hear Sadat because his message was not put in "a clear-cut Anglo-Saxon form."[38] Quite.

At the same time the State Department was overlooking Sadat's understated rejection of Geneva, the Egyptians were having an equally hard time because they overinterpreted Carter's straightforward statements. Fahmy describes the mistaken impression he received from some remarks made by the U.S. president at a meeting of the American and Egyptian delegations in September 1977. Carter's candor was a far cry from the devious, conspiratorial world of Middle Eastern discourse. Carter was commenting on Syrian and Palestinian objections to PLO representatives joining a Jordanian delegation in possible Arab-Israeli peace talks. Oblivious to the effect he was having on his listeners, Carter dismissed the issue in a few words. "Mr. Fahmy, I would like to know the Egyptian positions; you should not worry about the Syrian or Palestinian positions, let me handle this myself."

In typical Middle Eastern style, Fahmy erected an entire edifice of conjecture and suspicion on this seemingly trivial remark. He was stunned by Carter's words, because they implied that the United States had contacts with both Syria and the PLO, that Carter knew something about their positions unknown to the Egyptian government, and that he was "hiding important information from Egypt." The implications were staggering. "If this was really true, Egypt was no longer the leader in the peace process." After checking out the whole story, Fahmy concluded that Carter's remark was simply baseless "bravado." Although the episode is most revealing about Egyptian mistrust, it serves as a reminder of the need for precision in diplomatic exchanges with high-context individuals.[39]

Nehru's habit of understatement posed in its time an equal conundrum for U.S. diplomats. A classic failure of understanding, one of the most revealing I came across, occurred in February 1954. In what was to be a watershed in U.S.-Indian relations, the Eisenhower administration had decided to grant military aid to Pakistan. This moment was bitter for Nehru and the Indian government, and it marked a stunning diplomatic defeat. In the Indian worldview, Pakistan was the "enemy of the race," its arming by the United States a most alarming development. Before the public announcement of the deal, Ambassador Allen had been instructed to deliver a personal letter from President Eisenhower and to make clear that the American decision was not directed against India. It was hoped that friendly relations between the two countries would in no way be impaired. If the aid were misused for aggression against India, the United States would take action both through and outside the United Nations to thwart it. An Indian request for military aid would also be sympathetically considered.

Nehru carefully read the letter and the text of the forthcoming

announcement. When he had finished, "he smiled, studied his cig-
arette for a few moments, then said in a pleasant and almost con-
fidential tone, 'I have never at any moment, since the subject arose
two or three months ago, had any thought whatsoever that the U.S.
Government, and least of all President Eisenhower, wished to do
any damage to India.' " After expressing appreciation for the letter, Nehru proceeded to a judicious and calm explanation of his
concerns. "What disturbed him was not American motives but the
possible consequences of this action." He spoke of "small groups of
extremists among the Indian Muslims who did not conceal their
pleasure over Pakistan aid because they hoped it might lead to a
renewal of Muslim domination of India." Communal violence in
India and increased tension between India and Pakistan might follow. Moreover, although the present government of Mohammed
Ali in Pakistan was moderate, its political organization was weak,
and some successor might depart on a reckless adventure.

For all the dignity and restraint of his manner, Nehru was in fact
revealing his innermost fears. The American decision was a nightmare come true. Nehru had publicly expressed his opposition to
military aid for Pakistan, and the Indian government had officially
protested such a move. But Allen completely missed the true
meaning of Nehru's words. The ambassador commented on how
"surprisingly pleasant" the conversation had been and how Nehru
had "made a conscious effort to be agreeable." In an extraordinary
misjudgment, both of Nehru's reaction and of his policy of nonalignment, Allen concluded that Nehru "showed no adverse reaction to the President's offer to consider sympathetically any Indian
request for military aid, and it is possible that he was rather
pleased." The ambassador hoped that discussion on this subject
would diminish after a few days. "I do not anticipate any serious
public demonstrations."[40]

In fact, the Indian reaction was vehement. Particularly offensive
to India were the patronizing offer of military aid and the assurances that the deal was in no way directed against India—but that
if necessary the United States would thwart any aggression. As a
historian of U.S.-Indian relations has pointed out, Indians com-
plain about the 1954 episode to this day. "It may have done more
to complicate Indo-American relations than any other single
development."[41]

Except, perhaps, for one other: the disastrous 1971 meeting between President Nixon and Mrs. Gandhi. It was, Kissinger admits,
"a dialogue of the deaf." Describing their encounter in all its unpleasantness, Kissinger is convinced, however, that the breakdown

and prolonged dislocation in U.S.-Indian relations following the unexpected Indian invasion of East Pakistan was not the result of a subjective failure of understanding but of a traditional clash of irreconcilable interests. The two leaders, he claims, understood each other only too well.[42]

From the accounts of the principals themselves, however, it is doubtful they did. In fact, their mutual failure of understanding is uncannily reminiscent of Nixon's unfortunate 1969 meeting with Prime Minister Sato of Japan. Nixon received the impression that the Indian prime minister had given him some kind of implicit assurance that her country would not attack Pakistan. "India has never wished the destruction of Pakistan or its permanent crippling," he quotes her as saying. "Above all, India seeks the restoration of stability. We want to eliminate chaos at all costs."[43] Mrs. Gandhi tells a very different version. In her opinion, Nixon failed to grasp just how unbearable the situation was to India. "I told him, without mincing words, that we couldn't go on with ten million refugees on our backs, we couldn't tolerate the fuse of such an explosive situation any longer." Other European leaders with whom Mrs. Gandhi had spoken had understood, said Mrs. Gandhi to her interviewer, "but not Mr. Nixon."[44]

For an American diplomat, to turn from Indian understatement to Chinese indirection is to enter a new realm of semantic opacity. A sense of the dense and allusive Chinese communicatory style can be obtained from almost any account of diplomatic contact with China—not that U.S. officials always grasped what the Chinese were getting at. The well-documented account of an alert participant can be found in the pages of Kissinger's diplomatic memoirs. His description of the 1971–72 negotiations that resulted in the momentous Shanghai communiqué is particularly enlightening.

The first example to consider is Chinese prime minister Zhou Enlai's treatment of the Vietnam issue. (At the time, Kissinger was engaged in the Paris talks with a North Vietnamese delegation led by Le Duc Tho aimed at ending the Vietnam War.) Zhou conveyed the Chinese position on the Vietnam issue in the course of three separate meetings. This kind of rolling dialogue, in which the message is gradually unfolded over a period of time, is characteristic of Chinese diplomacy. On July 9, 1971, during Kissinger's first trip to Beijing, Zhou listened to his guest's account of the Paris talks but professed ignorance of them. As Kissinger appreciated, "it was a good device to avoid being pressed to take a position." It also hinted that Vietnam was not high on the list of Chinese concerns.[45]

A further revelation of the Chinese position came in nonverbal form on Kissinger's second trip to Beijing. On October 23, the U.S. diplomat was taken for an ostentatious public appearance at the Summer Palace. Tea was served on a boat on the lake in plain view of hundreds of Chinese spectators. Thus China conveyed messages that it was willing to commit itself in public to a profound shift in foreign policy, that it considered its American guests acceptable, and that it insisted that the U.S.-Chinese relationship was to be no hole-and-corner affair. The Vietnamese dimension of the occasion was not made clear to Kissinger until afterward. Among the spectators of the tea party, as Zhou later mentioned in an apologetic aside, was a North Vietnamese journalist taking photographs. Kissinger notes in passing that he "suspected" that Zhou was interested in North Vietnam getting the message of the incipient Sino-American relationship. But we can surely go further. If an observer for Hanoi was on the spot, it was not by accident. The Chinese orchestration of these occasions is meticulous. Zhou was surely signaling to North Vietnam—and ensuring that Washington grasped—that China would not permit North Vietnam to hinder a rapprochement with the United States. China had more important fish to fry.[46]

The final veil was removed during President Nixon's historic visit to China in February 1972. Zhou's treatment of the Vietnam issue, according to Kissinger, was a "masterpiece of indirection." He expressed "sympathy" for North Vietnam but explained Chinese support for that country on the basis of a historical debt rather than congruent national interests. The implication was that the U.S. connection, based on the perception of a common foe (the Soviet Union), was paramount. States do not go to the wall for historical debts. Zhou, as in July, declined to express his view on the Paris talks. Then, in a crucial but elliptical remark, he reiterated that "differences between China and the United States would be settled peacefully." This statement was interpreted by the U.S. delegation to mean that China would not intervene militarily in the war. The Vietnam issue was treated "largely in the context of long-term Soviet aspirations in Southeast Asia."[47] The covert message underlying the whole extended exchange was that China was effectively dissociating itself from its supposed North Vietnamese ally—a far-reaching development indeed. The actuality was confirmed before long.

The archetypal example of the Chinese conversational style is found in the famous Nixon-Mao meeting of February 21, 1972. The encounter was characterized by bantering and seemingly evanescent philosophical remarks by the Chinese leader, but later it could be seen to have laid down definitive guidelines for the new Sino-American relationship. Looking back, Kissinger refers to the "many-layered designs of Mao's conversation," comparing it to the "courtyards in the Forbidden City, each leading to a deeper recess distinguished from the others only by slight changes of proportion, with ultimate meaning residing in a totality that only long reflection can grasp."

On the question of trade, for instance, Mao conveyed his decision in the form of an explanation of Chinese slowness in responding to the Nixon administration's easing of export controls during the previous two years. China, he said, had been "bureaucratic" in insisting that the solution of major issues precede the resolution of smaller issues like trade and people-to-people exchanges. "Later on I saw you were right, and we played table tennis." In this disarming, understated way Mao gave his green light to progress on those matters at the summit. Other views were thrown out seemingly offhandedly, to avoid loss of face if the Nixon visit failed. Taiwan was placed on a subsidiary level as a relatively minor internal Chinese dispute. Banter and passing historical references hinted that the Chinese would solve the problem among themselves in their own good time.

In a discussion of Chinese security concerns, Mao made his point by omission: the threat of American or Chinese aggression, he opined, was "relatively small . . . You want to withdraw some of your troops back on your soil; ours do not go abroad." By a process of elimination, it was the threat from the Soviet Union that was to be feared. At the same time he had in a few words ("ours do not go abroad") touched on a whole list of American preoccupations. Anticipating Zhou, he eliminated the U.S. nightmare of Chinese intervention in the Vietnam War. He was also disclaiming any Chinese wish to challenge vital American interests in Japan and South Korea. But what of the ideological struggle? Mao disposed of the ringing anti-American slogans that had marked his rule with equal facility. Laughing uproariously, he dismissed them as the "sound [of] a lot of big cannons."[48] In sixty-five minutes, half of which were taken up by interpretation, Mao succeeded in providing a set of signposts for his American guests and the Chinese bureaucracy. Again and again, in the week of intensive negotiations that followed the Nixon-Mao meeting, Chinese officials would return to Mao's words. References that were originally obscure were later seen as significant. The dialogue, Kissinger sums up, had been conducted on the Chinese part "with extraordinary indirection and subtlety."

Nonverbal communication

Nonverbal communication embraces a vast area of human behavior, including facial expression, gestures, body contact, movement, use of space, costume, ceremony, and so on. Like language, it is a universal phenomenon with a great range of local variants. A gesture of approval in the United States may be taken for a very rude sign in Egypt. A smile in Japan may mask embarrassment rather than indicate enjoyment. Even when the act or expression itself—the frown, the gift—is common, rules of legitimate display may differ. What is an appropriate moment for tears in Egypt is one for self-restraint in the United States. An act of hospitality in Mexico City may be seen as a bribe in Washington. Many studies have documented this cross-cultural diversity.[49]

Actual misunderstanding—whether based on ignorance or misinterpretation—aside, the main difficulty for low-context individuals may simply be to appreciate the emphasis placed by their high-context counterparts on the nonverbal dimension of communication. Whereas the burden of meaning in low-context cultures is transmitted through the medium of words, high-context cultures are particularly sensitive to sign and symbol. The tendency of Foreign Minister Fahmy of Egypt to read more into American articulations than was justified has been noted. His memoirs also provide remarkable testimony of his attentiveness to American body language. In all his accounts of meetings with U.S. officials Fahmy describes their facial expressions and the emotions he read there. He provides meticulous detail about just when Nixon smiled or Kissinger lost his cool. The state of mind of his interlocutors was obviously of major importance to the Egyptian diplomat.

Although Egyptians do not make shows of anger, they have no inhibitions about exhibiting seemly (that is, socially acceptable) emotion in public. There is no shame attached to extreme expressions of grief or joy in the Arab world. On the contrary, Egyptians wear their emotions on their sleeves as a sign of social solidarity. To remain impassive while others grieve would be egoism of the worst sort. Fahmy's tendency to project this very Egyptian trait onto Americans is evident. He describes an indicative incident during the 1973 disengagement talks (immediately following the Yom Kippur War) in which Chief of Staff Gamasy, hearing that he would be permitted to retain only limited Egyptian forces on the East Bank of the Suez Canal, began to weep before the company of Egyptian and U.S. officials. "From the look on the faces of the American delegation," Fahmy writes, "one could easily see they too were upset by the injustice inflicted upon Egypt." It is easier to believe, and more likely, the Americans were disconcerted to see a senior army officer shedding tears in public. Egyptian and U.S. delegations met again in April 1974 in Alexandria. Secretary of State Kissinger had given President Sadat certain assurances about future U.S. arms supplies to Egypt. Fahmy was incredulous and detected the same reaction on the other side. "I watched the expressions on the faces of [Kissinger's] American colleagues; they were shocked and unbelieving . . ."[50]

Although Fahmy's interpretation of American reactions in these two cases was picturesque, it was of little consequence. More unfortunate was his reading of the U.S. response to Egyptian proposals brought to Washington in September 1977. To recapitulate, the Carter administration was in favor of convening the Geneva conference at an early date; the Egyptians were "in no hurry," believing it would lead nowhere. Furthermore, while the United States proposed a unified Arab delegation including Palestinian delegates, Egypt favored giving the PLO the option of participating. At an important meeting on September 21, Fahmy outlined the Egyptian position. He recalls that "Carter and his colleagues were listening attentively and I could see they understood and appreciated my points." The most authoritative American version has an exasperated Carter refuting the Egyptian proposals.[51] In the final analysis, neither side fully grasped the determination with which the other adhered to its own position.

The United States—founded in the Age of Reason, rigorously demarcating Church from State, and passionate in its belief in progress—has relegated ritual to the sidelines of public life. The national shrines and inaugural events that make up the so-called civil religion of the United States are a pale version of the pomp and circumstance that mark more traditional societies. Even private life is increasingly bereft of those intricate rites of passage that communities evolve to proclaim and sanctify the ages and stages of human growth. High-context cultures, steeped in tradition and placing crucial emphasis on the individual's standing in the group, reserve a central role for ceremony. Religious and civic activity alike revolve around ritual events and celebratory occasions, rich in costume and rite, dramatizing key events in the history and life of the society. Ceremony, in fact, is a key mechanism of group identity and cohesion.

High-context cultures, therefore, display acute awareness of the subtle messages about rank and reputation reflected and communicated in the fine detail of ritual and choreography. Of course, American officials strictly observe the rules and regulations of diplomatic etiquette, but they do not revel in it. It is simply something required so that meetings between government leaders can take place "with a minimum of misunderstanding."[52] Beyond that utilitarian function, it should be kept within strict bounds. "Protocol and striped pants," President Truman once wrote, "give me a pain in the neck."[53] Non-Western societies are not only skillful at manipulating protocol and ceremonial for political purposes, they are also prone to view political symbolism as something to be cherished in its own right.

Here lies fertile ground for confusion. In the early days of U.S.-Chinese contacts under President Nixon, the dense and allusive richness of Chinese political choreography was sometimes overlooked. For instance, U.S. observers entirely missed the most significant Chinese signal of reconciliation of all in the 1970–71 period. On October 1, 1970, Edgar Snow, the American journalist and author of sympathetic books on the Chinese revolution, was invited to stand next to Chairman Mao on top of the Gate of Heavenly Peace. This unprecedented gesture associated the Great Helmsman with the unfolding process of détente. Ruefully noting U.S. oversight, Kissinger concludes: "Excessive subtlety had produced a failure of communication."[54] The Chinese doubtless did not regard the gesture as particularly subtle.

Since its introduction to Chinese symbolic politics, U.S. diplomacy has become more familiar with this mode of communication. Alexander Haig, chief of staff in the Nixon White House, was conscious of the need for alertness during his stint as secretary of state from 1981 to 1982. Visiting Beijing in 1981 he was received by Deng Xiaoping in the Fujian Room of the Great Hall of the People. (Fujian is the province of China situated across from Taiwan.) Haig was unsure whether this was "happenstance or a subtle reminder." His hesitancy was unwarranted. Ten years before, Henry Kissinger had also been received by Zhou Enlai in that same room. But it was, Kissinger confesses, "a subtlety which—like the Snow interview—unfortunately was lost on me since I did not then know the name of the room nor to my shame would have recognized its significance. There is some advantage in invincible obtuseness. (Chou was obliged to point all of this out on a subsequent visit when we met in another room.)"[55]

The significance of meeting in the Fujian Room should therefore have been crystal clear to Secretary Haig. The United States (his hosts were saying) might temporarily support the Taiwan government but, situated thousands of miles away, would eventually loosen its attachment. For the People's Republic of China the link with Taiwan was not a political expedient but an immutable geographical and cultural bond that must eventually be consummated in reunification.

For years U.S. support of the Nationalist Chinese cause had been a painful thorn in the side of Beijing. During the Carter incumbency important progress had been made in resolving the issue, but in the Reagan era it threatened to reemerge. Running for office in 1980, Ronald Reagan, to Beijing's alarm, had expressed strong support for Taiwan. Chinese displeasure with this possible regression in U.S. policy was marked in various ways. During the election campaign vice presidential candidate George Bush, although a former ambassador to the People's Republic of China, was received with "reserve bordering on coldness." Now Haig was being made to understand that China had not abandoned its claim to Taiwan. At the airport the secretary of state was seen off by the vice foreign minister, not the foreign minister as protocol required. Haig understood that this slight indicated Chinese displeasure at President Reagan's remarks at a news conference that day that the Taiwan Relations Act (which formalized U.S. commitments to Taiwan's security) would be carried out as the law of the land.[56]

The American tendency to "obtuseness" (Kissinger's term) on symbolic matters is occasionally reflected in maladroit protocol. Presidential staffs tend to be more attuned to domestic political considerations, public relations, and security requirements than to foreign sensibilities. Matters are not helped by congressional and popular contempt for diplomatic fastidiousness. Diplomats are supposed to be hard-nosed operators, not bleeding hearts. U.S.-Indian relations were damaged in 1964 when an invitation to Prime Minister Shastri was abruptly withdrawn by President Johnson. There was no diplomatic reason for the cancellation; never very enthusiastic about protocol and its niceties, the president had simply decided that his calendar was too crowded. Plans for the visit were in full swing at the time. Worse, the announcement was first made in a news broadcast, with no prior warning to the Delhi embassy permitting it to soften the blow. Ambassador Bowles lamented that Shastri, an insecure and sensitive man, had been "rudely and publicly embarrassed." As a result, the government of India was deeply angered.[57]

In 1974 a presidential advance party, preparing for a visit by President Nixon to Cairo, was guilty of gross breaches of courtesy. The arrival of an advance party of several hundred people overwhelmed and disconcerted local officials. The arrogant behavior of the U.S. contingent in a host country was indefensible. The Cairo Hilton was evacuated of all guests; Egyptian arrangements were "sloughed aside"; Secret Service officers refused Egyptian transportation for the president and insisted that their own armored vehicle be brought in. When the Egyptians put their foot down on that demand, Nixon personally overrode the wishes of his security men.[58]

In 1969, in a similar incident in Delhi, Indian objections were overridden when Nixon's staff threatened that, if the Indians insisted on their own vehicle, the American president would not be allowed to stay at the Indian presidential residence. On this earlier occasion, Mrs. Gandhi conceded the point. She is supposed to have remarked, "If he's killed, it's his car!" On a visit by President Carter to Mexico City in 1979 one White House staffer, oblivious to Mexican feelings about the "lost provinces," had the bright idea that a Texas barbecue would be an appropriate event at which to entertain Mexican guests. Fortunately, the embassy overruled the suggestion.[59]

At the level of body language, the most noteworthy feature of Chinese, Indian, and Japanese behavior is their unusual (to Westerners' eyes) capacity for self-restraint and impassivity. These are enviable assets to bring to the negotiating table, where they deprive U.S. negotiators of highly desirable information about the interlocutors' true feelings. Imperturbable negotiators are able to conceal their eagerness for agreement, their interest in a particular concession, and any pressures to settle to which they might be subject.

Kissinger recalls seeing Zhou Enlai lose his massive composure on only one occasion. The Chinese prime minister epitomized the Confucian ideal of the cultivated person who strives to maintain perfect self-control, regardless of circumstances.[60] To this concept of virtue Japanese culture has added a remarkable aesthetic of silence, summed up in the Zen Buddhist motto, "Words are of no use." At negotiating sessions Japanese place great stress on clear-headed composure and listening rather than talking. Americans describe their astonishment at observing Japanese officials sitting in on meetings with their eyes closed.[61] Lest this be thought another hoary national stereotype, it should be remarked that the Japanese are themselves aware that they come across as "inscrutable" to the outside world and actually bemoan their lack of facility in intercultural communication.[62] Mitsuru Inuta has also written on his countrymen's tendency to disguise their real intentions beneath an agreeable, smiling appearance (*tatemae*).[63]

An experienced U.S. negotiator stressed the Indians' facility at masking their emotions. Like good poker players they were able, in his experience, to avoid "tipping their hand." He explained this ability by a combination of two factors: a sense, derived from the British, that to do so would be bad form; and conformity to the Hindu tradition of abjuring desire. Nehru's impassivity certainly misled U.S. diplomats on several occasions. Allen's failure in 1954 to detect Nehru's true reaction to the U.S.-Pakistani arms deal has already been described. Galbraith was also repeatedly led astray throughout the ill-fated Anglo-American attempt to mediate the Kashmir dispute. For instance, at one point Galbraith was instructed to try to sell the idea of partition to Nehru. "Nehru's face did not brighten perceptibly this evening when I brought up the idea," Galbraith writes, "but he did not throw me out." The ambassador quite wrongly concluded that the Indians did not "entirely rule out giving the Pakistanis some position in the [Kashmir] valley."[64] At this time India doubtless felt that it had no choice but to play along with the initiative. But the last thing the Indians had on their minds was transferring territory to their sworn enemies.

Nehru was also famous for his silences, which were always disconcerting to more loquacious Americans. During the period of deterioration in U.S.-Indian relations that followed the 1971 Indo-Pakistani war, India decided to close American libraries that had been set up in the provinces at the instigation of Chester Bowles. When the State Department sought in its files the documentary basis of the establishment of the libraries, it discovered that none existed. The agreement had simply derived from a conversation between Ambassador Bowles and the prime minister. Bowles had suggested the matter to Nehru and Nehru, without uttering a word, had given a brief inclination of the head.[65] Galbraith, too, confronted Nehru's impenetrable silences. "This left me stranded," the former ambassador writes.[66] Like father, like daughter. At their meetings, according to Kissinger, Mrs. Gandhi's "moody silences brought out all of Nixon's latent insecurities."[67]

✳ ✳ ✳

In the middle phase of negotiations there is much evidence to corroborate the antitheses suggested by my theoretical framework. A clear picture emerges of opposing and sometimes incompatible negotiating models. On the one hand, the United States, in the adversarial, can-do tradition, is confirmed as predominantly problem oriented, placing emphasis on concession and compromise, incremental progress, and the techniques of rational argument. On the other hand, non-Western subjects, in the consensual, face-salient tradition, are predominantly relationship oriented, eschewing bargaining on issues of high principle, not viewing compromise as an end in itself, minimizing techniques of confrontation and advocacy, and reflecting more hierarchical modes of government.

As far as communication is concerned, the low context–high context dichotomy is also strongly exemplified. American negotiators, true to the testamental origins of Judaism and Christianity, have inherited a literary legacy that ascribes peculiar value to the written word. Literal meanings and plain speaking are emphasized, and the opportunity to hammer out disagreement in open debate is welcomed. In contrast, non-Western negotiators possess less faith in the powers of the written word and are more inclined to value the spoken word as an instrument of social affect. Sensitive to questions of face and to the disruptive consequences an unguarded utterance may have for communal harmony, they display a preference for emollient rather than abrasive language, avoid harsh contradiction, and opt for a more allusive style of speech. Nonverbal cues acquire analogous importance as devices to express social solidarity; when necessary, they are kept under tight control lest offense be given inadvertently. By extension, particular weight is attached to symbolic politics.

nine

Bright Honor
End Game

As the end game is reached, American and non-Western philosophies of negotiation face off for a final settling of accounts. Unnecessary or premature concessions tilt the balance of advantage to one's opponent. What has been given away cannot be recalled. For one last time contrasting assumptions confront each other. Conceptions of time are crucial at this stage. Americans, viewing time as a wasting asset, are more likely to feel the pressure of approaching deadlines. Decisions have to be made about the form of the agreement, raising questions about the nature, scope, and finality of contracts: Americans, after all, spring from a tradition that seeks to regulate by contract certain relations that other cultures leave to ties of sentiment and obligation. Finally, the issue of face looms large: the need to present the accord in such a way that contrasting needs for intangible, and not merely material, gratification can be reconciled.

Issues of face

In shame cultures like Egypt and the other interdependent collectivistic societies discussed here, outward appearances are as important as substance. "Make your harvest look big," runs a popular

Egyptian saying, "lest your enemies rejoice." Better to starve and have others think you satisfied than to reveal a weakness. The modern Westerner may find it difficult to understand this philosophy of life because it flies in the face of the Western concept of material rationality. For any negotiated outcome to be acceptable in these circumstances, it must not only be good, it must also look good. Indeed, as we shall see, correct packaging may render palatable something otherwise unacceptable.

American negotiators do not display the obsession with face so characteristic of collectivistic cultures. In a study of the role of face in negotiation, Stella Ting-Toomey argues that negotiators from collectivistic backgrounds are concerned to honor face, whereas negotiators from individualistic cultures are adept at threatening face.[1] American diplomats are expected to behave honorably, that is, tell the truth; comport themselves with dignity; and negotiate within the framework of the law, constitution, and accepted moral principles of the United States. Subject to those provisos, the achievement of compromise (that is, equitable distribution of payoffs between the parties) is thought to constitute an inherently honorable outcome; there is certainly nothing shameful in having facilitated an agreement by meeting one's opponent halfway. Because the successful conclusion of a negotiation is in itself highly desirable, loss of prestige (probably a better word in this context than "face") would be felt to follow more from having "failed" to settle a problem than from this or that detail of the final accord. Hence the maxim that any agreement is better than no agreement.

For the representatives of interdependent cultures the experience of international negotiation is fraught with considerations of face. The very structure of the situation, in which competing parties pit their wills and skills against each other, is uncongenial to societies that see social harmony, not confrontation, as the desired state of affairs. Beyond the matter being negotiated, there exists an entire psychological dimension in which pride of place is given to considerations of psychic, not material, gains and losses. "While the discussion of tangible issues such as territorial rights, boundaries, and tangible scarce resources represents the substantive level of verbal, or written diplomatic exchange," Ting-Toomey argues, "intangible issues such as national representation, status, pride, honor, power, dignity, and face often reflect the hidden dimension of the overt negotiation process."[2]

Precedence and status inevitably loom large, both in the mechanics of the talks ("the shape of the table") and in the outcome.

To non-Western countries, any negotiation with the mighty United States is potentially redolent of challenges to national honor and perceived standing. When emotive topics like sovereignty, independence, and the defense of traditional values in the face of modernization are thought to be on the line, interlocutors of the United States may define success more in terms of resistance than agreement. To have withstood the United States may be perceived (or at least presented) as a prestigious outcome. Non-Western governments are invariably highly wary of appearing to have conceded cherished assets or bowed to American pressure. Face demands, therefore, that the agreement be defensible in the eyes of the group. We are back to appearances and presentation.

A classic illustration of the salience of symbolism in the end game is provided by the Connally-Kashiwagi talks of December 1971, held against the background of serious U.S. balance-of-payments problems. After months of preliminary negotiations on exchange rates, the moment of truth arrived in Washington. For Finance Minister Mizuta of Japan, the prospect of being pressured into concessions was too much. He canceled a meeting with his American counterpart because of an "upset stomach" (later admitted to be fictitious). At the crucial encounter he was replaced by his deputy Kashiwagi. Treasury Secretary Connally informed Kashiwagi that the United States insisted on a 17-percent upward revaluation of the yen and gave him until 10 A.M. the next day to reply.

Apparently unmoved by the ultimatum, Kashiwagi rejected the demand. Seventeen percent was unacceptable, he explained, because a Japanese finance minister had been forced to commit suicide in the 1930s after agreeing to a 17-percent revaluation. (Actually, the historical record was even bleaker: Finance Minister Junnosuke Inouye was assassinated in February 1932.) So it was the number that was taboo rather than the principle. Without more ado Connally suggested a revaluation of 16.9 percent, and Kashiwagi agreed. By proposing a substantively insignificant but symbolically crucial concession, the U.S. Treasury secretary had saved the honor of his counterpart.[3]

For China, as for Japan, considerations of face have long been decisive.[4] U.S.-Chinese relations amply demonstrate this point. Fortunately, American negotiators have been rather successful in addressing the issue. In the 1971–72 negotiations, face impinged on the diplomatic exchanges at various levels. First and most obvious, it was inherent in the very concept of an American presidential visit to Beijing, which, as many have pointed out, was uncannily reminiscent of past "pilgrimages" by "barbarians" to the Middle Kingdom. A Chinese leader did not visit the United States until 1979, following the formal normalization of diplomatic relations. The drafting of the announcement of the Nixon trip in July 1971 fully reflected Chinese requirements in this respect. The Chinese draft communiqué first submitted to Kissinger baldly implied that President Nixon was coming as a supplicant—that he had solicited an invitation. Put in this unembroidered way the text was unacceptable to the United States. But with only a slight alteration the communiqué that was finally agreed to carried very much the same implication. It read (Kissinger writes): "Knowing of President Nixon's expressed desire to visit the People's Republic of China, Premier Chou En-lai . . . has extended an invitation to President Nixon to visit China . . ." This wording left no doubt that the initial interest had come from the American, not the Chinese, side. The point is that from an American perspective (and within reason) the fact of the visit was perceived to be overwhelmingly more significant than the text of the invitation. Not so to the Chinese.

Chinese preoccupation with face was also reflected in the unique form of the crucial document that emerged from the Nixon visit, namely, the Shanghai communiqué. The initial American proposal, in Kissinger's words, "followed the conventional style, highlighting fuzzy areas of agreement and obscuring differences with platitudinous generalizations." This style, it transpired, was utterly unacceptable to the Chinese. If profound ideological differences were so easily papered over, what had been the purpose of China's years of struggle? At the express instructions of Mao, Zhou Enlai rejected the draft. "The communiqué had to set forth fundamental differences; otherwise the wording would have an 'untruthful appearance.'" Zhou's counterdraft set forth the Chinese position on the various issues in "extremely uncompromising terms," leaving room for the United States to insert its own contrary positions. This approach was utterly unconventional, but not only was it more truthful, it also ensured that neither side was seen to have sold out its principles for the sake of the rapprochement. The Shanghai communiqué, in fact, was a unique face-saving and also face-giving device. In substantive terms neither side made any concession to the other.[5]

Face, then, is very much about facades. The Shanghai communiqué was an elaborate artifice intended to free the parties to enter into a productive relationship. Above all, it ensured that neither side would be perceived to have lost, for such a perception would have been fatal for the continuation of the process. Sometimes honor is satisfied by a propitiatory formula, an original solution that effectively transcends the issue under contention or an ingenious device that either obscures reality or transforms it. All of these devices were resorted to at various times in the negotiations studied.

In the Tarapur negotiation with India of the early 1980s, one of the most contentious issues was the handling of nuclear waste. The United States insisted on intrusive safeguards to prevent a diversion of the material, while India rejected them as a violation of sovereignty. Nuclear waste, India argued, should either be returned to the United States or, if the latter did not want it, be left to India to do with as it saw fit. Finally both sides agreed on a third option involving adoption of the French process of caramelization, whereby waste products are injected into liquid glass, which can then be safely stored. Thus here an ingenious "technical fix," not completely satisfactory to either side, but going some way to meet the requirements of each, provided the way out of the conundrum.[6]

In the sensitive 1986–87 talks for the sale of a U.S. supercomputer to India, the same safeguards-sovereignty dilemma arose. Here the United States government needed safeguards against undesirable end use (for instance, application to nuclear weapons development) or the transfer of secret computer technology to the Soviet Union. The Indian government, as always, resisted the imposition of an intrusive supervisory regime; it had to be able to go before the Indian Parliament and credibly prove that sovereignty had not been compromised, that India was not falling under the control of a foreign power. In the end, the Indians proved very pragmatic in evolving language that went some way toward meeting U.S. concerns. In a classified memorandum—the form of the agreement was essential to its acceptability—the Indian government agreed not to network (meaning that users had to go in person to the computer) and accepted more intrusive monitoring than they had ever consented to before. Thus a compromise was reached away from the spotlights.[7]

As a mediator in the Egyptian-Israeli peace process the United States has displayed exceptional sensitivity and deftness in devising formulas to meet the Egyptian government's powerful need to protect its honor, both in the eyes of its own people and in the wider Arab community. In the November 1973 negotiations for a binding cease-fire agreement after the Yom Kippur War, it was vital to conceal the perilous state of the Egyptian Third Army and the fact that its very survival depended on Israeli forbearance. The presence of Israeli troops on the main road to Cairo did not at all conform with the triumphant picture that Sadat was attempting to project to the world. Accordingly, in return for certain concessions to Israel, a corridor would be opened up along the Cairo-Suez road to supply the encircled Egyptian forces. Although the route passed through Israeli-controlled territory, this fact would be disguised by placing the checkpoints under United Nations control.

In order to save Egyptian face, it was vital to obscure the precise details of this and other arrangements. As Kissinger understood, "too many public concessions would hurt [Sadat's] position with his Arab brethren." Acknowledgment of Israeli control of the Cairo-Suez road would have been deeply embarrassing, and a detailed schedule for the resupply of the army "would have brought home its plight to every Arab." If the cease-fire humiliated Egypt, what chance would there be of progress toward a political settlement?[8] The cease-fire agreement devised by the United States ensured that Egypt's reputation was *mastourah* (covered up against public censure).

To meet Mexico's psychological requirements has often required considerable technical ingenuity and material expense on the American part. In 1973 Mexico's principled insistence on water of quality equal to that enjoyed by U.S. farmers was sidestepped by American agreement to create fresh water through desalination. Similarly, one of the key elements in the Chamizal settlement was the relocation of the course of the Rio Grande, at a cost of $43.6 million. In the final stage of the 1963 negotiation, President Mateos of Mexico held out for more acreage than seemed feasible, given the lie of the land. He wished to be able to claim before his people, and history, that he had given away not even one square inch of territory. The solution of Boundary Commissioner Joseph Friedkin of the United States (who combined the talents of both diplomat and engineer) was a technical one. A new, deeper channel would be dug north of the Rio Grande's present course and set in concrete. This channel would not only solve the problem of flood control, it would also provide President Mateos with the extra land that he needed to gild his achievement.[9]

The symbols of success are so important that in the 1982 debt talks the Mexican team actually preferred a materially inferior agreement to one that bore the misleading appearance of a greater concession on its part. The short-term solution suggested by the U.S. Treasury to Mexico's liquidity crisis was a $2 billion loan. Mexican oil, to be sold to the U.S. strategic reserve under a fixed-term, renewable contract, would be the collateral for half that sum. The quid pro quo from the American point of view would be the concessionary price paid for the oil. Instead of the world price of $32 per barrel, the United States proposed to pay only $28. Finance Minister Silva Herzog of Mexico was dismayed by this proposal. The United States could not be permitted, Herzog argued, to appear to buy oil that still lay beneath Mexican soil. Doing so would entail the loss of the nation's patrimony. Moreover, a contract granting major price concessions to Washington was politically impossible. Despite the grave financial crisis, the president of Mexico could not appear to be capitulating to his mighty neighbor.

The Mexican counterproposal was for a loan with interest charged but no mention of the price of the oil. When the American experts came back with an arrangement that would entail an effective interest rate of 35 percent, the Mexicans were outraged. The device finally hit upon by the Department of the Treasury to cover Mexican concerns was an interest rate that would not look usurious but would be topped up by a front-end fee, or bank service charge. In principle, this was much more attractive to the Mexicans. After some haggling, a figure of $50 million was agreed upon. Under this arrangement Mexico would, in fact, be paid $27.40 for its oil, less than the $28 first proposed! As Chaudhuri notes, "With all their threats and break-offs the Mexicans had actually ended up with a worse deal."[10] The point is, of course, that the front-end fee concealed from observers back home the real price concession that had been made.

For a Mexican negotiator any public whiff of surrender would torpedo an agreement. Herbert Brownell, former attorney general and special negotiator with Mexico, stresses that Mexicans could never "appear to be giving in to the United States." Brownell's counterpart in the 1972–73 Colorado salinity talks was concerned about this point. It could even be "somewhat useful to have a fight with the United States," Brownell wryly observes. Mexicans are so convinced of their past exploitation and so preoccupied by present vulnerability that any agreement with Washington automatically comes under suspicion. Indeed, if an agreement can be presented as an American defeat, all Mexican psychological requirements are covered. "We got an agreement," a high-ranking Mexican official trumpeted at the end of the 1979 gas talks, "because the United

States suddenly agreed to our final offers. It was as simple as that. We are very pleased."[11]

Whether the official's boast reflected genuine satisfaction at having gained the upper hand over U.S. negotiator Warren Christopher, or wishful thinking, is an important question but hard to answer. It may be argued that, because face equals facade, cosmetic or symbolic adjustments rather than genuine concessions are sufficient to requite the honor of one's rival; it was so with the classic 16.9-percent solution of the yen revaluation conundrum, and in the debt crisis a rather flimsy disguise satisfied Mexican pride. Further comparative research is clearly required to determine if this point is true in general or only under certain conditions.

Forms of agreement

One face-saving device favored by non-Western negotiators is the informal, unwritten arrangement, which has several advantages. A formal treaty has a certain symbolic resonance as well as binding legal status. It is a solemn document signed at an appropriate ceremony, and it can be published for all to see. In short, it is an eminently public and tangible instrument. An informal arrangement lacks these weighty, irrevocable qualities of publicity. When an agreement is felt in some way to be discreditable or embarrassing, or to require unpleasant concessions, the unwritten understanding permits concealment, or at least minimization, of the accord. For those preoccupied by appearances there must be something psychologically reassuring about an agreement that has not been frozen in visible permanence, like a fly in amber.

American instincts, in contrast, militate against precisely those features of informal arrangements favored by high-context cultures. In the low-context tradition, obligations must be spelled out and (unintended) ambiguities resolved. Understandings based on the personal interpretation of the immediate negotiators are particularly suspect. All important transactions in the individualistic culture are based on contracts that explicitly set out the rights and duties of the parties and are backed up by the force of law, not by ties of sentiment. The tighter and more specific the accord, the less the likelihood, it is felt, of future misunderstandings. There should be no doubt what the signatories have actually committed themselves to. A good contract will try to cover all conceivable contingencies. Given the realities of international politics, American negotiators prefer formal agreements but may consent to informal arrangements where unavoidable. On occasion, however, the United States has been excessively formalistic, depriving itself of the substance of an arrangement by excessive insistence on legal form. There may also be a tendency to legalistic nit-picking, seeking to obviate all uncertainty in an uncertain world.

Military cooperation is an area of particular sensitivity, raising potent issues of sovereignty, independence, and alignment. When a formal defensive pact with the United States, with all it entails, is politically impossible, an informal arrangement may satisfy all the parties. In 1952, U.S.-Mexican negotiations for a military pact immediately broke down because Mexico was not prepared to undertake a formal obligation to commit its forces in hemispheric defense, let alone enter into a binding military alliance with the United States. Behind the scenes, however, Mexico was ready to be more helpful, and the United States discovered that it could gain in secret what it could not obtain publicly.[12]

This lesson has been repeated time and again. In June 1980 the Mexican oil well Ixtoc 1 blew out of control, spilling 30,000 barrels of oil a day into the Gulf of Mexico. Robert Krueger, the U.S. coordinator of Mexican affairs, announced demands for compensation for the pollution of Texas beaches. Mexico immediately published a categorical and irritable rejection. Krueger's heavy-handed tactics injured Mexican pride rather than encouraging compliance. But what Mexico could never agree to in public was acceptable if done discreetly. Out of the limelight, a cleanup operation did get under way, coordinated by U.S. and Mexican officials. The Mexicans agreed to U.S. Coast Guard ships entering Mexican waters to help with the operation on a low-key basis. This agreement would never have been possible had it gotten into the press. Mexico even offered to send teams to help clean up Texas beaches, although the United States declined this offer.[13]

What Mexico could offer of its own free will, as a gesture of good-neighborliness, could not be obtained by an explicit arrangement based on mutual consent. An agreement implies obligation, a curtailment of sovereignty; a unilateral act is an expression of free will. In the Israel-Egypt disengagement talks brokered by the United States after the 1973 Arab-Israeli war, Sadat made this point to Kissinger. "He could not accept a formal obligation to clear and reopen the Suez Canal. But he could tell me that if he could do so as his own decision—if Israel would only stop demanding it—he would begin clearance operations as soon as both armies had reached the lines foreseen in the disengagement agreement."[14]

In recent years much discreet U.S.-Egyptian cooperation in various security spheres has been made possible because it rested on informal arrangements. Landing rights for AWACS (Airborne Warning and Control System) planes, overflight rights in Egyptian air space, the joint "Bright Star" series of military exercises, and the use of Egyptian facilities in the 1981 Iran rescue mission were of this nature.[15]

The United States has run into trouble when pressing for more formal agreements; we have already seen an example in the ill-fated Ras Banas negotiations. Sadat's initial preference was for a rather general, indeed informal, understanding. The more detailed and formal the accord, the less likely it was to be acceptable. Only a low-profile, gentleman's agreement could evade Egyptian national sensibilities. The inescapable difficulty thus posed for the United States was nicely put by Representative Joseph Addabbo (D-N.Y.) following a visit of the House Subcommittee on Military Construction Appropriations to Egypt in 1981:

> If we are going to completely rebuild [Ras Banas]—we are talking about a billion dollars . . . In my meeting with President Sadat, he said no American flag, no agreement. Now, the American people, in our defense budget, with tax dollars, have gone to many bases. We have built bases in Libya, Vietnam, and Thailand. What guarantee do we have after we put in this untold millions of dollars . . . that they won't say, "thank you for building it. We will see you in 100 years and we will take over the bases."[16]

Strictly speaking, Addabbo's argument did not unambiguously strengthen the case for a formal guarantee. After all, the United States had been thrown off the Wheelus air force base in Libya despite the existence of an international agreement. Contracts, as *awase* negotiators know full well, cannot hold together an embittered relationship. Nor was it clear why Egypt would want to risk its partnership with the United States for a military camp it did not need at a godforsaken place like Ras Banas. But Addabbo was speaking as a representative and guardian of U.S. institutional and legal culture, and from this perspective it would have been inconceivable for the Congress to appropriate monies for the Ras Banas facility without some paper contract. For Sadat to imagine otherwise was unrealistic. Some things are nonnegotiable.

On occasion, the United States has gone beyond the bounds of proper form and strayed into the undergrowth of excessive formalism. It was surely so with the Defense Department's insistence on a privileges and immunities agreement to cover its naval and military medical research unit (see chap. 8). Because the unit had been permitted to work in safety even after the severance of U.S.-Egyptian diplomatic relations in June 1967, it is hard to understand what added benefit staff could derive from this new document. Here was an unworthy imputation on Egyptian hospitality.

Given the culturally grounded expectations and needs of the two sides, some negotiations appear foredoomed to failure. Ras Banas is one example. Another is the 1962–63 U.S.-Indian talks on air defense. The idea of a "tacit air defense pact" was first raised by the Indian government in December 1962 just after the Chinese withdrawal from Indian territory. India would provide the airfields and ground support, and the United States would send in planes to defend Indian cities in the event of an emergency, that is, a renewal of hostilities with China. Ambassador Galbraith seized on the proposal with enthusiasm, seeing it as a "great opportunity to bring India into much closer working association with the Western community." At the very outset, therefore, negotiations were dogged by an irreconcilable inconsistency: India wished for a "tacit" arrangement, Galbraith for "a virtual alliance." Almost at once the project began to unravel. The moment American views of the scheme became known to the Indians, they recoiled in predictable horror. Members of Parliament and the opposition press warned that the policy of nonalignment was threatened. Under fire, Nehru denied the idea altogether.[17]

In Sino-American relations special instruments of diplomacy have evolved. Differing fundamentally on the Taiwan issue, yet wishing to cooperate pragmatically in other areas, the two countries have been obliged to resort to forms of understanding not usually thought to possess the solemn, binding nature of the international treaty. Examples are the 1972 Shanghai communiqué, the parallel statements normalizing relations of 1978, and the 1985 Nuclear Cooperation Agreement. In effect, the United States has accommodated itself to Chinese practice. As Stanley Lubman points out, in the Chinese tradition a contract represents the beginning of a relationship and not its consummation. It defines the desired outcome of a transaction rather than the rights and obligations of the parties toward each other. The Chinese do not expect all contingencies to be anticipated and are particularly loath to consider the possibility of a breakdown in the partnership. Whereas Americans demand specificity, the Chinese are content with rather general language. They also view American contracts as overcomplex and prefer a simplicity that Americans find unsatisfactory.[18]

Japan, too, declines to view the written contract as the be-all and end-all of a relationship. Japanese business often relies much on unwritten agreements. Legal documents are the exception to the rule. "Just a lot of words" is how Masao Kunihiro sums up his compatriots' attitude to contracts. Moreover, as often as not contracts contain an escape clause ensuring that disagreement will be settled by consultation and not by litigation.[19] Mushakoji Kinhide adds that *awase* logic ensures that agreements are treated flexibly and broad-mindedly. "Japanese society operates by not making time exact and not paying strict attention to the provisions of contracts. Minor infringements are often overlooked (*ome ni miru*)."[20]

Americans do not take kindly to such a cavalier approach to contracts; infringements are not overlooked, but vehemently condemned as an unacceptable breach of trust. Donald Abelson, director of the Office of Trade Barriers in the Office of the U.S. Trade Representative, recalls with horror his own experience in this regard. In April 1979, Japan, together with the United States and other GATT (General Agreement on Tariffs and Trade) signatories, agreed on a standards code after years of negotiation. Before putting the code into law, Congress sought prompt assurances that U.S. trading partners would do likewise. Sadly, as Abelson notes, "in Japan quick agreements never seem to stick." The Japanese delegation went along with the U.S. request, apparently seeing it as no more than a sop to an overlegalistic Congress. After two negotiating sessions, they initialed an agreement, "drank champagne and that was it." They then, Abelson continues bitterly, "threw that initialed document into the waste-basket." The Japanese commitment turned out to be merely the first milestone on a long and weary road of further negotiation.[21]

Despite the flexibility of the United States in talks with China, it has still been unhappy about the Chinese willingness to tolerate loose ends. In 1978, for instance, the United States declined to discontinue the sale of arms to Taiwan. President Carter made this point absolutely clear to the Chinese representative in Washington in a statement on September 19. China did not like it but could live with it. Two days before the announcement of normalization, on December 13, Deng Xiaoping contented himself with a face-saving request to the United States not to sell arms to Taiwan in 1979, which surely implied his tacit acceptance of arms sales after 1979. On December 14 the United States acceded to Deng's request with the exception of sales already in the pipeline and replacement parts. Although nothing in the transcript of the conversation suggested that Deng contradicted the American position on arms sales, President Carter, advised by Vance and Brzezinski, felt that even greater clarity was called for. Ambassador Woodcock in Beijing was accordingly instructed to inform the Chinese that Carter's September 19 formulation still stood, notwithstanding the one-year moratorium. As anticipated by Woodcock, Deng was infuriated by American legalism and its mistrustful rejection of his own implicit, face-saving formula. Fortunately the meeting ended with the two sides agreeing to disagree.[22]

Calculated ambiguity is, in theory, an excellent device to paper over unresolved conflicts or to obscure embarrassing concessions. With the prospect of congressional scrutiny ahead, President Carter doubtless felt that it was not a practical way out. Similar formulas have also fallen through with Japan. In 1969 Japanese negotiators insisted that any agreement to restrain textile exports to the United States be conditional on there being "objective proof of injury" to U.S. industry. Complaints would be looked into by a multilateral agency. However, Japan let it be known that in practice a working group would ensure the application of export controls even if injury was not formally proved. That way Japanese domestic requirements would be met and face saved all around. Insisting on a watertight arrangement and not tacit assurances, the United States rejected the arrangement, thereby ensuring that the conflict continue festering for another two years.[23]

In recent years the United States does seem to have mellowed, however, in its attitude to informal international understandings. The 1985 Nuclear Cooperation Agreement went further than any other comparable accord to meet Chinese sensibilities. Permitting the sale and transfer of nuclear materials and equipment from the United States to the People's Republic, it was concluded only after far-reaching American concessions over "consent rights" and "safeguards."[24] In the past, the United States had required certain explicit commitments from its nuclear partners to ensure against the diversion of nuclear materials for the purpose of weapons production. Specifically, the cosignatory had to agree to request American consent before reprocessing spent U.S.-supplied fuel and also had to accept supervision of its reactors by the International Atomic Energy Agency (IAEA). Adherence to the Nuclear Non-

proliferation Treaty was also expected and was particularly perti-
nent in this case, given Chinese assistance to Pakistan's nuclear
weapons program.

China, however, was unwilling to make any formal commitments, although it had joined the IAEA, for two principal reasons:
first, because it argued that it was already a nuclear weapon state
and was therefore not obliged under the terms of IAEA member-
ship to accept supervision of materials provided by another nuclear weapon state. To do so would be to concede to the United
States control over the future course of its nuclear weapons development. Second, because China, like France, has always viewed the
Nuclear Nonproliferation Treaty as a discriminatory accord by
which the great powers seek to maintain their own nuclear weapons monopoly.

To overcome these objections demanded considerable flexibility
on the part of the United States and the display of maturity and
realism in its treatment of non-Western concerns. In place of "consent rights" Washington agreed to an elliptical and ambiguous provision in the treaty. Should China wish to reprocess fuel for peaceful purposes in the future, the parties would consult "immediately"
with a view to reaching agreement. For its part, the United States
would consider a Chinese request "favorably" and would avoid
"hampering" the latter's nuclear program or refrain from inhibit-
ing the "exploitation of nuclear energy for peaceful purposes."
The balancing Chinese assurance was contained in a vague clause
in which both parties agreed "to refrain from actions which either
party believes would . . . adversely affect cooperation under this
agreement." In the American view, this assurance provided the
United States with the equivalent of "consent rights," because
China was well aware that illegitimate diversion of fuel would most
certainly "affect cooperation under this agreement."

On the safeguards issue, the signatories agreed to "exchange information and visits." Here again the administration argued that
such an exchange was the equivalent of formal international supervision, because nuclear exports would not be licensed unless
the United States was satisfied that agreed arrangements came up
to IAEA standards.

The nonproliferation aspect was in some ways the trickiest issue
to resolve, because China refused any reference to the matter in
the treaty at all. The best that could be achieved was an oral pledge
made by Prime Minister Zhao Ziyang of China at a White House
reception. Raising his champagne glass in a toast, Zhao stated: "We

do not engage in nuclear proliferation ourselves, nor do we help other countries develop nuclear weapons."[25] The U.S. interpretation of this and other verbal Chinese assurances was contained in a classified State Department memorandum.[26]

Critics of the Nuclear Cooperation Agreement were dissatisfied that Chinese obligations were not explicitly spelled out in the text of the agreement. What if China declined in the future to agree with the U.S. interpretation? The ambiguity inherent in the accord would only foster misunderstanding and conflict. "There can only be one reason for these excursions into the netherworld of State Departmentese," Representative Edward Markey (D-Mass.) scathingly charged. "The Chinese are not prepared to commit to what the American law requires."[27]

In the end, however, the treaty was ratified. Congressional concerns were met by a joint resolution requiring the president, in advance of the issue of an export license, to provide certain defined assurances. Reciprocal arrangements on end use would have to be satisfactory and additional information provided on China's nonproliferation policies. When the debate subsided and the contestants departed, a complex structure of overlapping understandings was in place. In addition to the international treaty, there were oral Chinese assurances, a classified State Department memorandum of interpretation, explanations to the Congress, and a congressional resolution. All were required to reconcile the political and cultural needs of the two sides. The agreement was complicated, but Chinese honor and American propriety had been satisfied.

Pressures to settle

As the prospect of success or failure looms, pressures build up from the domestic constituency, from the opponent, and from oneself. Under the stress of this decisive encounter, the mettle and nerves of negotiators are tested to the utmost. Character is bound to be important. But, above all, the negotiating resources and assumptions of the group are put to the test. Americans enjoy one great advantage—their ingenuity and enterprising spirit—and suffer one major disability—their impatience.

From the tactical point of view, it is an unequal competition, for non-Western patience and persistence stand the negotiator in better stead than American habits of urgency. It is hard enough negotiating the issues; bargaining against the clock compounds the difficulty. Worse, the American negotiator joins an instinctive impatience to an overwhelming and barely concealed obligation to succeed; American culture, in the form of public opinion, career dictates, and government expectations, does not take kindly to failure. Therefore, in the final contest of wills, as the opposite numbers are well aware, Americans are at a disadvantage. Whereas they must bring matters to a prompt conclusion, their non-Western opponents—or, indeed anyone else free of stifling deadlines—can sit them out or, if necessary, credibly threaten to walk away from the bargaining table altogether. This freedom is an enviable asset.

The definitive statement on the tendency of the American negotiator to give ground in the face of an obdurate rival was made many years ago by the U.S. delegate to the Panmunjom armistice talks for ending the Korean War. Looking back on his experience, Ambassador Arthur Dean ruefully observes the asymmetry of pressures on the two sides:

> Communists are in no hurry. They have no timetable. They think time is on their side and that Americans, being optimistic, friendly, truthful, constructive and inclined to believe and hope for the best, will become discouraged. They believe that at a long-drawn-out conference the American negotiators will be forced by American public opinion to give in, in order to have a successful conference. Impatience mounts as no progress is reported. People ask: "What progress did you make today?" The Communists know this and utter rude, insulting, arrogant demands that the American negotiators stop their unconstructive stalling tactics.[28]

Alexis Johnson, the U.S. delegate at the ambassadorial talks with the People's Republic of China, described a similar experience: "During the almost 4 years that I was negotiating with the Chinese Communists at Geneva, between 1954 and 1958, what I found most annoying and frustrating was their supreme self-confidence that they need make no concessions of any kind and that if they just waited long enough we would be forced to make all the concessions to them."[29]

Now that some of the State Department papers on the ambassadorial talks are available to researchers, it is possible to document in greater detail the forces for concession to which Ambassador Johnson was subject. At least in the 1955 civilian repatriation talks, there is no evidence of a substantial gap between Johnson's personal judgment of what was attainable and that of officials back home. In a very few weeks, Johnson perceived that the Chinese refusal to agree to release all Americans on the mainland was irreducible. The talks had got under way on August 1. On August 18, the Chinese delegate made a great display of intransigence on the issue, resisting "persistent pressure" to provide assurances on the release of all the Americans. The battle continued for another two weeks, with Johnson pegging away with diminishing optimism.

According to Johnson's account, virtually the entire session of August 25 "centered around my continuing effort to obtain a definite statement on the definite period of time during which the remaining Americans would be released and Wang repeating this 'could never be done,' 'impossible' and repeating virtually verbatim his previous line in this regard." At the August 31 session, Johnson reported, the Chinese negotiator "showed no great sense of urgency," and Johnson doubted that the Chinese desire to move on to other matters was "strong enough to overcome their very strong reluctance to give up their position." He had already suggested that it would be difficult for the United States to maintain its original demands and suggested to the State Department that it might be "jeopardizing" the immediate release of more than half of the detained Americans by insisting that they all be freed. In its instructions of September 2, the State Department concurred, concluding that the agreed announcement was "as good as can be expected." [30]

The American propensity for self-induced deadlines was nowhere more evident than in the 1978 normalization talks with China. With admitted hindsight, it is clear that the haste with which these negotiations were pursued by the Carter administration was particularly inappropriate because time was actually working to the detriment of the People's Republic of China. There were tactical reasons why the United States wanted an agreement by the end of 1978—the looming debate over ratification of the Panama Canal treaties, the strategic arms limitation talks with the Soviet Union, and involvement in the Egyptian-Israeli peace process— but these were not insurmountable. But there were weighty, indeed inescapable, strategic considerations behind China's wish for early normalization: its planned attack on Vietnam and the need to neutralize the danger of Soviet involvement. Following the publication of the agreement on December 15, 1978, formal diplomatic relations were established on January 1, 1979, paving the way for the visit by Deng Xiaoping to the United States at the end of the month. On February 17 the People's Liberation Army attacked

Vietnam, Deng having cleverly obtained the appearance of U.S. complicity as a deterrent to Soviet intervention.

Nevertheless, despite the asymmetry of interest in a speedy resolution of the issue, China successfully concealed its own sense of urgency while the United States acted as though it faced an immutable deadline. At a meeting of top U.S. officials on June 20, 1978, it was first decided to aim for completion of the normalization negotiations by December 15, but the Chinese were not supposed to be informed of this target date. Secretary of State Vance argued that this timetable "would allow us to proceed with Peking at a reasonable pace and would have some negotiating advantages over a stretched-out process." However, National Security Adviser Zbigniew Brzezinski had already told Deng that President Carter was prepared to move as quickly as possible, and in September Carter openly stressed to the head of the People's Republic liaison office in Washington the desirability of a quick normalization. While the Chinese "hung tough" on their insistence that the United States terminate its arms relationship with Taiwan, Brzezinski made little attempt to conceal his own sense of urgency. He "told the Chinese Ambassador that if we missed this opportunity, we would have to delay normalization until far into 1979. The congressional schedule would be overloaded and we would have to move ahead on SALT and a possible meeting with Brezhnev." Brzezinski continued to be the main proponent of haste. Again on December 11, impatient with the slow pace of the Chinese response, he made the case for a speedy decision to Ambassador Chai.

The negotiating advantages to the Chinese of this artificially induced sense of urgency are obvious. It was made to appear, with no basis in the objective situation, that the United States was more eager for agreement than were the Chinese. As might be anticipated, there was a price to be paid for American impatience. The United States had concluded early that China would not be prepared to renounce officially its right to use force to reunify Taiwan with the mainland. Consequently, it was decided to settle on the device of an American statement of "interest in the peaceful resolution of the Taiwan issue," which would not be contradicted by a simultaneous Chinese statement. But on December 15, U.S. desires notwithstanding, the Chinese went ahead with a statement that did contradict the American position. The manner in which Taiwan would be brought "back to the embrace of the motherland," the People's Republic declared, "is entirely China's internal affair." It was a ringing slap in the face for Carter. To add insult to injury, in 1982 fresh negotiations on the problem of Taiwan produced a new agreement. In return for a remarkable U.S. commitment not to exceed past qualitative and quantitative levels of arms sales to Taiwan, China now pledged to seek a peaceful solution to unification. It had succeeded in selling the same horse twice.[31]

The axiom that some solution is better than no solution has also characterized U.S. negotiations with Mexico. Timothy Bennett felt that the American determination to solve problems led to a willingness to concede more than necessary in order to get a deal. Another State Department official agreed that Mexicans were better able to hold out for a more favorable bargain. In contrast to U.S. negotiators, Mexicans were "happy to go away without an agreement at a given session." In territorial disputes the key to a solution has invariably been U.S. acceptance of the Mexican position, even when the American case was a reasonable one (which it arguably was not, in the Chamizal talks). Joseph Friedkin, with years of experience negotiating with Mexico, observed that the resolution of the Presidio-Ojinaga land dispute simply depended on the State Department giving in. It did try for a compromise at first, but the Mexicans remained adamant that the contested area—the result of bewildering and uncharted changes in the course of the Rio Grande—had to be transferred to them. Mexico, Friedkin continued, was always "very patient." In the Presidio-Ojinaga case they "felt that if it couldn't be solved to their satisfaction, they'd just leave it pending."[32]

In the 1979 gas talks, the United States, which was paying $2.29 per thousand cubic feet for new domestic gas, finally settled on a new price of $3.625 after weeks of weary haggling with Mexico. The final rounds of bidding went as follows. On August 9, the United States was offering $3.40; Mexico held out for $3.75. Both sides dug their heels in at this point. Then on August 29–30, Under Secretary of State Warren Christopher met with Foreign Minister Castaneda of Mexico. While the United States upped its offer to $3.50, Mexico stuck at $3.75. If Christopher had expected a reciprocal concession by Castaneda, he was disappointed. The Mexican proved able to hang in longer. The final agreed price of $3.625 predictably split the difference between the two latter bids.[33]

According to Julius Katz, who had handled previous rounds of the negotiations, Christopher had indeed gone "over the edge," agreeing to an excessive price because of political considerations. In a haggle of this kind, Katz remarked, the United States is at an inevitable disadvantage. Because "you can't afford to fail" you say "let's let them have it." Now it may be legitimate to trade a marginal monetary concession for a more highly valued political advantage. But it should be noted that in this case the political considerations impinged absolutely symmetrically on the two sides. Both President Carter and President Portillo wanted an agreement in hand for their upcoming late September summit. Both welcomed the domestic benefits of a diplomatic success. Yet it was the American delegate who blinked first and proposed an unreciprocated concession on August 29.[34]

In the 1980–82 air service negotiations with Japan, the final outcome was the linear consequence of an error made at the outset. In its opening proposal the United States put forward a package that held nothing in reserve and put on the table almost everything on offer. Here was premature concession at its worst. Stubborn Japanese bargaining gained for Japan a major, unreciprocated concession in the final phase: the right to an all-cargo service to Chicago. The United States failed to achieve the objective that it had set its heart on—an additional landing point in Japan.[35] Obviously, one can never know if the Japanese delegation would ultimately have conceded the point in the face of reciprocal U.S. obduracy. But one thing is clear: having made major concessions at the beginning, the United States was left with insufficient bargaining chips at the end.

India's "geologic sense of time" and ready acceptance of delay were commented on by an experienced State Department official. He acknowledged that the weakness of the American approach to negotiation lay in its domestically conditioned habit of working under self-imposed time constraints. Officials jetting into Delhi from Washington for a few brisk days of talks totally miscalculate the time required. Ambassador Eilts and others confirmed that Egyptians were equally tough negotiators for Americans to deal with. They would stick stubbornly to their positions and accept a compromise only with difficulty.

Eilts's judgment is exemplified by Ellsworth Bunker's 1963 mission to mediate the cessation of Egyptian and Saudi intervention in the Yemeni civil war. Widely regarded as the greatest American negotiator of his generation, Ambassador Bunker faced a formidable opponent in President Nasser. The two men negotiated for three days after Bunker had already achieved a modification of the Saudi position. A key problem was the linkage of the suspension of Saudi aid to the royalists with the withdrawal of Egyptian forces. For three days Nasser did not yield an inch on this issue. Only at the close of their final meeting did the Egyptian president make a grudging concession in response to the American envoy's entreaties. "You know, Mr. President," Ambassador Bunker besought, "I have to be able to go back and say you actually withdrew some forces. Won't you give me just half a company? It isn't anything, half a company." Smiling somewhat, Nasser finally agreed.

Bunker had demonstrated rare judgment and patience, as subsequent events made clear. The fact is that half a company is not an independently viable military unit. One cannot withdraw half a company and leave it at that. The truth of the matter, as Bunker must have suspected, is that Nasser was prepared all along to withdraw at least a token force, knowing full well that without it there would be no agreement. He could not, however, give in too easily. When Bunker returned to Cairo from Jidda a week later, Nasser told him that he would like to withdraw two battalions within fifteen days of the commencement of disengagement and at least "one or two" companies simultaneous with the Saudi suspension of aid to the royalists. He had, in short, been holding out for reasons of tactics, not principle. A lesser negotiator than Ellsworth Bunker might have allowed himself to be discouraged.[36]

* * *

In the Bunker-Nasser encounter just described, the key to Bunker's success was a remarkable sensitivity to Nasser's psychological requirements. In a tour de force of creative negotiation, Bunker met each of the cultural requirements of high-context, face-salient interlocutors discussed in this chapter. He displayed infinite forbearance, being prepared to synchronize his negotiating pace with their more leisurely tempo. Like Kissinger years later, he patiently shuttled from Cairo to Jidda and back, allowing the task to dictate his timetable, and not the reverse. He also accommodated himself to the elliptical and implicit form of understanding preferred by Nasser. An oral assurance was all that was on offer. Most important was his shrewd willingness to allow Nasser to present his concession to Saudi Arabia as something of little importance, granted as a personal favor to the mediator. Had Bunker insisted on Nasser conceding two battalions and one or two companies up front, the agreement would have fallen through, for Nasser would have preferred proud intransigence to open compromise with his sworn enemies. By asking Nasser for half a company—"it isn't anything, half a company"—Bunker enabled the Egyptian leader to concede without loss of face. This was diplomacy of the highest order.

ten

In Search of Harmony
Conclusions

Culture has been called "the hidden dimension," unseen, yet exerting a pervasive influence on the behavior of individuals, groups, and societies. From this premise it has been but a short step for researchers to recognize the potential for misunderstanding in situations of intercultural communication. When interlocutors attempt to convey messages across linguistic and cultural barriers, meanings are lost or distorted in the process. What one culture takes to be self-evident, another may find bizarre. Strangely enough, international negotiation has, implicitly or explicitly, been excluded by many political scientists from this general tendency. In the cases investigated, involving the United States and a group of non-Western nations, it was seen that cross-cultural dissonances may strongly affect the conduct and outcome of diplomatic talks.

Negotiation theorists' dismissal of the effect of culture springs from the assumption that there is a single, universal paradigm of negotiation and that cross-national differences are stylistic and superficial. In opposition to that contention, the existence of two quite different paradigms of negotiation was confirmed by this study. One is associated with the predominantly verbal and explicit, or low-context, communicatory style of the United States. In a nutshell, it is infused with the can-do, problem-solving spirit, assumes a process of give-and-take, and is strongly influenced by

Anglo-Saxon legal habits. When theorists posit a universal para-digm of negotiation (usually involving such features as the "joint search for a solution," "isolating the people from the problem," and the "maximization of joint gains") they are in effect proposing an idealized version of the low-context, problem-solving model. No-tice the instrumental assumptions of rationality that underlie the paradigm: people are part of the problem, not the solution; each problem can be solved discretely; goals are defined in terms of ma-terial, not psychic, satisfactions.

An alternative, quite different, model of negotiation is just as self-consistent and valid in its own terms as the first. This model, associated with a nonverbal, implicit, high-context style of com-munication, predominates in interdependent societies that display a collectivistic, rather than individualistic, ethos. This paradigm was found to mark the negotiating behavior of the non-Western states examined. In contrast to the problem-solving, American model, it declines to view the immediate issue in isolation; lays par-ticular stress on long-term and affective aspects of the relationship between the parties; is preoccupied with considerations of symbol-ism, status, and face; and draws on highly developed communica-tion strategies for evading confrontation.

Putting the two paradigms together in the same room in an in-tercultural or interparadigmatic encounter produces some inter-esting reactions. American negotiators tend to be surprised by their interlocutors' preoccupation with history and hierarchy, pref-erence for principle over nitty-gritty detail, personalized and re-petitive style of argument, lack of enthusiasm for explicit and for-mal agreement, and willingness to sacrifice substance to form. They are frustrated by their partners' reluctance to put their cards on the table, intransigent bargaining, evasiveness, dilatoriness, and readiness to walk away from the table without agreement. Non-Western negotiators tend to be surprised by their interlocutors' ig-norance of history, preoccupation with individual rights, obsession with the immediate problem while neglecting the overall relation-ship, excessive bluntness, impatience, disinterest in establishing a philosophical basis for agreement, extraordinary willingness to make soft concessions, constant generation of new proposals, and inability to leave a problem pending. They are frustrated by their American partners' occasional obtuseness and insensitivity; ten-dency to see things and present alternatives in black-and-white, either-or, terms; appetite for crisis; habit of springing unpleasant surprises; intimidating readiness for confrontation; tendency to bypass established channels of authority; inability to take no for an answer; and obsession with tidying up loose ends and putting everything down on paper. Obviously, these are oversimplified depictions, but they do serve to highlight the main points of abrasion in the low context-high context encounter.

The historical record examined for this study provided persuasive evidence of the practical consequences of such intercultural disharmonies and incompatibilities. The chemical mixture obtained when the two paradigms joined in debate was shown to be highly volatile. In extreme cases, dissonance might have contributed to the failure of negotiations. However, it would be imprudent to claim that this factor was ever decisive by itself. In the 1950 civil aviation talks with Mexico, for example, Mexico resented not being treated as an equal, but substantive disagreement also separated the two sides. In the 1958 U.S.-Chinese ambassadorial talks over hostilities in the Taiwan Straits, at a time of widening Sino-Soviet discord, an opportunity to build upon some budding common interests was lost. Whereas Beijing insisted, in typical fashion, on prior U.S. agreement to a general renunciation of force, Washington pragmatically proposed to defuse hostilities step by step. Years later, in 1971, Mao surely hinted at past error when he told Nixon that the United States was right to propose tackling small issues before big ones. Lastly, cross-cultural incompatibilities seriously hindered the Ras Banas and General Motors negotiations with Egypt of the early 1980s, although there was potential for agreement in terms of significant shared interests and a good underlying relationship. In the Ras Banas affair the heavy-handed, legalistic approach of the Department of Defense frightened the Egyptians off when only a low-key accord to establish a modest facility was acceptable. As for General Motors, it was fatally discouraged by the labyrinthine and far from pristine maneuvers of the Cairo bureaucracy.

A second result of dissonance that has been illustrated was tactical rather than strategic, namely, it ensured that U.S. negotiators achieved less favorable terms than they might have otherwise. We saw that a common error of the United States was to offer premature concessions in the mistaken assumption that its opponent, driven by the same eagerness for compromise, would reciprocate in kind. This error placed the United States in an inferior position in the final round of negotiations. This tendency was observed in the 1955 civilian repatriation talks with China, when the United States made substantial concessions very soon and then, in the face

of Chinese obduracy, decided not to insist on the immediate release of all civilian detainees held on the mainland. Equally, in believing that holding hostages would achieve political benefit, China
(uncannily like Iran much later) sadly miscalculated the acute U.S.
sensitivity to human rights issues. As a result, relations were embittered for years. In the 1956–57 air transport talks, Mexico
achieved its major goals while the United States conceded its main
objectives, having long since—one-sidedly—exhausted its bargaining assets. Demonstrating the consistency of these tendencies, despite a change of cast and circumstances, a similar pattern appeared in the 1980–82 air service negotiations with Japan:
premature U.S. concessions in the face of Japanese reticence resulted in a final agreement more favorable to Japan. In the 1978
normalization talks with China, the United States naively informed
the Chinese that its opening position was not its last word. Playing
its hand closer to its chest, China withheld the assurance of a
peaceful resolution of the Taiwan issue, only to use that very trump
to obtain quite new concessions in 1982 discussions.

The most frequent consequence of intercultural misunderstanding that we saw was undramatic but pernicious: a spillover effect
spreading beyond the immediate negotiation and causing a loss of
credibility and damage to the wider relationship. This phenomenon has notably haunted U.S.-Japanese relations. On separate occasions in 1955, 1969, 1970, and 1987 the United States mistook
polite Japanese reluctance to offend for actual compliance. Having
failed to detect Japanese unhappiness, and foisted agreement on
its unenthusiastic ally, it then completely miscalculated the ability
of the Japanese political leadership to deliver the bureaucracy.
Such spurious accord, reached without the requisite process of
consensus building, was quickly repudiated in Tokyo. The result
was an all-round loss of confidence, with angry Americans and embarrassed Japanese. On two occasions the culprit was President
Nixon, who compounded cross-cultural insensitivity with classic
prejudice. In 1969 he completely misinterpreted the dismissive utterance of Prime Minister Sato of Japan ("I will do my best"); in
1971 he wrongly inferred from Mrs. Gandhi's elliptical and understated remarks that he had a pledge that India would not use military means to solve the Bangladesh crisis. When, in both cases,
"promises" were not kept, Nixon privately accused his interlocutors of being "liars." As a result of developments stemming from
the original misunderstanding, long-term harm was inflicted on
both relationships. The "broken pledge" syndrome also occurred
in 1979, when Ambassador Patrick Lucey took away the wrong im-

pression from a meeting with President Lopez Portillo of Mexico; and in 1987, when President Reagan and his advisers were misled by Prime Minister Nakasone of Japan.

Failure to read its negotiating partners' intentions correctly because of cross-cultural misunderstanding has also deprived the United States of the ability to foresee future moves and hence to take necessary preventive or remedial action. In 1954 Ambassador Allen completely misjudged Nehru's reaction to the U.S.-Pakistan arms deal. As a result, the American government was unprepared for the spasm of outrage that convulsed Indian opinion. Similarly, in 1977 the United States failed to grasp that behind President Sadat's lack of enthusiasm for a reconvening of the Geneva conference—"there was no rush"—lurked strong opposition to the scheme. Overlooking the Egyptian president's growing sense of desperation, the United States, albeit temporarily, lost complete control of the Middle East peace process. In 1962 Ambassador Galbraith also neglected to read between the lines of Nehru's tepid response to the Anglo-American Kashmir mediation. In the circumstances of India's border war with China, Nehru could hardly dismiss Western proposals out of hand. But misplaced American pressure on India to make concessions to Pakistan dissipated the considerable credit accruing to the U.S. government as a result of its timely military assistance. Again in 1984, agreement was foisted on a reluctant Egypt for the passage of nuclear warships through the Suez Canal. Having dragged its feet for years, the Egyptian government was loath to turn the United States down flat. But, as in the Kashmir example, credit was squandered and at the first opportunity Egypt repudiated the accord.

If cross-cultural dissonance can harm a relationship, the converse should be equally true: that cross-cultural harmony, based on careful attention to the other side's psychological needs, should prove beneficial. And indeed it has proved true. However, unless there are shared interests in an agreement, no amount of cross-cultural sensitivity will help. Rosalie Tung, in a survey of U.S. businessmen who had conducted trade negotiations with China, found that cross-cultural ignorance was "perceived as a primary factor responsible for the failure of negotiations." Cross-cultural knowledge, however, was a "necessary but insufficient condition for success" and had to "be combined with a genuine willingness to work toward a common goal."[1] Ambassador Samuel Lewis, a veteran of the U.S.-Egyptian-Israeli peace process, confirmed this point from his own experience.[2]

In the negotiations studied, some U.S. negotiators made a major contribution by carefully cultivating close personal relationships with their foreign counterparts. For example, in the 1962–63 Chamizal negotiation with Mexico, Ambassador Mann's long-standing friendship with Ambassador Tello proved invaluable. It is significant that the two ambassadors did their best work in informal settings. Many of the technical details were hammered out by officials of the International Boundary and Water Commission, who also had long experience of working together. Again in the 1973 Colorado salinity talks the close Brownell-Rabasa relationship was a great help; the breakthrough in negotiations came in a conversation while the two were out for a stroll. The role of the personal touch strongly emerges in a survey of U.S.-Egyptian relations since 1973; all major political successes have been facilitated by it. The Egyptian-Israeli disengagement agreements of 1974 and 1975, and the accords of 1978 and 1979, seem hardly conceivable without the intimate Kissinger-Sadat and Carter-Sadat relationships. To complete the picture it is worth recalling the personal rapport that obtained between President Lyndon Johnson and Mrs. Gandhi on Mrs. Gandhi's successful trip to Washington in 1966, when the two concurred on a reform package for the Indian economy that included a painful devaluation of the rupee. This thawing of relations took place despite the continuing U.S.-Pakistan alliance. So much for purely objective factors in international politics.

The salience of "personal chemistry" in international affairs may, of course, be overstated. After all, the ongoing conduct of foreign policy is in the hands of a great many agencies and officials. National leaders and high officials are engaged only intermittently. Nevertheless, consultations at the highest level can play a crucial role. Communication between heads of state and foreign ministers brings information authoritatively and promptly to the attention of their respective governments. Commitments are made, directions indicated, agendas set. Where that communication is easy and unencumbered, it may not be possible to brush aside unsurmountable differences, but misunderstanding of the other's intentions and gratuitous complications can be avoided. Moreover, without open channels of communication, opportunities to explore common interests may be missed.

A second factor facilitating harmony was the recognition by the United States that there are certain points of inviolable dogma that are nonnegotiable as far as a high-context interlocutor is concerned. However, once such axioms are conceded in principle, it may be possible, in a pragmatic fashion, to arrive at a satisfactory agreement on concrete issues. This approach involves true cross-cultural accommodation, in that it reconciles the deep-seated needs of both sides. It was this approach that underlay the 1962 Kennedy-Mateos accord paving the way for a resolution of the Chamizal dispute. Once the United States recognized the justice of the Mexican claim (conceded by international arbitration in 1911), Mexico was prepared to be utterly pragmatic in its practical implementation. An identical strategy was followed in 1973, when President Nixon committed the United States to a "just solution" of the Colorado River problem, thereby acknowledging the responsibility of the United States to ensure that usable water reached Mexican farmers. Similarly, in the 1969 Okinawa bases negotiations the United States wisely conceded the principle of "home-level reversion"—the return of the Ryukyu and Bonin islands to Japanese administration—thereby guaranteeing both continued U.S. use of the bases and future military cooperation. The 1972 Shanghai communiqué was yet another example of a generalized framework beneath the philosophical awnings of which pragmatic cooperation could proceed. In this case, remarkably, points of difference were not plastered over. But the two countries' opposition to hegemony (that is, Soviet ambitions) was proclaimed and the yawning gap over the Taiwan issue was bridged with the ingenious U.S. acknowledgment "that all Chinese on either side of the Taiwan Straits maintain there is but one China."[3]

A final ingredient in reaching agreement with high-context negotiators was scrupulous regard for their heightened sensitivity in matters of face. Any whiff of humiliation would doom an agreement to perdition. To obtain the substance of accord it was essential to preserve appearances: to maintain—if necessary, contrive—the impression that the accord was an achievement of the other side, concluded on the basis of mutual respect and equal standing, with no element of compulsion and no concession of principle. Striking examples of this pattern were found in the 1971 Japanese devaluation and the 1982 Mexican loan. In the first instance, a 17-percent devaluation of the yen was impossible, but 16.9-percent devaluation was acceptable. In the second case, Mexico was ready to receive a lower effective price for its oil than it could otherwise have obtained, because it rested on a face-saving arrangement. The vital importance of face was also observed in the 1971–72 talks with China, for example, in the terms of the invitation to President Nixon; and in the 1973 negotiations for a cease-fire following the

Yom Kippur War, when United Nations checkpoints on the Cairo-Suez road obscured the reality of the blockade of the Egyptian Third Army by Israeli forces. Finally, although it was not always feasible, something unacceptable as an explicit agreement might be palatable as an informal understanding. Over the years, many areas of cooperation, especially with Mexico and Egypt, have been assisted by this expedient.

It should be obvious by now that I do not believe that either Americans or their non-Western partners have a monopoly of wisdom when it comes to negotiation. As an outsider, I personally find much to commend in both the problem-oriented and relationship-oriented approaches. Learning that there is more than one way to go about things not only is enlightening but also enriches one's palette of alternatives. So it is neither possible nor desirable to lay down hard-and-fast, universal rules of how to negotiate. That depends on the issue, the circumstances, the opponent—and oneself. Nevertheless, there are certain obvious lessons to be drawn from this project. I present them here (for the benefit of the low-context individual faced by a high-context adversary) in the form of ten recommendations for the intercultural negotiator.

1. Prepare for a negotiation by studying your opponents' culture and history, and not just the issue at hand. Best of all, learn the language. Immerse yourself in the historical relationship between your two nations. It may explain more than you might expect.

2. Try to establish a warm, personal relationship with your interlocutors. If possible, get to know them even before negotiations get under way. Cultivating contacts and acquaintances is time well spent.

3. Do not assume that what you mean by a message—verbal or nonverbal—is what representatives of the other side will understand by it. They will interpret it in the light of their cultural and linguistic background, not yours. By the same token, they may be unaware that things look different from your perspective.

4. Be alert to indirect formulations and nonverbal gestures. Traditional societies put a lot of weight on them. You may have to read between the lines to understand what your partners are hinting at. Do not assume that they will come right out with it. Be ultra-careful in your own words and body language. They may read more into them than you intend.

5. Be aware of the emphasis placed by your opponents on matters of status and face. At a personal level, establish them as equals. Avoid the unmasked exercise of pressure. Do not express criticism

in public. Do not lose your temper. Avoid confronting them with prearranged solutions. Do not go over their heads. Avoid unpleasant surprises. Anything that leads to the loss of face is likely to be counterproductive.

6. Do not overestimate the power of advocacy. Your interlocutors are unlikely to shift their positions simply in response to good arguments. Facts and circumstances speak louder than words and are easier to comply with.

7. Adapt your strategy to your opponents' cultural needs. On matters of inviolable principle, attempt to accommodate their instinct for prior agreement with your preference for progress on practical matters. Where haggling is called for, leave yourself plenty of leeway. Start high, bargain doggedly, and hold back a trump card for the final round.

8. Flexibility is not a virtue against intransigent opponents. If they are concerned to discover your real bottom line, repeated concessions will confuse rather than clarify the issue. Nor is there merit in innovation for its own sake. Avoid the temptation to compromise with yourself.

9. Be patient. Haste will almost certainly mean unnecessary concessions. Resist the temptation to labor under artificial time constraints; they will work to your disadvantage. Allow your opponents to decide in their own good time. Their bureaucratic requirements cannot be short-circuited.

10. Outward forms and appearances may be as important as substance. For face-conscious negotiators, an agreement must be presentable as a prestigious outcome. On the other hand, symbolic gains may compensate them for substantive losses.

Notes

1. Prelude

1. Harold Nicolson, *Diplomacy,* 3d ed. (London: Oxford University Press, 1969), chap. 10.

2. Joseph C. Grew, *Ten Years in Japan* (London: Hammond, Hammond, 1944), 241.

3. U.S. Department of State, *Foreign Relations of the United States,* vol. 4, 1939 (Washington, D.C.: U.S. Government Printing Office, 1955), 455–62 (hereafter cited as *FRUS*).

2. Negotiation

1. Edward Burnett Tylor, *Primitive Culture* (New York: Harper and Row, 1958. Original ed. 1871).

2. Clyde Kluckhohn, "The Study of Culture," in D. Lerner and H. D. Lasswell, eds., *The Policy Sciences* (Stanford, Calif.: Stanford University Press, 1951), 86.

3. For a good discussion see Ogura Kazuo, "How the 'Inscrutables' Negotiate with the 'Inscrutables': Chinese Negotiating Tactics *Vis-à-Vis* the Japanese," *The China Quarterly* 79(1979):549.

4. Lucian Pye, *Chinese Commercial Negotiating Style* (Cambridge, Mass.: Oelgeschlager, Gunn, and Hain, 1982), 88–89.

5. For a review of the intercultural literature relevant to international relations, see Raymond Cohen, *Culture and Conflict in Egyptian-Israeli Relations: A Dialogue of the Deaf* (Bloomington: Indiana University Press, 1990), 8–13. See also idem, "International Communication: An Intercultural Approach," *Cooperation and Conflict* 22(1987):63–80; and idem, "Problems of Intercultural Communication in Egyptian-American Diplomatic Relations," *International Journal of Intercultural Relations* 11(1987):29–47.

6. For example: Mara B. Adelman and Myron W. Lustig, "Intercultural Communication Problems as Perceived by Saudi Arabian and American Managers," *International Journal of Intercultural Relations* 5(1981):349–63; Pierre Casse and Surinder Deol, *Managing Intercultural Negotiations* (Yarmouth, Me.: Intercultural Press, 1985); John L. Graham, "The Influence of Culture on the Process of Business Negotiations," *Journal of International Business Studies* 16(1985):81–96; Robert M. March, *The Japanese Negotiator* (Tokyo: Kodansha International, 1988); Lucian Pye, *Chinese Commercial Negotiating Style;* John Pfeiffer, "How Not to Lose the Trade Wars by Cultural Gaffes," *Smithsonian* 18(1988):145–56; Oded Shenkar and Simcha Ronen, "The Cultural Context of Negotiations: The Implications of Chinese Interpersonal Norms," *The Journal of Applied Behavioral Science* 23(1987):263–75; Rosalie L. Tung, "U.S.-China Trade Negotiations: Procedures and Outcomes," *Journal of International Business Studies* 13(1982):25–37; James R. Van De Velde, "The Influence of Culture on Japanese-American Negotiations," *The Fletcher Forum* 7(1983):395–99; Howard F. Van Zandt, "How to Negotiate in Japan," *Harvard Business Review* 48(1970):45–56.

7. Marie D. Strazar, "The San Francisco Peace Treaty: Cross-Cultural Elements in the Interaction between the Americans and the Japanese," in R. P. Anand, ed., *Cultural Factors in International Relations* (New Delhi: Abinhav, 1981), 63–76.

8. Hiroshi Kimura, "Soviet and Japanese Negotiating Behavior: The Spring 1977 Fisheries Talks," *Orbis* 24(1980):43–67.

9. Michael Blaker, *Japanese International Negotiating Style* (New York: Columbia University Press, 1977).

10. Richard H. Solomon, *Chinese Political Negotiating Behavior: A Briefing Analysis* (Santa Monica, Calif.: The RAND Corporation, 1985).

11. Hans Binnendijk, ed., *National Negotiating Styles* (Washington: Foreign Service Institute, 1987).

12. Samuel W. Lewis, impromptu comments at a United States Institute of Peace work-in-progress seminar, November 10, 1988.

13. Raymond F. Smith, *Negotiating with the Soviets* (Bloomington: Indiana University Press, 1989), 5–6.

14. Glen Fisher, *International Negotiation: A Cross-Cultural Perspective* (Yarmouth, Me.: Intercultural Press, 1980).

15. Now that we are in a "post-positivist" era, old-fashioned generalizations are back in fashion. See Yosef Lapid, "The Third Debate: On the Prospects of International Theory in a Post-Positivist Era," *International Studies Quarterly* 33(1989):235–54.

16. I. William Zartman and Maureen R. Berman, *The Practical Negotiator* (New Haven, Ct.: Yale University Press, 1982), 224–29.

17. Mark Zacher of the University of British Columbia suggested this point to me.

18. Robert F. Goheen, "Openings and Impediments in U.S.-India Relations" (speech to the International Council of Tulsa, April 28, 1988).

19. Glen Fisher, *Mindsets* (Yarmouth, Me.: Intercultural Press, 1988), 68–69.

20. Gilbert Winham, "Practitioners' Views of International Negotiation," *World Politics* 32(1979):117, 119.

3. Intercultural Dissonance

1. Lorand B. Szalay, "Intercultural Communication—A Process Model," *International Journal of Intercultural Relations* 5(1981):133–46.

2. Geert Hofstede, *Culture's Consequences* (Beverly Hills, Calif.: Sage, 1980).

3. See, for example, Harry C. Triandis, Richard Brislin, and C. Harry Hui, "Cross-Cultural Training Across the Individualism-Collectivism Divide," *International Journal of Intercultural Relations* 12(1988):269–89; Harry C. Triandis, Robert Bontempo, and Marcelo J. Villareal, "Individualism and Collectivism: Cross-Cultural Perspectives on Self-Ingroup Relationships," *Journal of Personality and Social Psychology* 54(1988):323–38.

4. Edward C. Stewart, *American Cultural Patterns* (Yarmouth, Me.: Intercultural Press, 1972), 68–72.

5. Edward T. Hall, *Beyond Culture* (New York: Anchor Press, 1976).

6. Stella Ting-Toomey, "Toward a Theory of Conflict and Culture," *International and Intercultural Communication Annual* 9(1985):71–86.

7. Edward T. Hall, *The Silent Language* (New York: Anchor Books, 1973), 157.

8. Ibid., 7.

9. *New York Times,* July 17, 1989.

10. Mushakoji Kinhide, "The Cultural Premises of Japanese Diplomacy," in Japan Center for International Exchange, ed., *The Silent Power: Japan's Identity and World Role* (Tokyo: Simul Press, 1976), 45–46.

11. Stanley Hoffmann, *Gulliver's Troubles, Or the Setting of American Foreign Policy* (New York: McGraw-Hill, 1968), 148.

12. Howard Raiffa, *The Art and Science of Negotiation* (Cambridge, Mass.: Harvard University Press, 1982).

13. Roger Fisher and William Ury, *Getting to Yes* (New York: Penguin, 1983).

14. Zartman and Berman, *The Practical Negotiator*, 144.

4. What Is Negotiable?

1. Herb Cohen, *You Can Negotiate Anything* (Secaucus, N.J.: Lyle Stuart, 1980).

2. William J. Burns, *Economic Aid and American Policy Toward Egypt, 1955–1981* (Albany: State University of New York Press, 1985), 152.

3. Norman D. Palmer, *The United States and India: The Dimensions of Influence* (New York: Praeger, 1984), 23.

4. *FRUS*, vol. 11, 1952–54, 1782.

5. *Jerusalem Post*, October 25, 1985.

6. Mohamed Riad, *The Struggle for Peace in the Middle East* (London: Quartet Books, 1981), 99.

7. Henry A. Kissinger, *The White House Years* (Boston: Little, Brown, 1979), 637.

8. Kenneth T. Young, *Negotiating with the Chinese Communists* (New York: McGraw-Hill, 1968), 348.

9. *FRUS*, vol. 14, pt. 1, 1952–54, 502.

10. Kissinger, *White House Years*, 689–90.

11. *FRUS*, vol. 2, 1950, 945.

12. John J. Jova, interview with author, January 13, 1989.

13. Kano Tsutomu, "Why the Search for Identity?" in Japan Center for International Exchange, ed., *The Silent Power*, 8, 9.

14. Leo J. Moser, "Cross-Cultural Dimensions: U.S.-Japan," in Diane B. Bendahmane and Leo Moser, eds., *Toward a Better Understanding: U.S.-Japan Relations* (Washington: Foreign Service Institute, 1986), 22.

15. I. M. Destler et al., *Managing an Alliance: The Politics of U.S.-Japanese Relations* (Washington: Brookings Institution, 1976), 12–23.

16. Robert Angel, "Meeting the Japanese Challenge, 1969–1971: Balance-of-Payments Problems Force the Nixon Administration to Act," *Pew Program in Case Teaching and Writing in International Affairs*, case 135, August 1988, 13–14.

17. Kissinger, *White House Years*, 762.

18. Gail E. Meyer, *Egypt and the United States: The Formative Years* (Cranbury, N.J.: Associated University Presses, 1980), 38–39.

19. *U.S. News and World Report*, August 13, 1954.

20. Account based on interview with former State Department official. Also see U.S. Congress, House Committee on Appropriations, *Military Construction Appropriations for 1982: Hearings before the Subcommittee on Mil-*

itary Construction Appropriations, 97th Cong., 1st sess., 1981, pt. 5 (Washington, D.C.: U.S. Government Printing Office, 1981).

21. Kissinger, *White House Years*, 326.

22. Destler et al., *Managing an Alliance*, 23–35.

23. *FRUS*, vol. 6, pt. 2, 1951, 2142, 2153.

24. *FRUS*, vol. 11, 1952–54, 1710–11, 1714–15.

25. John Kenneth Galbraith, *Ambassador's Journal: A Personal Account of the Kennedy Years* (Boston: Houghton Mifflin, 1969), 393, 419, 423–24.

26. Robert F. Goheen, interview with author, April 6, 1989; Palmer, *The United States and India*, 234–35.

27. Alan Riding, *Distant Neighbors: A Portrait of the Mexicans* (New York: Vintage Books, 1986), 463; Governor Patrick Lucey, telephone interview with author, January 31, 1989; U.S. Congress, Senate Committee on Foreign Relations, *Situation in Mexico: Hearings before the Subcommittee on Western Hemisphere Affairs*, 99th Cong., 2d sess., May 13, June 17, and June 26, 1986 (Washington, D.C.: U.S. Government Printing Office, 1986).

28. *FRUS*, vols. 9, 1945, 1160; 2, 1949, 675–77; 2, 1950, 951.

29. Surya Prakash Sinha, "The Axiology of the International Bill of Human Rights," in Pace University School of Law, *Yearbook of International Law*, vol. 1, 1989, 26.

30. Ibid., 28, 55.

31. Hermann F. Eilts, interview with author, October 17, 1988.

32. Ismail Fahmy, *Negotiating for Peace in the Middle East* (Baltimore: The Johns Hopkins University Press, 1983), 188.

33. *Time*, October 21, 1985.

34. *FRUS*, vols. 14, pt. 1, 1952–54, 478, 474–5, 479–80, 1030; 3, 1955–57, 7, 23, 64–5.

35. Young, *Negotiating with the Chinese Communists*, 322–23.

5. Setting Out the Pieces

1. Zartman and Berman, *The Practical Negotiator*, chaps. 3, 4, 5.

2. Daniel Druckman, "Stages, Turning Points, and Crises: Negotiating Military Base Rights, Spain and the United States," *Journal of Conflict Resolution* 30(1986):327–60.

3. See Masao Kunihiro, "The Japanese Language and Intercultural Communication," 58, 61, and Kinhide, "The Cultural Premises of Japanese Diplomacy," 45–46, in Japan Center for International Exchange, ed., *The Silent Power*.

4. Kinhide, "Japanese Diplomacy," 43–45.

5. I. William Zartman, "Prenegotiation: Phases and Functions," in

Janice Gross Stein, ed., *Getting to the Table* (Baltimore: The Johns Hopkins University Press, 1989), 5.

6. Brian W. Tomlin, "The Stages of Prenegotiation: The Decision to Negotiate North American Free Trade," in Stein, *Getting to the Table*, 18–43.

7. Zartman, "Prenegotiation," 10.

8. Kinhide, "Japanese Diplomacy," 44.

9. Angel, "Meeting the Japanese Challenge," 34–37.

10. *The Economist*, October 27, 1984.

11. Solomon, *Chinese Political Negotiating Behavior*, 2.

12. Ibid., 10.

13. Zbigniew Brzezinski, *Power and Principle: Memoirs of the National Security Adviser 1977–1981* (New York: Farrar, Strauss, Giroux, 1983), 227.

14. Kazuo, "How the 'Inscrutables' Negotiate," 540.

15. Fisher, *International Negotiation*, 30–31.

16. Thomas Mann, telephone interview with Lewis Rasmussen, March 6, 1989; Joseph Friedkin, telephone interview with Lewis Rasmussen, March 16, 1989.

17. Hermann F. Eilts, interview with author, August 19, 1985.

18. John S. Badeau, *The Middle East Remembered* (Washington: The Middle East Institute, 1983), 189.

19. Joseph S. Sisco, interview with author, August 14, 1985.

20. Jimmy Carter, *Keeping Faith: Memoirs of a President* (New York: Bantam Books, 1982), 418. Quoted in Janice Gross Stein, "Prenegotiation in the Arab-Israeli Conflict: The Paradoxes of Success and Failure," in *Getting to the Table*, 194.

21. Clement Henry Moore, "Clientelist Ideology and Political Change," in Ernest Gellner and John Waterbury, eds., *Patrons and Clients in Mediterranean Societies* (London: Duckworth, 1977), 255–73.

22. Cohen, *Culture and Conflict*, 63.

23. Henry A. Kissinger, *Years of Upheaval* (Boston: Little, Brown, 1982), 640.

24. Ibid., 694

25. Carter, *Keeping Faith*, 284.

26. Cyrus Vance, *Hard Choices* (New York: Simon and Shuster, 1983), 175.

27. Fisher, *International Negotiation*, 18.

28. Michael K. Blaker, "Probe, Push, and Panic: The Japanese Tactical Style in International Negotiations," in Robert A. Scalapino, ed., *The Foreign Policy of Modern Japan* (Berkeley: University of California Press, 1977), 59–60.

29. Ibid.

30. Thomas P. Bernstein, "The Negotiations to Normalize U.S.-China Relations," *Pew Program in Case Teaching and Writing in International Affairs,* case 426, August 1988, 23.

31. Blaker, "Probe, Push, and Panic," 60–61.

32. Kissinger, *White House Years,* 330–31.

33. Thomas Mann, telephone interview with Lewis Rasmussen, March 6, 1989.

34. Larman C. Wilson, "The Settlement of Boundary Disputes: Mexico, the United States, and the International Boundary Commission," *International and Comparative Law Quarterly* 29(1980):49.

35. Herbert Brownell and Samuel D. Eaton, "The Colorado Salinity Problem with Mexico," *The American Journal of International Law* 69(1975):255–71.

36. Steven Lande, interview with author, January 27, 1989.

37. *FRUS,* vol. 11, 1946, 993–96.

38. Account based on Richard B. Craig, "Operation Intercept: The International Politics of Pressure," *Review of Politics* 42(1980):556–80.

39. Patrick Lucey, telephone interview with author, January 31, 1989.

40. Robert Wilcox, interview with author, January 27, 1989.

41. Janice Gross Stein, "Getting to the Table: The Triggers, Stages, Functions, and Consequences of Prenegotiation," in idem, *Getting to the Table,* 257.

6. Let the Contest Commence

1. Leo J. Moser, "Negotiating Style: Americans and Japanese," in Bendahmane and Moser, *Toward a Better Understanding,* 43.

2. Daniel M. Kasper, "Holding Over Tokyo: U.S.-Japan Air Service Negotiations," *Pew Program in Case Teaching and Writing in International Affairs,* case 104, 1988, 5. Dr. Kasper served on the American delegation.

3. Paul Kreisberg, interview with author, January 15, 1989.

4. Kazuo, "How the 'Inscrutables' Negotiate," 541.

5. Brzezinski, *Power and Principle,* 225.

6. Ibid.

7. Ibid.

8. Bernstein, "U.S.-China Relations," 30–31.

9. Angel, "Meeting the Japanese Challenge," 30.

10. Hiroshi Kimura, "Soviet and Japanese Negotiating Behavior: The Spring 1977 Fisheries Talks," *Orbis* 24(1980):48.

11. Destler et al., *Managing an Alliance,* 109.

12. Fisher, *International Negotiation*, 41.

13. *FRUS*, vol. 6, 1943, 611, 613–14, 615.

14. Herbert Brownell, interview with author, January 19, 1989. See also Brownell and Eaton, "Colorado Salinity Problem."

15. Adhip Chaudhuri, "The Mexican Debt Crisis, 1982," *Pew Program in Case Teaching and Writing in International Affairs*, case 204, 1988, 1, 6–7.

16. Ibid., 9–11; Peter Wallison, interview with author, January 18, 1989.

17. Carter, *Keeping Faith*, 340–41.

18. Hermann F. Eilts, interview with author, October 17, 1988.

19. *FRUS*, vol. 6, 1951, pt. 2, 2127.

20. Chester Bowles, *Promises to Keep: My Years in Public Life 1941–1969* (New York: Harper and Row, 1971), 526.

21. William J. Barnds, "India and America at Odds," *International Affairs* 49(1973):379.

22. Phyllis J. Rolnick, "Charity, Trusteeship, and Social Change in India," *World Politics* 14(1962):439–60.

23. Bernard S. Cohn, *India: The Social Anthropology of a Civilization* (Englewood Cliffs: Prentice Hall, 1971), 131–32.

24. Paul Kreisberg, interview with author, February 5, 1989.

25. R. V. R. Chandrasekhara Rao, "Searching for a Mature Relationship," *Round Table* 263(1976):249–60.

26. Kazuo, "How the 'Inscrutables' Negotiate," 532–34.

27. Solomon, *Chinese Political Negotiating Behavior*, 11.

28. Vance, *Hard Choices*, 82.

29. George T. Crane, "The Sino-U.S. Textile Trade Agreement of 1983: The Anatomy of a Trade Battle," *Pew Program in Case Teaching and Writing in International Affairs*, case 109, 1988, 2–5.

30. Shenkar and Ronen, "Cultural Context of Negotiations," 270.

31. Doris Meisner, interview with author, January 25, 1989.

32. Timothy Bennett, interview with author, January 27, 1989.

33. Riding, *Distant Neighbors*, 281.

34. George W. Grayson, *The United States and Mexico: Patterns of Influence* (New York: Praeger, 1984), 81–82.

35. Edmund Glenn et al., "Cultural Styles of Persuasion," *International Journal of Intercultural Relations*, 1(1977):52–66.

36. Solomon, *Chinese Political Negotiating Behavior*, 8.

37. Pye, *Chinese Commercial Negotiating Style*, 26–27, 41.

38. Ibid.

39. Young, *Negotiating with the Chinese Communists*, 166, 178.

40. Quoted in Solomon, *Chinese Political Negotiating Behavior,* 19.

41. Kissinger, *White House Years,* 745–46.

42. Mohamed Hassanein Heikal, *The Cairo Documents* (New York: Doubleday, 1973), 238.

43. Kissinger, *Years of Upheaval,* 215.

44. Ibid., 823, 825.

45. Department of State *Bulletin* 71(1974):92–93.

46. Hermann F. Eilts, interview with author, October 17, 1988.

47. William B. Quandt, *Camp David: Peacemaking and Politics* (Washington: The Brookings Institution, 1986), 136.

48. Thomas Mann, telephone interview with Lewis Rasmussen, March 6, 1989.

49. *Washington Post,* September 6, 1979.

50. Account based on George W. Grayson, "The U.S.-Mexican Natural Gas Deal and What We Can Learn from It," *Orbis* 24(1980):573–607; and Julius Katz, interview with author, January 11, 1989.

51. Kinhide, "Japanese Diplomacy," 46.

7. On Tactics and Players

1. I. William Zartman, "Negotiation as a Joint Decision-Making Process," *Journal of Conflict Resolution* 21(1977):619–38.

2. William B. Quandt, "A Strong Sense of National Identity," in Binnendijk, *National Negotiating Styles,* 118–20.

3. Fuad I. Khuri, "The Etiquette of Bargaining in the Middle East," *American Anthropologist* 70(1968):700.

4. Kissinger, *White House Years,* 747.

5. Raiffa, *Art and Science of Negotiation,* 48.

6. Kissinger, *Years of Upheaval,* 829, 832.

7. Fisher, *International Negotiation,* 48.

8. Timothy Bennett, interview with author, January 27, 1989.

9. Adolfo Aguilar, interview with author, December 21, 1988.

10. *FRUS,* vol. 6, 1955–57, 707–8.

11. Ibid., 739–41. Agreement in *U.S. Treaties and Other International Agreements (UST),* (1957), vol. 8, 306–16.

12. Daniel Druckman et al., "Cultural Differences in Bargaining Behavior: India, Argentina, and the United States," *Journal of Conflict Resolution* 20(1976):413–52.

13. *FRUS,* vol. 11, 1952–54, 1708, 1709.

14. Ibid., 1722, 1723.

15. Ibid., 1735.

16. Nathaniel B. Thayer and Stephen E. Weiss, "Japan: The Changing Logic of a Former Minor Power," in Binnendijk, *National Negotiating Styles,* 67–68.

17. Moser, "Negotiating Style," 46.

18. Destler et al., *Managing an Alliance,* 106.

19. Blaker, "Probe, Push, and Panic," 81.

20. Timothy J. C. O'Shea, "The U.S.-Japan Semiconductor Problem," *Pew Program in Case Teaching and Writing in International Affairs,* case 139, September 1988, 58, 62, 63, 64, 67.

21. Thomas P. Rohlen, "Three Snapshots of Japan," in Bendahmane and Moser, *Toward a Better Understanding,* 18.

22. O'Shea, "Semiconductor Problem," 64.

23. Solomon, *Chinese Political Negotiating Behavior,* 6.

24. Shenkar and Ronen, "Cultural Context of Negotiations," 270.

25. Young, *Negotiating with the Chinese Communists,* 389.

26. Vance, *Hard Choices,* 79, 81–82.

27. This quotation and remaining ones on the repatriation talks are from *FRUS,* vol. 3, 1955–57.

28. Nancy Adler, *International Dimensions of Organizational Behavior* (Boston: Kent, 1986), chap. 6; Martin W. Simpson III, "Cultural Influences on Foreign Policy," in Charles F. Hermann, Charles W. Kegley, Jr., and James N. Rosenau, eds., *New Directions in the Study of Foreign Policy* (Boston: Allen and Unwin, 1987), 384–405.

29. Lucius Battle, interview with author, August 13, 1985.

30. Hermann F. Eilts, interview with author, October 17, 1988.

31. Fahmy, *Negotiating for Peace,* 153, 52, 75.

32. Quandt, *Camp David,* 116.

33. Riding, *Distant Neighbors,* 474.

34. Grayson, "U.S.-Mexican Natural Gas Deal," 582, 586–88.

35. O. P. Dwivedi and R. B. Jain, "Bureaucratic Morality in India," *International Political Science Review* 9(1988):208–9.

36. N. Ram, "India's Nuclear Policy: A Case Study in the Flaws and Futility of Non-Proliferation," *IDSA Journal* 14(1982):504.

37. Paul Kreisberg, interview with author, February 5, 1989.

38. Hermann F. Eilts, interview with author, October 17, 1988.

39. Kissinger, *White House Years,* 1056.

40. Solomon, *Chinese Political Negotiating Behavior,* 7.

41. Vance, *Hard Choices,* 117.

42. Chihiro Hosoya, "Characteristics of the Foreign Policy Decision-Making System in Japan," *World Politics* 26(1974):353–70.

43. In Bendahmane and Moser, *Toward a Better Understanding,* 40.

44. Destler et al., *Managing an Alliance,* 15.

45. Kissinger, *White House Years,* 336–39.

46. Ellis S. Krauss, "Under Construction: U.S.-Japan Negotiations to Open Japan's Construction Markets to American Firms, 1985–1988," *Pew Program in Case Teaching and Writing in International Affairs,* case 145, 1989, 25–26.

8. Sounds, Signals, Silence

1. Quoted in Kunihiro, "Japanese Language," 60–61.

2. Roger W. Benjamin, "Images of Conflict Resolution and Social Control: American and Japanese Attitudes Toward the Adversary System," *Journal of Conflict Resolution* 19(1975):123–37.

3. Joseph Friedkin, telephone interview with Lewis Rasmussen, March 16, 1989.

4. Herbert Brownell, interview with author, January 19, 1989.

5. Badeau, *Middle East Remembered,* 214.

6. Ibid., 75–77.

7. Lucius Battle, interview with author, August 13, 1985.

8. Interview with State Department official.

9. Palmer, *United States and India,* 22–23.

10. *FRUS,* vol. 11, 1952–54, 1645.

11. Ibid., vol. 8, 1955–57, 278.

12. Hermann F. Eilts, interview with author, August 19, 1985; John J. Jova, interview with author, January 13, 1989.

13. U.S. Congress, *Situation in Mexico,* 81, 89, 90–91, 49.

14. *Washington Post,* August 14, 1980, 32–33.

15. Cohen, "Egyptian-American Diplomatic Relations," 34–35.

16. John S. Badeau, *The American Approach to the Arab World* (New York: Harper and Row, 1968), 73.

17. Heikal, *Cairo Documents,* 204.

18. Bowles, *Promises to Keep,* 491.

19. Galbraith, *Ambassador's Journal,* 406, 447.

20. Ibid., 493, 494.

21. Ashok Kapoor, *International Business Negotiations: A Study in India* (New York: New York University Press, 1970), 156–60, 170.

22. Clyde Haberman, "Japanese Have a Way (Out) with Words," *International Herald Tribune,* March 26–27, 1988.

23. *The Economist,* September 14, 1985.

24. Kunihiro, "Japanese Language," 64.

25. Burns, *American Policy Toward Egypt*, 61.

26. Quandt, "National Identity," 119.

27. Interview with former State Department official.

28. Interview with State Department official.

29. Quandt, "National Identity," 119.

30. Galbraith, *Ambassador's Journal*, 385. My emphasis.

31. Craig, "Operation Intercept," 559–60, 564–65.

32. Masao Kunihiro, "U.S.-Japan Communications," in Henry Rosovsky, ed., *Discord in the Pacific: Challenges to the American-Japanese Alliance* (Washington: Columbia Books, for the American Assembly, 1972), 167.

33. Krauss, "Under Construction," 40.

34. Richard Parker, interview with author, October 25, 1988.

35. See Bernard Reich, *Quest for Peace* (New Brunswick, N.J.: Transaction Books, 1977), 93.

36. Quandt, *Camp David*, 132, 92, 115.

37. Ibid., 124.

38. Harold Saunders, interview with author, October 27, 1988.

39. Fahmy, *Negotiating for Peace*, 206.

40. *FRUS*, vol. 11, 1952–54, 1738–39. Definite and indefinite articles restored by me.

41. Palmer, *United States and India*, 24.

42. Kissinger, *White House Years*, 878–82.

43. Richard M. Nixon, *The Memoirs of Richard Nixon* (London: Arrow Books, 1978), 525.

44. Oriana Fallaci, *Interview with History* (Boston: Houghton Mifflin, 1976), 161.

45. Kissinger, *White House Years*, 749.

46. Ibid., 779.

47. Ibid., 1073.

48. Ibid., 1061–62.

49. I. Eibl-Eibesfeldt, "Similarities and Differences between Cultures in Expressive Movements," in R.A. Hinde, ed., *Nonverbal Communication* (Cambridge: Cambridge University Press, 1972), 297–314; P. Ekman, "Universals and Cultural Differences in Facial Expressions of Emotion," in J. Cole, ed., *Nebraska Symposium on Motivation, 1971* (Lincoln: University of Nebraska Press, 1971), 201–83; Aaron Wolfgang, ed., *Nonverbal Behavior: Perspectives, Applications, Intercultural Insights* (Lewiston, N.Y.: C.J. Hogrefe, 1984).

50. Fahmy, *Negotiating for Peace*, 42, 45, 48, 73, 157, 207, 237.

51. Ibid., 207; Quandt, *Camp David*, 115.

52. James W. Symington, *The Stately Game* (New York: Macmillan, 1971), 27.

53. Charles Thayer, *Diplomat* (London: Michael Joseph, 1960), 217.

54. Kissinger, *White House Years,* 699.

55. Ibid., 750.

56. Alexander M. Haig, *Caveat: Realism, Reagan and Foreign Policy* (New York: Macmillan, 1984), 206, 207, 208.

57. Bowles, *Promises to Keep,* 498.

58. Hermann F. Eilts, interview with author, August 19, 1985.

59. Governor Patrick Lucey, telephone interview with author, January 31, 1989.

60. Kissinger, *Years of Upheaval,* 696; Shenkar and Ronen, "Cultural Context of Negotiations," 267.

61. Kunihiro, "U.S.-Japan Communications," 163; Bendahmane and Moser, *Toward a Better Understanding,* 17.

62. Umesao Tadao, "Escape from Cultural Isolation," in Japan Center for International Exchange, ed., *The Silent Power,* 28.

63. *The Economist,* September 14, 1985.

64. Galbraith, *Ambassador's Journal,* 474.

65. Interview with State Department official.

66. Galbraith, *Ambassador's Journal,* 406.

67. Kissinger, *White House Years,* 848.

9. Bright Honor

1. Stella Ting-Toomey and Mark Cole, "Intergroup Diplomatic Communication: A Face-Negotiation Perspective," in Felipe Korzenny and Stella Ting-Toomey, eds., *Communicating for Peace: Diplomacy and Negotiation* (Newbury Park, Calif.: Sage, 1990), 83.

2. Ibid., 78.

3. Angel, "Meeting the Japanese Challenge," 45–46.

4. H. C. Hu, "The Chinese Concept of Face," *American Anthropologist* 44(1944):45–64.

5. Kissinger, *White House Years,* 751, 759, 781–82. On the concept of face giving, see Stella Ting-Toomey, "Intercultural Conflict Styles: A Face-Negotiation Theory," in Young Yun Kim and William B. Gudykunst, eds., *Theories in Intercultural Communication* (Beverly Hills, Calif.: Sage, 1988), 213–38.

6. Robert F. Goheen, interview with author, April 6, 1989; interview with State Department official.

7. Interview with State Department official.

8. Kissinger, *Years of Upheaval,* 641–54.

9. Robert Sayre, interview with author, January 30, 1989.

10. Roger S. Leeds and Gale Thompson, "The 1982 Mexican Debt Negotiations," *FPI Case Studies* 4, 1987, 25; Chaudhuri, "Mexican Debt Crisis," 10–11.

11. *Washington Post,* September 22, 1979; Herbert Brownell, interview with author, January 19, 1989.

12. *FRUS,* vol. 4, 1952–54, 1327, 1328, 1330, 1351.

13. Interview with State Department official.

14. Kissinger, *Years of Upheaval,* 825.

15. Interview with State Department official.

16. U.S. Congress, *Military Construction Appropriations,* 133.

17. Galbraith, *Ambassador's Journal,* 439, 463, 476, 478.

18. Stanley B. Lubman, "Negotiations in China: Observations of a Lawyer," in Robert A. Kapp, ed., *Communicating with China* (Yarmouth, Me.: Intercultural Press, 1983), 60–61, 64–65, 67–68.

19. Kunihiro, "U.S.-Japan Communications," 159, 166.

20. Kinhide, "Japanese Diplomacy," 42–43.

21. Donald S. Abelson, "Experiencing the Japanese Negotiating Style," in Bendahmane and Moser, *Toward a Better Understanding,* 54, 56.

22. Bernstein, "U.S.-Chinese Relations," 35–37.

23. Destler et al., *Managing an Alliance,* 115.

24. The account is based on James Reardon-Anderson, "U.S.-China Nuclear Cooperative Agreement," *Pew Program in Case Teaching and Writing in International Affairs,* case 110, 1989.

25. *Forbes,* June 4, 1984, 153.

26. Daniel Horner and Paul Leventhal, "The U.S.-China Nuclear Agreement," *The Fletcher Forum* (Winter 1987):113.

27. Reardon-Anderson, "U.S.-China Nuclear Cooperative Agreement," 3.

28. Young, *Negotiating with the Chinese Communists,* 352.

29. Ibid.

30. *FRUS,* vol. 3, 1955–57, 46, 62, 64, 73–74, 75. Definite and indefinite articles restored by me.

31. Account based on Bernstein, "U.S.-China Relations."

32. Interviews with author: Timothy Bennett, January 27, 1989; and State Department official. Joseph Friedkin, telephone interview with Lewis Rasmussen, March 16, 1989.

33. Grayson, "U.S.-Mexican Natural Gas Deal," 600–601.

34. Julius Katz, interview with author, January 11, 1989.

35. Kasper, "Holding Over Tokyo," sequel A, 1–2.

36. Christopher J. McMullen, *Resolution of the Yemen Crisis, 1963: A Case Study in Mediation* (Washington: Institute for the Study of Diplomacy, 1980), 32–37; Badeau, *Middle East Remembered*, 212.

10. In Search of Harmony

1. Rosalie L. Tung, "U.S.-China Trade Negotiations: Practices, Procedures, and Outcomes," *Journal of International Business Studies* 13(1982):34.

2. Samuel W. Lewis, impromptu comments at a United States Institute of Peace work-in-progress seminar, November 10, 1988.

3. Kissinger, *White House Years*, 1492.

Bibliography

Abelson, Donald S. "Experiencing the Japanese Negotiating Style." In Diane B. Bendahmane and Leo Moser, eds., *Toward a Better Understanding: U.S.-Japan Relations.* Washington, D.C.: Foreign Service Institute, 1986.

Adelman, Mara B., and Lustig, Myron W. "Intercultural Communication Problems as Perceived by Saudi Arabian and American Managers." *International Journal of Intercultural Relations* 5(1981):349–63.

Adler, Nancy. *International Dimensions of Organizational Behavior.* Boston: Kent, 1986.

Angel, Robert. "Meeting the Japanese Challenge, 1969–1971: Balance-of-Payments Problems Force the Nixon Administration to Act." *Pew Program in Case Teaching and Writing in International Affairs.* Case 135, August 1988.

Badeau, John S. *The American Approach to the Arab World.* New York: Harper and Row, 1968.

———. *The Middle East Remembered.* Washington, D.C.: The Middle East Institute, 1983.

Barnds, William J. "India and America at Odds." *International Affairs* 49(1973):371–84.

Bendahmane, Diane B., and Moser, Leo, eds. *Toward a Better Understanding: U.S.-Japan Relations.* Washington, D.C.: Foreign Service Institute, 1986.

Benjamin, Roger W. "Images of Conflict Resolution and Social Control: American and Japanese Attitudes Toward the Adversary System." *Journal of Conflict Resolution* 19(1975):123–37.

Bernstein, Thomas P. "The Negotiations to Normalize U.S.-China Relations." *Pew Program in Case Teaching and Writing in International Affairs.* Case 426, August 1988.

Binnendijk, Hans, ed. *National Negotiating Styles.* Washington, D.C.: Foreign Service Institute, 1987.

Bibliography

Blaker, Michael K. *Japanese International Negotiating Style.* New York: Columbia University Press, 1977.

———. "Probe, Push, and Panic: The Japanese Tactical Style in International Negotiations." In Robert A. Scalapino, ed., *The Foreign Policy of Modern Japan.* Berkeley: University of California Press, 1977.

Bowles, Chester. *Promises to Keep: My Years in Public Life 1941–1969.* New York: Harper and Row, 1971.

Brownell, Herbert, and Eaton, Samuel D. "The Colorado Salinity Problem with Mexico." *The American Journal of International Law* 49(1975):225–71.

Brzezinski, Zbigniew. *Power and Principle: Memoirs of the National Security Adviser 1977–1981.* New York: Farrar, Strauss, Giroux, 1983.

Burns, William J. *Economic Aid and American Policy Toward Egypt, 1955–1981.* Albany: State University of New York Press, 1985.

Carter, Jimmy. *Keeping Faith: Memoirs of a President.* New York: Bantam Books, 1982.

Casse, Pierre, and Deol, Surinder. *Managing Intercultural Negotiations.* Yarmouth, Me.: Intercultural Press, 1985.

Chaudhuri, Adhip. "The Mexican Debt Crisis, 1982." *Pew Program in Case Teaching and Writing in International Affairs.* Case 204, 1988.

Cohen, Herb. *You Can Negotiate Anything.* Secaucus, N.J.: Lyle Stuart, 1980.

Cohen, Raymond. "International Communication: An Intercultural Approach." *Cooperation and Conflict* 22(1987):63–80.

———. "Problems of Intercultural Communication in Egyptian-American Diplomatic Relations." *International Journal of Intercultural Relations* 11(1987):29–47.

———. *Culture and Conflict in Egyptian-Israeli Relations: A Dialogue of the Deaf.* Bloomington: Indiana University Press, 1990.

Cohn, Bernard S. *India: The Social Anthropology of a Civilization.* Englewood Cliffs, N.J.: Prentice Hall, 1971.

Craig, Richard B. "Operation Intercept: The International Politics of Pressure." *Review of Politics* 42(1980):556–80.

Crane, George T. "The Sino-U.S. Textile Trade Agreement of 1983: The Anatomy of a Trade Battle." *Pew Program in Case Teaching and Writing in International Affairs.* Case 109, 1988.

Destler, I. M.; Sato, Hideo; Clapp, Priscilla; and Fukui, Haruhiro. *Managing an Alliance: The Politics of U.S.-Japanese Relations.* Washington, D.C.: The Brookings Institution, 1976.

Druckman, Daniel. "Stages, Turning Points, and Crises: Negotiating Military Base Rights, Spain and the United States." *Journal of Conflict Resolution* 30(1986):327–60.

Druckman, Daniel; Benton, A. A.; Ali, F.; and Bagur, J. S. "Cultural Differences in Bargaining Behavior: India, Argentina and the United States." *Journal of Conflict Resolution* 20(1976):413–48.

Dwivedi, O. P., and Jain, R. B. "Bureaucratic Morality in India." *International Political Science Review* 9(1988):205–14.

Eibl-Eibesfeldt, I. "Similarities and Differences between Cultures in Expressive Movements." In R. A. Hinde, ed., *Nonverbal Communication.* Cambridge: Cambridge University Press, 1972.

Ekman, P. "Universals and Cultural Differences in Facial Expressions of Emotion." In J. Cole, ed., *Nebraska Symposium on Motivation, 1971.* Lincoln: University of Nebraska Press, 1971.

Fahmy, Ismail. *Negotiating for Peace in the Middle East.* Baltimore: The Johns Hopkins University Press, 1983.

Fallaci, Oriana. *Interview with History.* Boston: Houghton Mifflin, 1976.

Fisher, Glen. *International Negotiation: A Cross-Cultural Perspective.* Yarmouth, Me.: Intercultural Press, 1980.

———. *Mindsets.* Yarmouth, Me.: Intercultural Press, 1988.

Fisher, Roger, and Ury, William. *Getting to Yes.* New York: Penguin, 1983.

Galbraith, John Kenneth. *Ambassador's Journal: A Personal Account of the Kennedy Years.* Boston: Houghton Mifflin, 1969.

Glenn, Edmund; Wikmeyer, D.; and Stevenson, K. "Cultural Styles of Persuasion." *International Journal of Intercultural Relations* 1(1977):52–66.

Graham, John L. "The Influence of Culture on the Process of Business Negotiations." *Journal of International Business Studies* 16(1985):81–96.

Grayson, George W. "The U.S.-Mexican Natural Gas Deal and What We Can Learn from It." *Orbis* 24(1980):573–607.

———. *The United States and Mexico: Patterns of Influence.* New York: Praeger, 1984.

Haig, Alexander M. *Caveat: Realism, Reagan and Foreign Policy.* New York: Macmillan, 1984.

Hall, Edward T. *The Silent Language.* New York: Anchor Books, 1973.

———. *Beyond Culture.* New York: Anchor Books, 1976.

Heikal, Mohamed Hassanein. *The Cairo Documents.* New York: Doubleday, 1973.

Hoffman, Stanley. *Gulliver's Troubles, or the Setting of American Foreign Policy.* New York: McGraw-Hill, 1968.

Hofstede, Geert. *Culture's Consequences.* Beverly Hills, Calif.: Sage, 1980.

Horner, Daniel, and Leventhal, Paul. "The U.S.-China Nuclear Agreement." *The Fletcher Forum* 11(1987):105–122.

Hosoya, Chihiro. "Characteristics of the Foreign Policy Decision-Making System in Japan." *World Politics* 26(1974):353–70.

Hu, H. C. "The Chinese Concept of Face." *American Anthropologist* 44(1944): 45–64.

Japan Center for International Exchange, ed. *The Silent Power: Japan's Identity and World Role.* Tokyo: The Simul Press, 1976.

Kamel, Mohamed Ibrahim. *The Camp David Accords.* London: KPI, 1986.

Kapoor, Ashok. *International Business Negotiations: A Study in India.* New York: New York University Press, 1970.

Kasper, Daniel M. "Holding Over Tokyo: U.S.-Japan Air Service Negotiations." *Pew Program in Case Teaching and Writing in International Affairs.* Case 104, 1988.

Kazuo, Ogura. "How the 'Inscrutables' Negotiate with the 'Inscrutables': Chinese Negotiating Tactics *Vis-à-Vis* the Japanese." *The China Quarterly* 79(1979):529–52.

Khuri, Fuad I. "The Etiquette of Bargaining in the Middle East." *American Anthropologist* 70(1968):698–706.

Kimura, Hiroshi. "Soviet and Japanese Negotiating Behavior: The Spring 1977 Fisheries Talks." *Orbis* 24(1980):43–67.

Kinhide, Mushakoji. "The Cultural Premises of Japanese Diplomacy." In Japan Center for International Exchange, ed., *The Silent Power.* Tokyo: The Simul Press, 1976.

Kissinger, Henry A. *The White House Years.* Boston: Little, Brown, 1979.

———. *Years of Upheaval.* Boston: Little, Brown, 1982.

Kluckhohn, Clyde. "The Study of Culture." In Daniel Lerner and Harold D. Lasswell, eds., *The Policy Sciences.* Stanford, Calif.: Stanford University Press, 1951.

Krauss, Ellis S. "Under Construction: U.S.-Japan Negotiations to Open Japan's Construction Markets to American Firms, 1985–1988." *Pew Program in Case Teaching and Writing in International Affairs.* Case 145, 1989.

Kunihiro, Masao. "U.S.-Japan Communications." In Henry Rosovsky, ed., *Discord in the Pacific: Challenges to the American-Japanese Alliance.* Washington, D.C.: Columbia Books, for the American Assembly, 1972.

———. "The Japanese Language and Intercultural Communication." In Japan Center for International Exchange, ed., *The Silent Power.* Tokyo: The Simul Press, 1976.

Lakos, Amos. *International Negotiations: A Bibliography.* Boulder, Colo.: Westview Press, 1989.

Lapid, Yosef. "The Third Debate: On the Prospects of International Theory in a Post-Positivist Era." *International Studies Quarterly* 33(1989):235–54.

Leeds, Roger S., and Thompson, Gale. "The 1982 Mexican Debt Negotiations." *FPI Case Studies* #4, 1987.

Lubman, Stanley B. "Negotiations in China: Observations of a Lawyer." In Robert A. Kapp, ed., *Communicating with China.* Yarmouth, Me.: Intercultural Press, 1983.

March, Robert M. *The Japanese Negotiator.* Tokyo: Kodansha International, 1988.

McMullen, Christopher J. *Resolution of the Yemen Crisis, 1963: A Case Study in Mediation.* Washington, D.C.: Institute for the Study of Diplomacy, 1980.

Meyer, Gail E. *Egypt and the United States: The Formative Years.* Cranbury, N.J.: Associated University Presses, 1980.

Moore, Clement Henry. "Clientelist Ideology and Political Change." In Ernest Gellner and John Waterbury, eds., *Patrons and Clients in Mediterranean Societies.* London: Duckworth, 1977.

Moser, Leo J. "Cross-Cultural Dimensions: U.S.-Japan." In Diane B. Bendahmane and Leo Moser, eds., *Toward a Better Understanding: U.S.-Japan Relations.* Washington, D.C.: Foreign Service Institute, 1986.

——. "Negotiating Style: Americans and Japanese." In Diane B. Bendahmane and Leo Moser, eds., *Toward a Better Understanding: U.S.-Japan Relations.* Washington, D.C.: Foreign Service Institute, 1986.

Nixon, Richard M. *The Memoirs of Richard Nixon.* London: Arrow Books, 1978.

O'Shea, Timothy J. C. "The U.S.-Japan Semiconductor Problem." *Pew Program in Case Teaching and Writing in International Affairs.* Case 139, September 1988.

Palmer, Norman D. *The United States and India: The Dimensions of Influence.* New York: Praeger, 1984.

Pfeiffer, John. "How Not to Lose the Trade Wars by Cultural Gaffes." *Smithsonian* 18(1988):145–56.

Pye, Lucian. *Chinese Commercial Negotiating Style.* Cambridge, Mass.: Oelgeschlager, Gunn, and Hain, 1982.

Quandt, William B. *Camp David: Peacemaking and Politics.* Washington, D.C.: The Brookings Institution, 1986.

——. "Egypt: A Strong Sense of National Identity." In Hans Binnendijk, ed., *National Negotiating Styles.* Washington, D.C.: Foreign Service Institute, 1987.

Raiffa, Howard. *The Art and Science of Negotiation.* Cambridge, Mass.: Harvard University Press, 1982.

Ram, N. "India's Nuclear Policy: A Case Study in the Flaws and Futility of Non-Proliferation." *IDSA Journal* 14(1982):445–538.

Rao, R. V. R. Chandrasekhara. "Searching for a Mature Relationship." *Round Table* 263(1976):249–60.

Reardon-Anderson, James. "U.S.-China Nuclear Cooperative Agreement." *Pew Program in Case Teaching and Writing in International Affairs.* Case 110, 1989.

Reich, Bernard. *Quest for Peace.* New Brunswick, N.J.: Transaction Books, 1977.

Riad, Mohamed. *The Struggle for Peace in the Middle East.* London: Quartet Books, 1981.

Riding, Alan. *Distant Neighbors.* New York: Vintage Books, 1986.

Rohlen, Thomas P. "Three Snapshots of Japan." In Diane B. Bendahmane and Leo Moser, eds., *Toward a Better Understanding: U.S.-Japan Relations.* Washington, D.C.: Foreign Service Institute, 1986.

Rolnick, Phyllis J. "Charity, Trusteeship, and Social Change in India." *World Politics* 14(1962):439–60.

el-Sadat, Anwar. *In Search of Identity.* London: Fontana, 1977.

Shenkar, Oded, and Ronen, Simcha. "The Cultural Context of Negotiations: The Implications of Chinese Interpersonal Norms." *The Journal of Applied Behavioral Science* 23(1987):263–75.

Simpson, Martin W. III. "Cultural Influences on Foreign Policy." In Charles F. Hermann, Charles W. Kegley, Jr., and James N. Rosenau, eds., *New Directions in the Study of Foreign Policy.* Boston: Allen and Unwin, 1987.

Sinha, Surya Prakash. "The Axiology of the International Bill of Human Rights." Pace University School of Law: *Yearbook of International Law,* vol. 1, 1989.

Smith, Raymond F. *Negotiating with the Soviets.* Bloomington: Indiana University Press, 1989.

Solomon, Richard H. *Chinese Political Negotiating Behavior: A Briefing Analysis.* Santa Monica, Calif.: The RAND Corporation, 1985.

Stein, Janice Gross, ed. *Getting to the Table: The Process of International Prenegotiation.* Baltimore: The Johns Hopkins University Press, 1989.

———. "Getting to the Table: The Triggers, Stages, Functions, and Consequences of Prenegotiation." In idem, *Getting to the Table.* Baltimore: The Johns Hopkins University Press, 1989.

Stewart, Edward C. *American Cultural Patterns.* Yarmouth, Me.: The Intercultural Press, 1972.

Strazar, Marie D. "The San Francisco Peace Treaty: Cross-Cultural Elements in the Interaction between the Americans and the Japanese." In R. P. Anand, ed., *Cultural Factors in International Relations.* New Delhi: Abinhav, 1981.

Symington, James W. *The Stately Game.* New York: Macmillan, 1971.

Szalay, Lorand B. "Intercultural Communication—A Process Model." *International Journal of Intercultural Relations* 5(1981):133–46.

Tadao, Umesao. "Escape from Cultural Isolation." In Japan Center for International Exchange, ed., *The Silent Power: Japan's Identity and World Role.* Tokyo: The Simul Press, 1976.

Thayer, Charles. *Diplomat.* London: Michael Joseph, 1960.

Thayer, Nathaniel B., and Weiss, Stephen E. "Japan: The Changing Logic of a Former Minor Power." In Hans Binnendijk, ed., *National Negotiating Styles.* Washington, D.C.: Foreign Service Institute, 1987.

Ting-Toomey, Stella. "Toward a Theory of Conflict and Culture." *International and Intercultural Communication Annual* 9(1985):71–86.

———. "Intercultural Conflict Styles: A Face-Negotiation Theory." In Young Yun Kim and William B. Gudykunst, eds., *Theories in Intercultural Communication*. Beverly Hills, Calif.: Sage, 1988.

Ting-Toomey, Stella, and Cole, Mark. "Intergroup Diplomatic Communication: A Face-Negotiation Perspective." In Felipe Korzenny and Stella Ting-Toomey, eds., *Communicating for Peace: Diplomacy and Negotiation*. Newbury Park, Calif.: Sage, 1990.

Tomlin, Brian W. "The Stages of Prenegotiation: The Decision to Negotiate North American Free Trade." In Janice Gross Stein, ed., *Getting to the Table*. Baltimore: The Johns Hopkins University Press, 1989.

Triandis, Harry C.; Bontempo, Robert; and Villareal, Marcelo J. "Individualism and Collectivism: Cross-Cultural Perspectives on Self-Ingroup Relationships." *Journal of Personality and Social Psychology* 54(1988): 323–38.

Triandis, Harry C.; Brislin, Richard; and Hui, C. Harry. "Cross-Cultural Training across the Individualism-Collectivism Divide." *International Journal of Intercultural Relations* 12(1988):269–89.

Tsutomu, Kano. "Why the Search for Identity?" In Japan Center for International Exchange, ed., *The Silent Power: Japan's Identity and World Role*. Tokyo: The Simul Press, 1976.

Tung, Rosalie L. "U.S.-China Trade Negotiations: Procedures and Outcomes." *Journal of International Business Studies* 13(1982):25–37.

Tylor, Sir Edward Burnett. *Primitive Culture*. New York: Harper and Row, 1958. Original ed. 1871.

U.S. Congress, House Committee on Appropriations, *Military Construction Appropriations for 1982: Hearings before the Subcommittee on Military Construction Appropriations*, 97th Cong., 1st sess., 1981, pt. 5. Washington, D.C.: U.S. Government Printing Office, 1981.

U.S. Congress, Senate Committee on Foreign Relations, *Situation in Mexico: Hearings before the Subcommittee on Western Hemisphere Affairs*, 99th Cong., 2d sess., 13 May, 17 June, and 26 June 1986. Washington, D.C.: U.S. Government Printing Office, 1986.

U.S. Department of State. *Foreign Relations of the United States*, vols. 6, 1943; 9, 1945; 11, 1946; 2, 1949; 2, 1950; 6, pts. 1 and 2, 1951; 4, 11, 1952–54; 3, 6, 8, 1955–57. Washington, D.C.: U.S. Government Printing Office, different dates.

Van De Velde, James R. "The Influence of Culture on Japanese-American Negotiations." *The Fletcher Forum* 7(1983):395–99.

Vance, Cyrus. *Hard Choices*. New York: Simon and Shuster, 1983.

Van Zandt, Howard F. "How to Negotiate in Japan." *Harvard Business Review* 48(1970):45–56.

Wilson, Larman C. "The Settlement of Boundary Disputes: Mexico, the United States, and the International Boundary Commission." *International and Comparative Law Quarterly* 29(1980):38–53.

Winham, Gilbert. "Practitioners' Views of International Negotiation."
World Politics 32(1979):111–35.

Wolfgang, Aaron, ed. *Nonverbal Behavior: Perspectives, Applications, Intercultural Insights.* Lewiston, N.Y.: C. J. Hogrefe, 1984.

Young, Kenneth T. *Negotiating with the Chinese Communists.* New York: McGraw-Hill, 1968.

Zartman, I. William. "Negotiation as a Joint Decision-Making Process." *Journal of Conflict Resolution* 21(1977):619–38.

———. "Prenegotiation: Phases and Functions." In Janice Gross Stein, ed., *Getting to the Table.* Baltimore: The Johns Hopkins University Press, 1989.

Zartman, I. William, and Berman, Maureen R. *The Practical Negotiator.* New Haven: Yale University Press, 1982.

Index

Jennings Randolph Program for International Peace

As part of the statute establishing the United States Institute of Peace, Congress envisioned a fellowship program that would appoint "scholars and leaders of peace from the United States and abroad to pursue scholarly inquiry and other appropriate forms of communication on international peace and conflict resolution." The program was named after Senator Jennings Randolph of West Virginia, whose efforts over four decades helped to establish the Institute.

Since it began 1987, the Jennings Randolph Program has played a key role in the Institute's effort to build a national center of research, dialogue, and education on critical problems of conflict and peace. Through a rigorous annual competition, outstanding men and women from diverse nations and fields are selected to carry out projects designed to expand and disseminate knowledge on violent international conflict and the wide range of ways it can be peacefully managed or resolved.

The Institute's Distinguished Fellows and Peace Fellows are individuals from a wide variety of academic and other professional backgrounds who work at the Institute on research and education projects they have proposed and participate in the Institute's collegial and public outreach activities. The Institute's Peace Scholars are doctoral candidates at American universities who are working on their dissertations.

Institute fellows and scholars have worked on such varied subjects as international negotiation, regional security arrangements, conflict resolution techniques, international legal systems, ethnic and religious conflict, arms control, and the protection of human rights. These issues have been examined in settings throughout the world, including the Soviet Union, Europe, Latin America, sub-Saharan Africa, and South Asia.

As part of its effort to disseminate original and useful analyses of peace and conflict to policymakers and the public, the Institute publishes book manuscripts and other written products that result from the fellowship work and meet the Institute's high standards of quality.

Michael S. Lund
Director

DATE DUE

CENTER FOR PEACE LEARNING
GEORGE FOX COLLEGE
NEWBERG OR, 97132